THE GREAT WAR

CAROLYN HOLBROOK is an Australian Research Council DECRA Fellow at Deakin University, Director of Australian Policy and History and the author of *Anzac: The unauthorised biography* (NewSouth, 2014).

KEIR REEVES is professor of Australian history at Federation University Australia.

THE GREAT WAR

AFTERMATH AND COMMEMORATION

Edited by Carolyn Holbrook & Keir Reeves

UNSW PRESS

A UNSW Press book

Published by
NewSouth Publishing
University of New South Wales Press Ltd
University of New South Wales
Sydney NSW 2052
AUSTRALIA
newsouthpublishing.com

© Carolyn Holbrook and Keir Reeves 2019
© In individual chapters retained by authors.
First published 2019

10 9 8 7 6 5 4 3 2 1

This book is copyright. While copyright of the work as a whole is vested in Carolyn Holbrook and Keir Reeves, copyright of individual chapters is retained by the chapter authors. Apart from any fair dealing for the purpose of private study, research, criticism or review, as permitted under the Copyright Act, no part of this book may be reproduced by any process without written permission. Inquiries should be addressed to the publisher.

 A catalogue record for this book is available from the National Library of Australia

ISBN   9781742236629 (paperback)
         9781742244679 (ebook)
         9781742249162 (ePDF)

Design Josephine Pajor-Markus
Cover design Hugh Ford

All reasonable efforts were taken to obtain permission to use copyright material reproduced in this book, but in some cases copyright could not be traced. The editors welcome information in this regard.

CONTENTS

Acknowledgments vii
1 The Great War: Aftermath and commemoration 1
   Carolyn Holbrook and Keir Reeves

WAR'S END

2 Conscription and the strange case of Captain Father Thomas O'Donnell 21
   Anne Beggs-Sunter
3 The 1918 Armistice and the civilian experience of war 32
   Bart Ziino
4 Bringing the AIF home: The organisation of repatriation 1918–19 45
   Meleah Hampton
5 The veteran challenge: Repatriation benefits for Australian soldiers 58
   Martin Crotty
6 Australian naval activities in the Pacific at the end of the Great War 69
   David Sutton
7 Plans for peace, fears of war: Defending Australia in 1919 79
   Honae Cuffe

SOCIAL, POLITICAL AND PERSONAL LEGACIES

8 Anzacs and Australasians 91
   Marilyn Lake
9 Australian politics in the wake of the First World War 100
   Frank Bongiorno
10 'They should at least be given a voice': Aboriginal veterans and the RSSILA 113
   Richard Trembath

11 Anzac trauma and frontier violence? Re-examining
    the Coniston Massacre   124
    Thomas J Rogers
12 Remembering the resilient   135
    Joan Beaumont
13 William Roy Hodgson and the aftermath of the
    First World War   154
    Keir Reeves, Kathryn Avery and David McGinniss

REPRESENTING THE GREAT WAR

14 'A suitable memorial'? Painting, memory and the
    Great War   167
    Margaret Hutchison
15 Staging history in Brisbane's Anzac centenary   179
    Geoffrey AC Ginn
16 Remembering and forgetting the First World War at
    the Sir John Monash Centre   193
    Bruce Scates

COMMEMORATING THE GREAT WAR

17 Remembrance Day: The poor cousin of Australian
    war commemoration   211
    Romain Fathi
18 What is wrong with Anzac?   224
    Henry Reynolds
19 Honest History: Lessons in the politics of history   232
    David Stephens
20 Making sense of the Great War centenary   244
    Carolyn Holbrook

Notes   254
Contributors   281
Index   289

ACKNOWLEDGMENTS

The production of this book has been a collective effort. Special thanks to all the contributing authors, our publisher Phillipa McGuinness, the team at UNSW Press particularly Sophia Oravecz and Joumana Awad, editor John Mapps and cover designer Hugh Ford. Thanks also to the staff and members of the board at Creative Clunes who helped to expedite the project, particularly Richard Mackay-Scollay, Dr Tess Brady, Professor Andrew Reeves, Lesley Falkiner-Rose, Tim Nolan and Lily Mason. Thank you also to members of the Clunes RSL for hosting and generously providing their time and facilities for the tie-in exhibition guest-curated by Dr Michael Taffe. The ANZAC Centenary Fund generously financed the exhibition titled 'Fighting for Peace', launched by Dr Carolyn Holbrook, as well as this publication examining how the notions of fighting for peace in the context of aftermath and commemoration have occurred over the past hundred years from regional, national and international perspectives. Special thanks to Featherstone Book Town members Peter Biggs and Lincoln Gould for their insights and suggestions at the Clunes Book Town Festival in 2018. Professor Keir Reeves also acknowledges the staff and members of the Collaborative Research Centre in Australian History and the School of Arts at Federation University Australia as well as Graham Hannaford, Jaclyn Wood and Benedict Coyne for their contribution to the Hodgson chapter. Dr Carolyn Holbrook acknowledges members of the Contemporary Histories Research Group at Deakin University, particularly Dr Bart Ziino, Associate Professor Clare Corbould and Professor David Lowe.

Carolyn Holbrook and Keir Reeves

1

THE GREAT WAR: AFTERMATH AND COMMEMORATION

Carolyn Holbrook and Keir Reeves

Late in 1988, a veteran of the Second World War called Bill Hall met with the Defence Minister, Kim Beazley, at Parliament House in Canberra. Hall was the patron of the New South Wales World War One Veterans' Association and he suggested to Beazley that the government sponsor a group of old diggers to travel to Gallipoli for the seventy-fifth anniversary of the landing in 1990. Beazley thought the idea had merit and took it to Prime Minister Bob Hawke, who agreed. Here was an opportunity to marshal the unifying national spirit that had eluded the government during the Bicentenary, hampered as that celebration was by Aboriginal resentment and the desire not to offend non-British Australians.

The Hawke government's decision to fund the Gallipoli pilgrimage, as it became known, was calculated and astute. The government had discerned growing public sympathy towards the Anzac mythology during the 1980s, in contrast to the apathy and hostility that had characterised the 1960s and 1970s. According to Beazley, the 'emotional outpouring' of the Australian public when veterans of the Vietnam War were formally welcomed home in 1987 'contributed to a willingness to go big on the 75th anniversary of the landing'.

The Hawke government also determined that the Anzac legend aligned with its broader policy agenda: 'What made us receptive was the strong reassertion of Australian nationalism as a theme of government in the 1980s', Beazley recalled:

> The notion that we punched above our weight featured strongly in defence and foreign policy. Initiatives such as the South Pacific Nuclear-Free Zone, APEC, the peace settlement in Cambodia, defence self-reliance as a fundamental strategy of government, all had strands of this nationalist sentiment in them. We turned our attention to the national icons that we traditionally felt made us distinctive and Gallipoli fell into that category.[1]

The Gallipoli pilgrimage was a great success. Fifty-two old diggers aged between 93 and 104, many of them too frail to walk independently, travelled to Turkey. They mixed affably with former Turkish enemies and lingered among the graves of former comrades. Hawke, who later described the trip as 'one of the most moving experiences of my prime ministership', riffed effortlessly with old soldiers and young backpackers alike.[2] Coverage was beamed live by satellite to ABC television audiences for five hours, and relayed to commercial television channels. Domestic press reports remarked upon the revival of Anzac Day and its superiority over Australia Day as the national day of celebration. A *Sydney Morning Herald* editorial noted that the Anzac spirit was 'more to do with mateship and sacrifice than conquest and power'.[3]

The lineage of this book can be traced all the way back to that commemorative baptism on the shores of Gallipoli in 1990. As the political class stepped into the breach created by the decline of the RSL, the modern version of Anzac – Anzac 2.0 – was born. A grassroots Anzac revival had been discernible since the 1970s, in the activities of family historians, and the popularity of books and films like Bill Gammage's *The Broken Years* (1974), Patsy Adam

The Great War: Aftermath and commemoration

Smith's *The Anzacs* (1978) and Peter Weir's *Gallipoli* (1981), which drew heavily from Gammage's book. This new form of Anzac was noticeably different from its discredited predecessor. It had shed its imperialist and racist connotations, and its tendency to trumpet the martial ability of Australian soldiers. Anzac 2.0 spoke in the modern idiom of mateship, suffering and sacrifice; its heroes were not the old codgers who got embarrassingly drunk each Anzac Day, but naive young men, like Archie Hamilton from the film *Gallipoli*, whose sacrifice gave birth to Australian nationhood. Once the authority of the prime minister and the resources of the state swung behind this kinder, gentler version of Anzac, it developed an unstoppable momentum.

Prime Minister Paul Keating did not share his predecessor's emotional attachment to the Gallipoli campaign. For Keating, Gallipoli was a catastrophic defeat, from which Australians had fashioned a national myth that symbolised subservience to the imperial master. Moreover, Keating argued, the First World War had swung a wrecking ball through the progressive reforms that characterised the early Commonwealth:

> Much of the radical nationalist sentiment which had been so strong at the turn of the century died with the diggers in the First World War. The Labor Party, the bearer of the radical nationalist tradition, was torn apart ... The new nationalism, based on the heroic sacrifice of the First AIF, was a conservative amalgam of pride in Australia and devotion to the British Empire.[4]

Keating's term in office coincided with the 50th anniversary of several significant Pacific battles of the Second World War. With the help of rhetoric crafted by his historian-speechwriter Don Watson, Keating sought to reorient Anzac commemoration towards these anniversaries. On Anzac Day in 1992, Keating travelled to Papua New Guinea, where he gave a speech invoking the war-time Labor Prime Minister, John Curtin:

> He took the Anzac legend to mean that Australia came first – that whatever the claims of Empire on the loyalty of those who died in the Great War, the pre-eminent claim had been Australia's. The Australians who served here in Papua New Guinea fought and died not in defence of the old world, but the new world. Their world. They died in defence of Australia, and the civilisation and values which had grown up there. That is why it might be said that, for Australians, the battles in Papua New Guinea were the most important ever fought.[5]

Keating's historical revisionism was highly controversial, but it did succeed in directing more attention to the Asian battles of the Second World War. It did not, however, diminish popular regard for Gallipoli.

Keating's successor, John Howard, was the most enthusiastic prime ministerial advocate that Anzac has ever had. The war that had shackled Australia to Britain and thwarted its independence in the mind of Paul Keating, had for Howard (and Hawke and Beazley before him), the very opposite connotation. It was the moment at which Australians experienced for the first time their distinctiveness from Britons. Howard spoke of the 'feeling of separate identity' that was entrenched in Australians during the Great War by virtue of: 'Pride in battlefield successes, the magnitude of our losses, sometime dismay at British High Command decision making and some starkly different attitudes held by Australians and their British cousins in respect to class and discipline'.[6] Howard's prime ministership coincided with the peak of Gallipoli backpacker tourism, and he made the trip to Turkey for the dawn service in both 2000 and 2005.

Howard encouraged the flag-waving nationalism that has become commonplace in Australia now, and frequently evoked Anzac as a bedrock of the national identity.

The 2005 Gallipoli dawn service at which Howard spoke attracted a record crowd of 30 000 people, the majority of them young backpackers from Australia and New Zealand.[7] Many Australians were perturbed in the lead-up to the 90th anniversary, when the Turkish government undertook work on the peninsula to widen roads and increase parking for tour buses. These works had disturbed the gravesites of Australian soldiers, and prompted a Senate inquiry that was critical of the government for being insufficiently attentive to the issue. The Commonwealth walked a fine line between acknowledging the national sovereignty of the Turkish government and calming those Anzac adherents at home whose hackles were raised. Hackles rose again in the aftermath of the dawn service when reports emerged that the overnight program of Australian and New Zealand rock and pop music included the Bee Gees hits 'Tragedy' and 'Stayin' Alive'. When journalists wrote that overcrowding had left people reclining against gravestones, and the national park strewn with rubbish, critics wondered whether Anzac had morphed from commemoration to entertainment.[8]

Historians had been watching the growing cultural salience of the Anzac legend with varying degrees of curiosity and alarm since the 1990s. By the time of the 'Anzactainment' controversy of 2005, they were armed with a bunch of questions – why had Anzac commemoration defied the widely held expectation that it would endure only as long as the last of the old soldiers? What drove tens of thousands of young Australians to travel to Gallipoli on Anzac Day, and what caused them to shed tears for men they never knew, most of whom died decades before they were born? Most worryingly, did this unexpected Anzac resurgence carry with it the risk of obscuring the tragedy of war, or even glorifying it?

Bruce Scates was among the first historians to respond to the Anzac revival. Spurred by his own visit to the Somme in the mid-1990s, he examined the phenomenon of Australian battlefield tourism in *Return to Gallipoli* (2006). Using evidence from 700 interviews, Scates sought to understand the motivations and impressions of modern-day battlefield 'pilgrims'. He concluded that these travellers, many of them young backpackers, formed deep emotional attachments to the Gallipoli landscape. Their understanding of the war transcended 'the shallow rhetoric of the media and the politicians', and far from romanticising the conflict, they deplored its 'tragic, brutal waste'.[9]

Other historians took a different view of the phenomena they observed. Mark McKenna and Stuart Ward were not so sure that young backpackers travelling to Gallipoli for the Anzac dawn service were merely responding to the landscape in front of them:

> Like pilgrims to Jerusalem or Lourdes, the Australians are 'moved' to tears at the sight of holy ground, the place where the sacred stories of Anzac began. They believe that their emotional response is immediate, elicited by the sight of Australian gravestones (the sprigs of wattle placed carefully at their feet) and the sudden realisation of so many young lives lost. It is as if all prior knowledge of Gallipoli counted for nothing when weighed against the experience of 'being there' ... Remarkably, few pilgrims pause to ask themselves whether their profound emotional investment in the Anzac legend is discovered 'on site' or brought with them from Australia.[10]

The authors decried the 'sentimental nationalism' (is there any other kind?) that motivated the tourists' attachment to the Anzac legend. Their real concern, however, appeared to be the conservative political values that were being attached to the Anzac legend so effectively by the Prime Minister, John Howard.[11] McKenna and Ward thought that 'the pilgrimages may have less and less to do with "history" and more and more to do with the commerce and politics of nationalism in John Howard's Australia'.[12]

The 'top-down' interpretation, which characterises the Anzac revival as the product of political puppet mastery, found its most expansive and influential form in a book called *What's Wrong with Anzac?* (2010), by Marilyn Lake, Henry Reynolds, Mark McKenna, Joy Damousi and Carina Donaldson. The authors argued that 'For several years now Australia has seen the relentless militarisation of our history':

> Political leaders of all persuasions, government departments led by the Department of Veterans' Affairs, national institutions such as the Australian War Memorial, mass media, opinion makers, publishers and schools in every state and territory now either actively fund or promote the commemoration of Australians at war, whether at Gallipoli, Fromelles or Kokoda, in Korea and Vietnam …[13]

The authors of *What's Wrong with Anzac?* were concerned that this 'khaki armband' version of Australian history obscured our understanding of other important aspects of the past, such as the frontier wars and the range of pioneering social reforms that characterised the post-Federation nation. Furthermore, the authors were concerned that the 'cult of the warrior stands in the way of critical appraisal of Australian engagement in overseas wars'; that critics who question our troops' involvement in Iraq and Afghanistan, for example, are at risk of being labelled as unpatriotic traitors to the Anzac legend.[14]

The thesis of *What's Wrong with Anzac?* did not go unchallenged. In similar vein to Bruce Scates, Inga Clendinnen, Ken Inglis and

Graeme Davison it claimed that Anzac was an historically based mythology, to which many Australians felt attached, quite apart from the propagandising efforts of the state.[15] The sociologist Jim McKay argued that a filter existed between state propaganda and its audience: 'teachers and students do not have messages about Anzac injected hypodermically into their brains from resources produced by the Department of Veterans' Affairs', he wrote. McKay believed the popularity of Anzac was driven by a complex range of emotional motivations and transnational attitudes and interactions, complemented by the rise of 'dark tourism'.[16] Jo Hawkins analysed the rise and decline of Gallipoli backpacker tourism in her study of the commodification of Anzac; a phenomenon that dates all the way back to 1915. Her *Consuming Anzac* showed how commercial interests such as the Australian Football League and Carlton and United Breweries dip their snouts in the Anzac trough for great financial gain.

In 2013 Christina Twomey broke free from the polarity of the top-down versus bottom-up debate with an original explanation for the revival of Anzac. Twomey doubted that the popularity of Anzac could be explained by state propaganda alone: 'Despite the vast sums of government money spent on war memorials, commemorative events and education kits for schoolchildren, state initiative alone seems an unlikely explanation for the popular embrace and emotive power of Anzac'. Nor did she think that the emphasis on Anzac equated to the 'militarising of Australian history'. Instead, Twomey linked the revival of Anzac commemoration to the increased salience of trauma in Western cultures: by the 1980s 'the suffering of soldiers in war and the potential for them to be traumatised by it became a central trope in the public discussion of Anzac', she wrote.[17] The psychological turn was double-edged; by tempering tendencies towards glorification with reminders of the suffering caused by war it has allowed the state an acceptable space within which to perpetuate Anzac commemoration. Conversely, the emphasis placed by many academics and artists on the trauma and suffering of war looks very much like the old anti-war movement clothed in contemporary rhetoric.

The Great War: Aftermath and commemoration is informed by our conviction that the Anzac legend is a complex and dynamic phenomenon, whose popularity defies simple explanation. While the thread of political patronage connects the 1990 Gallipoli pilgrimage to the 2015 Anzac centenary, political benefaction does not explain everything about the commemorative explosion. Anzac 2.0 is the product of a conjunction of many factors, including the rise of family history and genealogical studies driven by familial war records, political patronage and battlefield tourism, and its compatibility with the trauma zeitgeist, so often associated with the memory of conflict. We recognise that potent cultural phenomena like Anzac are multi-faceted and subjective; that people attach different meanings to the Anzac legend according to their own experience and needs. Though Anzac is sometimes invoked by jingoists and racists, it would be overly simplistic to conflate Anzac commemoration with excessive, celebratory nationalism. Just as Anzac triggers concerns for many Australians about the fetishisation of war, there are plenty of decent, thoughtful people who feel a sentimental attachment to Anzac; who take inspiration from its appeals to service, comradeship, stoicism, duty (a concept that has slipped from fashion) and good humour in the face of extreme adversity and defeat.

The scholarship in *The Great War: Aftermath and commemoration* reflects the complexity of the war and its legacy. The contributors possess a wide range of expertise and varied points of view. They include eminent senior historians, whose work has shaped the field of Great War and Anzac historiography, and emerging historians, applying innovative analysis to previously unexamined archives. The book examines the interwoven themes of aftermath and commemoration; one of the war's most telling legacies has been its influence on the national identity, as expressed through commemorative practices. But we are mindful that the contemporary ubiquity of Anzac has siphoned historiographical attention into the war and its commemoration, at the expense of important and highly pertinent issues pertaining to the post-war world. The first two sections of the book examine the aftermath of war and invite us to consider how the First World War shaped the development of Australian society, politics and international relations. Sections three and four consider themes of representation and commemoration of the war.

One of the most enduring legacies of the First World War was the animosity generated by the conscription campaigns of 1916 and 1917 between Catholics and Protestants. The quasi-heroic lens through which Australians typically view the First World War not only obscures events on the home front, but blurs understanding of the extent to which our fate was bound to what was happening overseas. Anne Beggs-Sunter uses the intriguing case of Father Thomas O'Donnell to exemplify the fortunes of Irish-Australians during the First World War, and the extent to which they were affected by events in Ireland. The Catholic priest began the war as an ardent loyalist and advocate of conscription. After observing the British government's ruthless response to the 1916 Easter Rising in Dublin, O'Donnell's sympathies shifted, to the extent that he was charged with treachery and briefly imprisoned in the Tower of London. This tumultuous personal transformation is poignantly illustrative of one of the most divisive episodes in Australian history, which greatly increased hostility and prejudice between Protestants and Catholics.

Like Beggs-Sunter, Bart Ziino seeks to invert the conventional emphasis on the battlefront; an emphasis, he notes, that characterises Australian war memory now as much as it did then. He uses the Armistice of 11 November 1918 as a window through which to glimpse a different experience of war on the home front. His chapter shows that news of the Armistice prompted celebration, but also immense relief that the anxieties that had so characterised the war were coming to an end. Ziino examines those expressions of relief in the streets, but also in Australia's various parliaments, where politicians attempted to give meaning to the war. Despite the willingness of politicians to lionise the Anzacs over the course of the war in order to court public support, jingoism came very much second to expressions of relief and gratitude in November 1918.

Among the immediate challenges faced by those who surveyed the post-war world was the task of repatriating soldiers. Repatriation was an immensely difficult undertaking, both logistically and strategically. Done poorly it could result in restless soldiers being stuck overseas for extended periods of time. It also had implications domestically, as Australia confronted the rapid return of so many servicemen. Meleah Hampton's chapter examines the scheme, overseen by Sir John Monash, that saw 150 000 Australians returned home at the end of the war. Hampton concludes that it was Monash's skilled leadership of the demobilisation and repatriation process that enabled Australia to avoid the civil unrest from aggrieved veterans that was experienced in other countries, including the United States, during the 1920s.

Martin Crotty provides an assessment of the benefits available to Australian veterans after the First World War. He compares the Australian repatriation scheme with those of other countries, including the Soviet Union, Britain, New Zealand and the United States. Crotty challenges the common view that Australian veterans were ill-treated, claiming they were better provided for than any other group, arguably apart from United States veterans after the Second World War. Most returned men went on to live productive lives. If some never recovered from their war experience, Crotty argues, it was not for want of effort by the Australian government and the public.

Chapters 6 and 7 consider geo-political legacies of the war. David Sutton uses the tale of two naval expeditions to illustrate the ways in which Australia pursued an emboldened defence policy, which simultaneously sought to position the nation as a regional power and an agent of the British Empire within the Pacific region. The mission of HMAS *Fantome* to the New Hebrides, which took retribution for the murder of a French planter, showed that Australia was prepared to use deadly force to enforce British colonial rule. While the HMAS *Encounter* mission to provide medical assistance to Samoa in an outbreak of Spanish flu was 'ostensibly carried out in the spirit of genuine altruism', Sutton discerns ulterior, strategic motives.

Honae Cuffe's chapter calls for a reassessment of Australian aims at the Paris Peace Conference. Scholarship has tended to focus on Billy Hughes' prickly demeanour and assertive nationalism. Cuffe argues, however, that Hughes' attitude needs to be viewed within the context of Australia's strategic defence aims. Throughout the war Australian political and defence circles feared that Japan was potentially the source of the next great conflict. The peace-making diplomacy that emerged during the Paris Peace Conference was not just about the punitive imposition of post-war justice on the Central Powers, but also geared towards containing Japanese expansion in the Asia-Pacific region. Cuffe's chapter suggests there was considered strategic thinking behind the racism and assertiveness displayed by Hughes in Paris.

Section two probes the social, political and personal legacies of the war. Marilyn Lake examines the paradox that lies at the heart of the Anzac legend: how was a transnational military formation, the Australian and New Zealand Army Corps, reimagined by Australians as a national story and put into service as the foremost symbol of national distinctiveness? She argues that the exclusion of New Zealand from the Gallipoli story is part of a much wider and deeply significant act of forgetting. Prior to the First World War, 'Australasia' was recognised internationally as a leader of progressive social reform. Lake argues that the omission of New Zealand from the Anzac formulation corresponded with the decline of the progressive 'Australasian world' and the victory of conservative imperialism in post-war Australia.

Frank Bongiorno surveys the post-war political landscape with less pessimism than Marilyn Lake. He challenges the highly influential interpretation that contrasts the policy stasis of that period with the progressive reform of the years following Federation. Initiatives such as the abolition of the Queensland upper house, the introduction of a form of preferential voting and compulsory voting, and the election of women to parliament indicate that the inter-war period was not as conservative and unimaginative as is commonly supposed. Bongiorno argues that the war's greatest political legacy was the emergence of the Country Party as a response to the economic disruption caused by the conflict.

Increased recognition of Indigenous soldiers has been one of the striking trends to emerge from the Great War centenary. Approximately 1300 Aboriginal men served in the war, despite being officially banned by the *Defence Act*. Richard Trembath describes how those Aboriginal men who returned from the war were excluded from the soldier settlement scheme, the burgeoning Anzac legend and much of the camaraderie among returned men. He traces the efforts of the RSSILA (the predecessor of the RSL) to advocate on their behalf during the war. Trembath finds that the patchy efforts of the lobby group in helping Indigenous men receive repatriation benefits, including them in social activities and publicising their role in the war reflect a broader failure in inter-war Australian society to pay more than intermittent interest to the welfare of Aboriginal people.

Chapters 11–13 confront one of the most common images evoked by the First World War, that of the traumatised soldier. The trauma zeitgeist leads us to attribute post-war dysfunction to war service. But has the pendulum swung too far? Thomas Rogers scrutinises the adequacy of war trauma as an explanation for the behaviour of William George Murray, a returned soldier turned policeman who killed 31 (and likely many more) Aboriginal people at Coniston in Central Australia in 1928. To what extent was the massacre, which was deemed by an official inquiry to be an act of self-defence, a result of Murray's war service, as some historians have implied? Rogers argues that Murray's actions are better understood in the context of the 'frontier attitude' he developed during his police service, rather than any trauma he suffered in 1914–18. He contrasts the deluge of knowledge in popular culture about the First World War (including the psychological state of soldiers) with the lack of information about the frontier wars and the motivations of those who perpetrated violence.

The dominance of the trauma discourse has also caused historians to overlook the evidence of resilience among returned soldiers, Joan Beaumont argues. Using the examples of two very well-known returned soldiers, General Pompey Elliott and Hugo Throssell VC, and the lesser known Charles Hawker, Beaumont probes the complexities associated with veterans' adjustment to life after the First World War. Both Elliott and Throssell committed suicide – though not until the Great Depression – while Hawker, the most severely wounded of the three, prospered in post-war life, until his untimely death in a plane crash in 1938. While it may be difficult to be conclusive about the sources and prevalence of resilience, Beaumont argues that we need to acknowledge that for many returned soldiers this is a more appropriate framing of their post-war life than trauma and victimhood.

Keir Reeves, Kathryn Avery and David McGinniss tell the story of William Roy Hodgson, who landed at Gallipoli on 25 April 1915 and sustained a near-fatal injury a few days later. After the war,

Hodgson worked in military intelligence, before rising to the top of the External Affairs Department. He later served at the United Nations and had a direct hand in drafting the Universal Declaration of Human Rights (UDHR), as part of the UDHR Drafting Committee chaired by Eleanor Roosevelt. Like Rogers and Beaumont, the authors challenge the well-rehearsed conceit of the damaged soldier. Not only did Hodgson lead a fruitful post-war life, but he traced his stellar success to his experience in the First World War.

Section three of *The Great War: Aftermath and commemoration* considers how the Great War has been represented in the mediums of painting, theatre and museums. Margaret Hutchison examines the Australian official war art scheme, which emerged in 1916 and was managed by military officers and public servants working in London. From the outset, the Australian scheme emphasised the military experiences of infantry troops, at the expense of life behind the lines and on the home front. By comparing the Australian scheme to those of Britain and Canada, Hutchison shows how the Australian program complemented and consolidated a broader pattern of nationally focused war remembrance in Australia.

Geoffrey AC Ginn describes the development and production of two plays about the Great War that were performed in Brisbane during the centenary, *A Lost Story of the Great War* and *The Blood Votes: An historical drama*. As one of the project leaders for *The Blood Votes*, together with colleagues, Ginn wanted to challenge the dominance of the Anzac warrior myth. By introducing a range of historical characters, including Women's Peace Army activist Margaret Thorp and Prime Minister Billy Hughes, *The Blood Votes* captured the high emotion of the conscription debates, while simultaneously encouraging audiences to think critically about the war. Ginn argues that documentary theatre offers a highly effective means of presenting the public with a complex version of Australian experience in the Great War.

THE GREAT WAR

Bruce Scates presents a searing critique of the $100 million Sir John Monash Centre (SJMC) in Villers-Bretonneux, France. Injecting into the chapter his own short-lived experience as an historical adviser to the project, Scates compares the SJMC with the Historial de la Grande Guerre museum in France. While the Historial is a sombre place that emphasises the tragedy and complexity of the war, Scates claims that the SJMC presents an heroic, Australian-centred perspective; that it strives for emotional affect over considered analysis and conflates war with entertainment. While Europe has fashioned a complex, transnational understanding of the war, Scates concludes that Australia continues to replicate the discredited belief that war is a measure of the greatness of a nation.

The final section of the book looks at issues of commemoration and public memory. Australia spent more than any other combatant nation on commemorating the First World War centenary; Honest History's David Stephens puts the total at around $600 million when Commonwealth, state and corporate contributions are tallied up. The Sir John Monash Centre, which opened at Villers-Bretonneux in April 2018, signalled the post-1990 commemorative culture's annexation of France. The $498 million expansion of the Australian War Memorial, championed by memorial director Brendan Nelson, has taken the commemorative splurge to new heights of excess. The project was funded in the 2019 Budget, having been waved through by a Labor opposition that feared being accused of that most treacherous of political crimes: being anti-Anzac – and, by implication, unAustralian.

While Bart Ziino examines attitudes to the Armistice in 1918, Romain Fathi considers the history of Armistice Day – later restyled as Remembrance Day – ever since. He describes the origins of the commemoration and its early forms, including the minute's silence. Fathi demonstrates how Remembrance Day has always held less meaning for Australians than other Allied combatants. While most nations found the solemnity and mourning of Armistice Day resonated with their experience of the war, Australians have preferred the patriotic and celebratory overlays of Anzac Day.

Henry Reynolds tallies up the price Australians pay for what he describes as 'the militarisation of our history'. Reynolds traces the beginning of the Anzac obsession to John Howard's instigation of the 'culture wars'. The conservative prime minister achieved what Reynolds describes as a 'counter revolution in Australian historiography', masterfully turning the focus away from the emerging historiography of frontier violence, towards an overseas military campaign. The emphasis on the Anzac legend provided ballast for Howard's desire to promote a triumphant view of the Australian past, Reynolds argues. The consequences of this military bias, the chapter claims, include widespread ignorance of the aspects of Australian history that are most distinctive, including the welfare reforms and equality of wealth distribution in the early 20th century.

One of the most interesting phenomena to emerge from the Anzac centenary, and one that will no doubt interest future historians, is the Honest History network. Led by political scientist and former bureaucrat David Stephens, the group was formed in 2013 to push back against what it perceived as the rising tide of Anzackery – jingoistic, often politically sponsored, forms of Anzac commemoration. Stephens' chapter describes the origins of Honest History and weighs its success in combating Anzackery. The author offers his reflections after leading Honest History in its attempt to balance Anzac with other aspects of Australian history.

Carolyn Holbrook's chapter attempts a first draft of the history of the Anzac centenary. She argues that political and commercial interests misjudged the nature of popular interest in Anzac commemoration. Expensively produced television shows that invited Australians to be both entertained and educated about the First World War returned disappointing ratings, and the public flinched over blatant and clumsy attempts to cash in on the Anzac bonanza, such as Woolworths' 'Fresh in Our Memories' campaign. Yet huge crowds turned out for dawn services on 25 April 2015. Holbrook concludes that Anzac's status as a quasi-religion in contemporary Australia obviates the desire for intellectual engagement and recoils against the exploitation and denigration of the sacred. Like formal religions, Anzac has its ritual in the dawn service, and its holy text in Peter Weir's film *Gallipoli*.

It is not hard to understand why so much historiographical energy has been devoted to the First World War and the Anzac legend, given the amount of public resources allocated to commemoration in the last thirty years. The $498 million Australian War Memorial expansion and the obscene sponsorship of the Memorial by weapons manufacturers are proof that the commemorative colossus demands constant vigilance. The end of the centenary, however, provides a fitting moment at which to take stock, and consider future historiographical directions. As Henry Reynolds has emphasised, Australian history did not begin with the Great War; neither did it end with it. The crowds that greeted the Armistice with gratitude and relief could not have known that economic depression and another catastrophic global conflict lay just down the track. Contributors to *The Great War: Aftermath and commemoration* have laid out a number of challenging new interpretations about the aftermath of the war in Australia. It is time for the historiographical lens to pull back from 1914–18, to help us better understand how the First World War shaped the century ahead, and how we live with its legacies still.

WAR'S END

2

CONSCRIPTION AND THE STRANGE CASE OF CAPTAIN FATHER THOMAS O'DONNELL

Anne Beggs-Sunter

In February 1918, the Reverend Father Thomas O'Donnell embarked for France as a chaplain in the First Australian Imperial Force (AIF). O'Donnell was a Catholic priest from Tasmania who had been a prominent advocate of conscription. He served with distinction in France, but a bizarre twist to his service came in 1919, when he was court-martialled for 'disloyalty' to the king. When visiting Ireland, O'Donnell had been overheard supporting Irish independence while wearing his AIF uniform. He was temporarily incarcerated in Dublin and then in the Tower of London, tried at court martial, and found not guilty. O'Donnell's conversion from imperial loyalist to outspoken Irish nationalist is part of the sectarian story of the First World War, which is so often hidden in the shadow of the ubiquitous Anzac legend.

Irish-Australians comprised between a quarter and a third of the population in 1914, and they enlisted in the First AIF roughly in proportion to their eligibility. Historian Jeff Kildea has shown how the Irish-Australian soldier's experience of war mirrored that of the wider AIF.[1] The story on the home front was different, however. The pre-eminent historian of Irish Australia, Patrick O'Farrell, argued that the issue of Irish self-determination deeply divided the Irish-Australian community by the end of the war. Whereas Home

Rule for Ireland within the British Empire had been the general desire of Irish-Australians before 1916, after the Dublin Rising of Easter 1916, interests began to shift gradually to the cause of Irish independence, with rising support for the nationalist Sinn Féin movement.[2] The end of the war saw Australia deeply divided along the lines of class, ethnicity and religion.[3]

Nineteenth-century Irish immigrants to Australia strongly supported the cause of Irish Home Rule. Typical of these immigrants were Moses and Mary O'Donnell, who owned a small farm on the outskirts of Buninyong, near the thriving goldfield city of Ballarat. Their son, Thomas Joseph O'Donnell, was born in 1876, one of five children.[4] Thomas secured a good education, and with a vocation to the priesthood, was sent to the Sacred Heart Monastery at Kensington in Sydney to undertake his initial training. By 1905, O'Donnell was in Tasmania, from where Archbishop Murphy of Hobart sent him to All Hallows College, Dublin, to complete his studies. In 1907, before his ordination, O'Donnell was writing for the Melbourne *Advocate* on Catholic affairs in Europe. Among O'Donnell's articles was a column concerning French seminarians being forced to undertake national service prior to ordination.

O'Donnell returned from Dublin in 1914 to a country that was grappling with issues of sectarianism, including the long-running debate about whether the Catholic Church should receive funding to assist in operating parish schools, which had been unleashed by the free, secular and compulsory education acts of the 1870s. The historians Elizabeth Malcolm and Dianne Hall described sectarian conflict as being 'institutionalised in the new Australian Commonwealth's political culture'.[5] In an interview conducted in 1919, O'Donnell reflected on his time as a seminarian at All Hallows, claiming that he came to love the Irish people, and the people's cause of Home Rule.[6] However, Marilyn Lake recorded that the newly ordained priest in the diocese of Hobart, fast gained 'a reputation as a political demagogue', and a strong supporter of the British war effort.[7]

O'Donnell was one of the few Catholic clerics to speak in favour of conscription in the 1916 referendum campaign. Indeed, 'the famed Irish priest' was much in demand as a public speaker for his 'fervent oratory such that people paid to hear him' and his speeches received extensive coverage in leading newspapers.[8] O'Donnell's support for conscription was at odds with the views of his family. A letter from his brother Frank claimed that none of his siblings supported compulsion and the 'Prussianising of Australia'.[9]

O'Donnell's statements in support of conscription seemingly drew the admiration of Prime Minister William Morris 'Billy' Hughes. When the 1917 referendum campaign was in full swing, the priest appeared on platforms in Melbourne as a Catholic counterweight to that turbulent and eloquent opponent of conscription, Archbishop Daniel Mannix. The 1917 campaign saw a dramatic escalation in sectarianism, with Hughes declaring in newspaper advertisements that opponents of conscription were nothing more than Sinn Féinners, led by Mannix.

On 14 December 1917, Father O'Donnell appeared on the platform of a pro-conscription meeting in Melbourne. He obfuscated on the issue of Irish Home Rule, stating that 'the people of Australia want to do what is right in regard to Ireland, and … would do all they could to satisfy and rectify the trouble which the people had in Ireland'.[10] O'Donnell voiced his strong support for the troops at the front and Prime Minister Hughes, and reiterated his opposition to the anti-conscriptionist position of Archbishop Mannix. He declared that he had just been to the Victoria Barracks for a medical examination, and if he was not accepted as an army chaplain, he would enlist in any way he could.

Father O'Donnell was accepted as a chaplain, with the rank of captain, on 22 February 1918. O'Donnell was 40 years of age, and was then living in the Ballarat district. His voluminous file in the National Archives explains much about him. On his file it is noted that his Chaplain-General, Archbishop Mannix, had given him permission to enlist. He was attached to the 11th Battalion of the 3rd Infantry Brigade, and arrived in France on 21 May 1918, and saw action on the Hindenburg Line, assisting the battalion surgeon with casualties. He was recommended for a Military Medal, and later made public statements to the effect that the Australians had saved the day when General Gough's army ran away from the Germans in March 1918.

While O'Donnell served with distinction in the First AIF, sectarianism was mounting in Australia. The failed republican rising in Dublin of Easter 1916 had been initially condemned by Irish-Australians, but sympathy for Sinn Féin grew with reports of executions and imprisonments following the rebellion.[11] The growing support for Sinn Féin among Irish-Australians was demonstrated by the large crowds at meetings and parades on St Patrick's Day in March 1918. The Hibernian Australasian Catholic Benefit Society held a St Patrick's Day breakfast at the Melbourne Exhibition Building, which was attended by 8000 Irish-Australians. Archbishop Mannix received a standing ovation at the event for his defence of Irish independence and condemnation of the failure of the British government to deliver the Home Rule it had promised Ireland in 1914. Protestant loyalists condemned the appearance of Sinn Féin flags at these events and urged the Prime Minister to deport Mannix.[12] Urged on by loyalists and abetted by the rabidly anti-Catholic governor-general, Sir Ronald Munro Ferguson, Hughes' Nationalist government banned the carrying of Sinn Féin flags and discussions at Irish clubs, under the provisions of the *War Precautions Act*.[13] The editor of the Ballarat *Evening Echo*, James Scullin, a future Labor Prime Minister, reported the ban under the headline:

Conscription and the case of Captain Father Thomas O'Donnell

HYSTERICAL LOYALTY
GOVERNMENT'S NEW STANDARD
WHO MAY ESCAPE?
SOME AMAZING REGULATIONS.[14]

As the war entered a crucial phase in early 1918, Britain was urged by its allies to resolve the Irish question. Pressure from the United States government saw the British establish an Irish Convention in Dublin, with the object of designing a new Irish Home Rule constitution. The initiative was doomed to failure, however, as the British Cabinet required that decisions of the Convention be unanimous, never a realistic possibility given the presence of the Protestant Ulster Unionists under Sir Edward Carson.[15] At the beginning of March 1918, the Irish Home Rule leader John Redmond died, leaving a void in leadership of the Irish cause, which was immediately filled by Sinn Féin.[16]

Over the course of 1918, several Sinn Féin candidates won seats in by-elections for the British parliament. At the general election held in December 1918, Sinn Féin candidates secured all the Irish seats in the parliament. The victorious candidates refused, however, to take their seats in Westminster. They met instead at the Mansion House in Dublin, calling themselves the Dáil Éireann and declaring a sovereign Irish republic. Their leader, Éamon de Valera, hoped that United States President Woodrow Wilson and other representatives at the Paris Peace Conference would fight for the recognition of small nations, including Ireland. But de Valera was disappointed; the British military asserted its authority over Ireland. In 1919 a state of undeclared war existed between Irish republicans and the British government, represented by the paramilitary Black and Tans and Auxiliaries.[17]

When the war ended in November 1918, Reverend Thomas O'Donnell was in Belgium. While awaiting repatriation, he wrote many eloquent letters to the Tasmanian press expressing his views on the demobilisation of Australian troops, the plight of Australian war horses, and the treatment of small nations at the coming Peace Conference. O'Donnell visited Ireland in October 1919, hiring a car to travel through the countryside and visit relatives and clerical friends. He was carrying a pistol that had belonged to John Mitchel, the Young Ireland leader who had been transported to Bermuda and then Van Diemen's Land in the 1840s for treason, and who escaped to the United States in 1853. The fact that O'Donnell took the pistol with him from Australia in February 1918 indicates his strong sympathy with Ireland. While in Dublin, he met Arthur Griffith, the founder of Sinn Féin, and presented him with the souvenir pistol. This meeting drew the attention of the Irish Special Branch, which placed him under surveillance. O'Donnell subsequently remarked that he felt he was being watched by agents of the British government as he travelled around.

On 10 October 1919, O'Donnell stayed at the International Hotel in Killarney, where he entered into conversation with an Ulster businessman at dinner. O'Donnell was reported to have spoken very loudly and excitedly about the current political troubles.[18] In the room were several others, including a British army officer, who eavesdropped on the conversation of the Australian, and took notes of his utterances. The British officer reported O'Donnell to the military authorities in Dublin, who arrested and imprisoned him, without any specific charge, other than mention of him using seditious language in a public place. O'Donnell was held for ten days in Dublin gaol before being escorted to London by an AIF officer and placed in the Tower of London. The following day he was allowed to leave on 'open arrest', under the authority of the Australian military authorities. He began to talk to the press and organise legal assistance. He also cabled Prime Minister Hughes for support in his plight.

Conscription and the case of Captain Father Thomas O'Donnell

The sensational news of O'Donnell's arrest was first published in the Melbourne *Herald* on 20 October 1919. The news precipitated Irish-Australians to begin lobbying on his behalf. The most prominent of O'Donnell's advocates was Archbishop Mannix, who told a large gathering in Melbourne:

> I can say for Father O'Donnell that before he left this land he was a priest without blemish. He went to the front of his own freewill, as he was entitled to do. He had done everything a chaplain could do, and he went to Ireland one of the most loyal men Mr. Hughes had ever met. When Father O'Donnell went there his eyes were opened, and he threw in his lot with those with whom we are prepared to throw in our lot. The authorities took him by the neck and threw him into a felon's cell, and these are the people who expect us here, in Australia and in America, to believe in them. But they are beyond belief.[19]

On 26 November 1919, O'Donnell faced a court martial at the Westminster Guildhall, before a packed public gallery. It was alleged that on 10 October 1919 at the International Hotel in Killarney he had used 'disloyal words regarding the Sovereign'. While at the hotel, in his AIF uniform, he had been overheard saying:

> We Australians fought for the Independence and right to self-government to small nations which is being denied to the finest and oldest little country in the world by a few satellites of King George who are filling their own pockets at the expense of the people and whose hands are red with the blood of Irish patriots.[20]

The trial lasted three days, during which O'Donnell was represented by three Irish barristers he had retained in London. He was found not guilty, much to the joy of the Melbourne Catholic *Advocate*, which declared that 'there is not a Catholic who does not rejoice at the triumph of Fr. O'Donnell over English militarism in Ireland'. Not only Catholics, but 'all lovers of fair play' were pleased that Fr. O'Donnell has come through without a stain on his character, and 'with a dignity becoming his office', the paper claimed.[21] O'Donnell was granted leave with pay and allowances and was demobilised in England in December 1919. He travelled to Rome and the United States before returning to Tasmania in 1920, just as Archbishop Mannix was preparing to travel to the United States, Rome and Ireland.

The situation in Ireland was becoming increasingly tense, after its case for self-determination was not raised at the Paris Peace Conference in 1919. The Lloyd George government proved unable to resolve the Irish question. The path to a solution was obstructed by a powerful minority of Ulster Unionists, who insisted on the partition of Ireland in any legislation.

Daniel Mannix was feted by the press and large crowds in New York, where he met with Éamon de Valera.[22] After the success of his American visit, Mannix sailed for Ireland where he intended to reunite with his aged mother. His ship, the *Baltic*, was dramatically intercepted by a British Navy destroyer off the coast of Ireland and the archbishop was landed at Penzance, England. He was ordered not to visit Ireland, or the cities of Manchester, Liverpool and Glasgow, where there were large Irish Catholic populations.

It was Father O'Donnell's turn to speak out publically in support of Archbishop Mannix. An article in the *Launceston Examiner* on 13 August 1920 presented 'FATHER O'DONNELL'S VIEW':

> When interviewed in New York, the Rev. Thos. O'Donnell, chaplain of the 3rd Brigade, 1st Division, Australians, who is returning from Ireland, said: 'I think the Government

Conscription and the case of Captain Father Thomas O'Donnell

is pursuing wrong tactics regarding Dr. Mannix. Had they allowed him to go to Ireland he would not have been able to address meetings, since public meetings were forbidden. They took him off the ship instead, and advertised his mission everywhere'.

As O'Donnell anticipated, Britain's treatment of Mannix earned the archbishop great publicity and sympathy. There were huge protests in England, the United States and Australia. At a meeting in Ballarat it was reported that 'England had gone into the great war for the reason that Germany poured her troops through Belgium, and England should realise that what was good enough for Belgium, Poland, Romania, and Servia in the way of self-determination was good enough for Ireland'.[23] It is instructive that the conservative *Ballarat Star*, which had stood so strongly in favour of conscription, now appeared to be supporting the cause of Irish Home Rule.

Upon his return to Tasmania in 1920, O'Donnell was immediately active with his pen, writing to local newspapers about his experiences. He described his visit to Rome to meet the Pope, who was 'a wonderful man and a great diplomat. Just the man for the times'. He related how the British government had made great efforts to get the Pope to denounce the Sinn Féin movement, but had failed: 'Times have changed, and the mighty British Government finds that it has not the same influence as it had in the days gone by. And it never will have that influence again', wrote O'Donnell.[24]

O'Donnell continued to be a thorn in the side of Protestant loyalists. In January 1921 'the well-known AIF chaplain, who was arrested in Ireland and imprisoned in the Tower of London' spoke in Adelaide during a lecture tour on the 'The Agony of Ireland and Her Struggle against British Militarism'. According to the Catholic *Southern Cross* newspaper, O'Donnell was a 'brilliant Australian orator', who would 'relate his experiences with the "Diggers" and also his experiences in Ireland, and will expose the misrule and brutality of the British Government in that country. The admission is only 1/'.[25]

In his lectures, O'Donnell pondered how best to respond to the Irish situation; through the granting of Home Rule, or the Sinn Féin position of complete independence. He preferred Home Rule along the lines of the self-determination that had been granted to the settler dominions, but was prepared to accept the republican position, given the intransigence of Edward Carson and the Ulsterites. O'Donnell was suspicious of the British government, which had 'made no definite concrete offer. All that they have offered is a mongrel measure which divides the country and gives powers which if offered to us here we would reject with scorn'.[26]

O'Donnell's suggestion of a solution to the Irish question was innovative and dominion-focused. In an article published in Hobart's labour newspaper, the *World*, he proposed a conference of representatives of the dominions, chaired by the Prince of Wales. The conference would outline a set of principles for Irish independence, which would then be put to a referendum of the Irish people. O'Donnell suggested that the solution of the Irish problem might provide a model for solving the issue of Indian governance. Just as Australians had stood for self-determination, so they must as loyal citizens support the cause of Ireland, O'Donnell claimed. With rhetorical flourish, he wrote that 'the blood of sixty thousand of our sacred dead was shed to consecrate it anew. They died to make the world safe for democracy, and for the triumph of right over might. May right and democracy soon triumph in Ireland'.[27]

O'Donnell was delighted to receive news on 7 December 1921 that a treaty had been signed between Sinn Féin representatives and the British government. He was optimistic that a bright independent future for Ireland had at last opened up. O'Donnell's hopes and the hopes of all Irish-Australians were blighted by the civil war that erupted in Ireland between 1922 and 1923 over the deficiencies of the treaty.[28]

Thomas O'Donnell served out his priesthood in Tasmania, always an eloquent and opinionated speaker. In later life he became increasingly conservative in his views on Australian politics, but retained a great affection for Ireland. The strange case of O'Donnell's trial for sedition came at a dramatic moment at the end of the Great War. For Ireland, it was not 'war's end', but rather the beginning of a period of repression, rebellion and civil war before an Irish republic was finally achieved.

For Irish-Australians, the war had seen a dramatic rise in sectarian bitterness between Catholics and Protestants.[29] The charismatic Irishman, Archbishop Mannix, had asked the question of where national loyalty lay – with Australia, or with the empire? His linking of the Easter Rising to the issue of conscription, and to the quest for self-determination for small nations at war's end, led for repeated calls in Protestant circles for him to be arrested for sedition. Irish-Australian opinion gradually united behind Mannix, as exemplified in the case of Father O'Donnell, crystallising in a move away from empire loyalty to national sovereignty. At the end of the war, Catholic Irish-Australians were characterised as suspect members of the British Empire, and they would suffer abuse and discrimination over the next decade.

3

THE 1918 ARMISTICE AND THE CIVILIAN EXPERIENCE OF WAR

Bart Ziino

Tuesday was the saddest day I have passed for a long time – the great victory seems to mean so little for me, which to the great bulk of people was so joyful.

Arthur Fry, 14 November 1918

Sydney man Arthur Fry experienced the end of the Great War in a way that might not be immediately familiar to us. He had lost two sons to the war, and the moment of victory did little to alleviate his pain. His story reminds us that this war was fought on the battlefields and in private homes. One of the intriguing things about the Anzac tradition, however, is the way in which it was actively shaping understandings of the war of 1914–18 even as the conflict continued. From the moment of the Gallipoli landings, the cultural work of divining the meaning of war for Australians was refracted through that event. But Anzac's power to shape conceptions of the war was never absolute. Rather did Anzac contend with experiences of the Great War that did not fit easily within a narrative emphasising the achievements and sacrifices occurring at the front. We might think here of the anti-war sentiments articulated by a minority. In a broader sense, however, a civilian experience of war – an experience of extended strain and endurance at home – looms much larger.

The 1918 Armistice and the civilian experience of war

This was a war characterised by a deep interrelationship between fighting at the front and the will to sustain the effort among home populations. Civilians invested in the war carried an enormous burden of anxiety and fear, and they struggled to find the resilience to cope. During the war, Anzac worked to remobilise the civilian population's commitment, through appeals to the achievements of the men at the front. In future, Anzac continued to lionise those achievements, linking them ever more firmly to conceptions of national identity. Civilians' own experiences of war would struggle for recognition within that rubric. So powerful and painful had those experiences been, however, that civilians could not concede their importance entirely in the face of the battlefront. Even as civilians themselves were active in privileging soldiers' experiences over their own, one event permitted widespread expression of their long trial. This was the moment of the Armistice, in November 1918.

The declaration of the Armistice was an occasion on which appeals to the primacy of the Australian soldiers' deeds and character were themselves subordinated to widespread and genuine expressions of relief from the torment and pain that had so defined the war for civilians. This chapter seeks to recover the potency and urgency with which that experience of war surged into public at the moment the fighting stopped. In the streets, and indeed in the nation's parliaments, Australians demonstrated their relief, and at the same time drew attention to the emotional strain so central to their war experience. The intensity of that feeling might have faded quickly from public view, especially as soldiers returned, but it was never entirely subsumed by Anzac. Reminders of that experience emerged in public occasionally, for instance, in women's efforts to have their own sacrifices memorialised, and in September 1939, when a new war prompted Australians to recall their torment of 1914–18 as a sign of what was coming. The terms of public remembering today have, however, tended to submerge civilian experience once again. The Anzac centenary in Australia extended the scope of its commemorations beyond 1918, to encompass other conflicts, but its program struggled to expand the breadth of Australians' understanding of the Great War itself, especially in terms of how the vast bulk of Australians experienced this profoundly difficult event. An analysis of reactions to the Armistice of 1918 offers an opportunity to see more clearly that experience and, perhaps, to reassert its importance in how we contemplate the Great War today.

In November 1918 two sentiments were very much alive in an Australian community that had already been anticipating the end of the war for several weeks. Excitement at the prospect of victory over Germany was certainly one of them. The other was an ongoing anxiety surrounding the fate of loved ones still at the front. For those who felt that anxiety daily, its effects were repressive and debilitating. For over four years, the war at home had pressed itself into Australians' minds; in late 1918 it was no less potent. Thus even as military prospects improved, hopes centred on the survival of loved ones. Sydney woman Isabella Parkes exhibited those priorities in writing to her son at the end of September 1918: 'War news is almost too good to be true – but peace is in sight we are told. When will you be coming marching home laddie'?[1]

Anticipation of the war's end was exciting: it meant that the war these people had so committed themselves to winning would end in victory. But the end of the conflict also meant that loved ones would be safe. When it finally did end, urban and rural Australians alike poured into the streets to mark the occasion as loudly as they could. Just what that behaviour expressed is worth closer examination. This was not simply the exultation of victory. Even as the Melbourne *Age* reported the 'boisterous processions', its reporter noted that '[t]he horror of war had been lifted, the dread days were over, and here was a whole morning, afternoon and night for rejoicing'.[2] This public – and sanctioned – outpouring of emotion was at heart a response to the relief from years of anxiety, fear and longing that finally promised to end.

Given that politicians had been so prominent in extolling the virtues of the Anzacs since 1915, one might expect to find in the nation's various parliaments the most willing reassertion of that rhetoric as the war came to an end. And yet from politicians came some of the most powerful reminders that the experience of the Great War had not been confined to the battlefield, but had engaged entire populations in the emotionally draining effort to sustain the fight. So anticipated was the end to that trial that rumours of an Armistice swirled about persistently for weeks prior. Indeed, the Western Australian parliament thought it had confirmation of the Armistice on 7 November, and its members commenced to make speeches on the subject. In Sydney the following day, the premature reports provoked a major outbreak of celebration in the streets. The news spread largely by virtue of sound: locomotive whistles up and down the train lines, ferries in the harbour and then the noise of the crowds themselves brought other people into the streets. Factory and shop workers walked out, obliging their employers to close for the day, while others emerged from their homes and headed into the city centre.

Inside the New South Wales parliament, members could hear the sounds in the streets, and were chafing to get out, despite the Minister of Public Instruction insisting that no official news had arrived. 'There is absolutely no foundation at present for what is going on in the city', he told the Assembly.[3] Official or not, the news had commenced the release of four years of tension. Members demanded adjournment:

> We are now in a state of excitement. The war has been going on for over four years, and it is in in our minds that it is finished, and you cannot stem that conviction. We are jubilant

at the fact that human life has ceased to be sacrificed, and naturally everyone wants to jubilate.[4]

Observing the mood, the minister conceded, and released members to join the throng outside.

An extraordinary scene confronted them. Crowds and vehicles jammed the streets, producing an overwhelming noise. Social reformer Jessie Street was in its midst: 'every second person had a hooter, bell, rattle, whistle, or some other instrument—were working it for all they were worth. Kerosene tins were never so popular before'.[5] It was not just the noise, but also the feeling in the crowd that drew Street's attention. Where some in authority had expected crowds to misbehave, most accounts emphasised their good temper. They had something for which to be glad. Street insisted that 'it really did you good to see everybody so simply bursting with happiness elderly and staid men and women, grandparents … radiating benevolence and sincerity at everyone'.[6]

Days later Australians repeated those scenes across the country, as official news came to hand. Again, despite that outward excitement, inside the various parliaments we begin to see very quickly the difficulty the nation's leaders had in articulating their feelings, and explaining the meaning of the day. The chauvinism of Anzac offered little guidance: it spoke neither to what civilians had endured, nor to the global scale of events, in which Australia's contribution was relatively small. Some spoke of Gallipoli and its importance. In the Commonwealth parliament, the Minister for Repatriation, Senator Edward Millen, declared that 'this war, amongst other things, has made Australia a nation in a sense that it was not before. It has given us a new conception of national life'.[7] Nevertheless, the tenor of speeches, including Millen's, was very much more about acknowledging that Australians owed greater debts to those who had suffered the war more immediately. In particular this meant Britain, and of course Australians could see themselves as part of the British Empire's success in the war. Acting Prime Minister William Watt declared that while the community was proud to be Australian, 'we are proud, too, and at this time especially, to be Britishers; proud of our blood and our race and of our partnership in the Empire'.[8] But invoking greater debts also meant acknowledging allies like France and Belgium, on whose soil the war had been fought, and the decisive intervention by the United States, even if it took Americans longer than it should have to realise that they 'could no longer stand apart from civilisation and humanity'.[9]

This was why Victoria's Nationalist Premier, Harry Lawson, spoke in terms of 'unbounded gratitude' when the news came.[10] Like other Australians, he recognised that defeat had been a distinct possibility, especially when the Germans made their extraordinary advance in April 1918, pushing the Allies back over the ground they had struggled to win over the previous two years. Victory in this 'stupendous struggle' remained difficult to grasp given how recently the result had been uncertain. 'We feel', said South Australian Premier Archibald Peake, 'that the world has been involved in a tremendous catastrophe, from which it has escaped by the skin of its teeth'.[11] Here was a moment not for boasting, but instead relief and recognition of the event's broadest significance.

In acknowledging how much had been at stake, and how close Britain and its allies had come to defeat, Australia's parliamentarians also found room to acknowledge how painful the experience of war had been. As in the broader community, in all parliaments were members whose sons were at the war. They knew the war not only in its military dimensions, but as an ordeal of waiting and worrying, of constantly fearing the worst. In South Australia's Legislative Council, Liberal member David Gordon had a son in the Australian Flying Corps. Gordon insisted that it had been a 'terrible ordeal' not only for those at the front, 'but for those who have had to endure at home the agonies of suspense'.[12] It could be difficult to articulate one's feelings under the circumstances. Western Australia's leader of the opposition, Philip Collier, certainly struggled to do so:

> I feel that I should like to make a speech, but my feelings are rather of a mixed nature. In fact, I feel that I should like to make a speech; but, on the other hand, I feel utterly unable to make one.[13]

The problem here was not just the scale and importance of the events, but that emotions were entirely mixed, between pride, gratitude, relief and – of course – sorrow, even on the very day of victory. Victoria's Solicitor-General, Arthur Robinson, declared that the end had come to an 'era of doubt and fear, of trembling and hope, of anticipation and triumph, and it leaves us all with feelings so bewildered that we are at present unable to fully realize the stupendous victory which has been achieved'.[14] His political opponent, John Percy Jones, simply declared that 'I do not know how this war has affected honorable members, but it has kept me in a condition of mental agony. I am hardly able to realize even yet that the fearful times through which we have been passing are now over'.[15]

Where they could realise it, speakers commonly spoke of the breaking of daylight after the long period of darkness. New South Wales President of the Legislative Council John Garland declared that 'we have passed through that black dark period – the last four years – when the sun refused to emerge from the blackest of skies, and our hopes had almost been lost, but, thank God, to-day the sun shines again'.[16] That black dark period might have been a time of heroism, but the word was less on the lips of speechmakers than was the pain of those years. They had been years, the conservative politician George Ritchie said in the South Australian Assembly, 'of hard fighting, cruelty, slaughter, broken homes, broken hearts, broken lives, and almost a broken world'.[17] Victorian Labor leader Walter Manifold described it more luridly but no more sincerely as 'a hideous time, a long drawn-out agony of four and a quarter years'.[18] The Armistice had brought that agony to a close, though it could not restore the world as it had once been. Nevertheless, the ardent empire patriot Sir Joseph Carruthers in New South Wales was glad to see the end of the war, as it offered 'some recompense for all the pain, anguish, and suffering one has gone through during the last four years'.[19]

Those on the streets now embraced their first opportunity to cast off some of the restraint that had characterised the war years. While some of that restraint had been externally imposed, for instance in the cancelling of sporting fixtures, or even of the dance season, so much of it had been socially imposed in the face of so much anxiety and loss. People had not felt willing or able to show happiness at a time of so much suffering. As Melbourne woman Jacoba Palstra would put it to her son, the Christmas that followed the Armistice represented 'the first time in years that one dared to be happy and show it too'.[20] Palstra's reticence was based not only on a consideration for others in their suffering: she had two of her own sons serving in France, and well understood what it had meant to endure the war and its precarious line between hope and the desolation of grief. Suddenly, Australians could release the feelings they had so repressed. Standing in the streets, Sydney man William Jones felt it happen. 'In less than an hour', he wrote to his soldier-son the following day, 'the pent up feeling of four years was let loose'.[21] While the poet John le Gay Brereton had seen in the crowd good humour, he was also sensitive to what he called the 'deep feeling' of the event in Sydney. Specifically, he meant 'the relief which had to express itself or burst, and the tense undermood of sorrow for what could be no more. Tears and laughter struggled for pre-eminence in that great day'.[22]

As the Armistice eased emotional restraint in the community, thoughts turned quickly to when loved ones might begin returning home. At the same time, however, there were many who felt awkward about their own relief from the war's torment. They were thinking of those for whom the Armistice eased nothing of their pain, but rather increased their awareness that the war had cost them the lives of their own loved ones. Rose Keast of Broken Hill had suffered terrible anxiety over her son, on service in France and then Mesopotamia. She found in the Armistice 'a much lighter heart'. And yet she was all too aware of those whose loved ones would not be returning. 'After my joy', she told her son,

> I begun to think what this terrible war meant to some just think of the poor mothers that have lost their all there what all this blowing of whistles and ringing bells meant to them it would only make them feel their sorrow more.[23]

For their part, some of the bereaved found vindication for their sacrifice in the Armistice. In Melbourne, Reuben Hallenstein declared it 'a great consolation to even those of us who have lost our dear ones to know that the sacrifice has not been in vain'.[24] Western Australia's Minister for Works, WJ George, had lost a son, but was generous enough to think more of those whose anxiety persisted: '[f]rom them at least the dark pall of sorrow and anxiety has been lifted, and I can rejoice with them that they will see their boys again, although I shall not see mine'.[25]

But Rose Keast was right: there were those who found the Armistice a painful affirmation that their loved ones were not returning, and that the war had robbed them of the future they had anticipated. Sydney parliamentarian George Black saw in the people an undercurrent of emotion that prevented him celebrating the Armistice as he might otherwise have done. '[F]or myself', he said, 'I could not enjoy it ... because of the sadness which I knew was in many hearts. I feel greatly for men and women who have lost those dear to them, for the fathers and mothers who have sent sons to the war who may never return'.[26] In Sydney, Arthur Fry affirmed Black's instincts. Having lost two sons to the war, Fry insisted that the day of the Armistice 'was the saddest day I have passed for a long time – the great victory seems to mean so little for me, which to the great bulk of people was so joyful'. The 'buffoonery' of the celebrations 'hurt a bit', he said, though he understood the need.[27]

If politicians spoke with full hearts across their respective chambers, the divisive politics of the war at home were still much in evidence at the very moment it ended. Victorian Premier Harry Lawson hoped that politicians and the community alike would work to 'remove from public life that discord and bitterness of spirit which have kept us asunder'.[28] But it was too much to hope for. In the federal parliament the antipathies surrounding the conscription issue were still playing out even as senators were offering thanks for the victory. At the end of speeches in favour of sending a congratulatory message to the king, senators sang the national anthem and gave three cheers. Then, on the call of a senator, three cheers for France's Field Marshal Foch; then from Labor Senator Maughan three cheers for 'our volunteer Army'. And from the other side of the chamber, from Maughan's one-time Labor comrade, came a call in response for three cheers for 'The conscript armies of our Allies'.[29]

In the streets, too, those tensions were being felt, as participants divided fellow citizens into those who deserved and those who did not deserve to enjoy the relief and release of the end of the war. Ada Jones told her son that 'those that made the most noise, was the fellows who stayed at home, the returned men as a whole took things very quiet'.[30] Jones probably was not in a position to appreciate that even those who determinedly opposed war could share her sense of relief at its end. Yet the sentiment was certainly shared. Brisbane labour activist Margaret Thorp, for instance, thought that the cessation of hostilities was 'wonderful news' that would mean 'a gloriously happy Xmas for everybody'. In Sydney, Mary Boote – whose estranged husband Henry edited the *Worker* newspaper – joined in ringing bells and blowing whistles, though she distinguished herself from those she saw giving in to patriotic excess, by insisting that 'we're rejoicing because the guns have at last stopped belching murder'.[31]

If such distinctions were lost even in November 1918, perhaps we should not be surprised that civilian experiences of the war itself largely yielded before an idea of the war that emphasised soldiers and their achievements. Of course, civilian experiences of the war were not simply forgotten. Communities of remembrance formed, by which to assert the value of one's experiences and especially one's sacrifices. Joy Damousi and Tanja Luckins have each shown how various groups – especially women – sought to have their particular sacrifices recognised in public. They found that the failure of women's sacrifices to endure in public memory of the war produced efforts to reassert the legitimacy of their experience. Their efforts could be fuelled as much by anger and resentment at their own neglect as by their determination to remember those whom the war had taken from them.[32] In this way, a civilian experience of war could find expression, though as Luckins observes, any sense in which civilians might be seen to be memorialising their own experiences of loss, as opposed to the sacrifices of soldiers, could attract criticism.[33] Sanctioned space opened again, however, as Hannah Muirhead has shown, when the outbreak of a second world war in September 1939 provoked public recall of experiences of enduring its predecessor. As the Red Cross established new branches, for instance, its leadership emphasised not only the achievement of the organisation between 1914 and 1918, but also recalled the difficulty of that period.

The 1918 Armistice and the civilian experience of war

Muirhead quotes 'Miss Midnight's' advice from her aunt in the September 1939 *Australian Women's Weekly*:

> It doesn't do any good just sitting about worrying, and it's much better for everybody to go about as cheerfully as possible. And Aunt Julia should know because she admits she remembers the Great War.[34]

Aunt Julia's memory owed little to what the Anzac tradition might say about 1914–18; the recrudescence of war in 1939 opened a space in which civilian memories of war once again achieved legitimacy, even if they would be subsumed once again beneath the events of 1939–45.

If total war is characterised by the integral relationship between the home and battlefronts, remembering it has been characterised by a much more exclusive emphasis on the battlefront. A whole other experience of war, linked to the battlefield but not of the battlefield, has receded, where once, if briefly, its magnitude had been on show to all. Just as news of the Armistice drew a multitude of people into Australian streets in November 1918, so were their responses to the end of the war much more complex than the joyful faces appearing in the illustrated papers suggested. As much as the Armistice was the instrument of victory over Germany, it was also the sign that a long confrontation with fear and anxiety in Australia was coming to an end. Where Australians had so often fought that war in the seclusion of private homes, or in small supportive groups, the Armistice brought those people into public to express their relief, and to begin to expend what one observer called 'the war-strickened-nervous energy of the people'.[35] That first Armistice Day in Australia revealed just how deeply the war had become part of everyday existence, and the profound relief Australians felt that its presence might soon begin to recede. Indeed the Armistice produced a rather singular moment, which exposed the nationalist rhetoric of Anzac as inadequate in capturing the meaning of the event to those who had experienced the war at home. Our sense of the enormity and uniqueness of that war experience for civilians has similarly receded; without it we risk a too shallow understanding of the roots of our own commemoration of the trauma of 1914–18.

4

BRINGING THE AIF HOME: THE ORGANISATION OF REPATRIATION 1918–19

Meleah Hampton

> It is a gross, but common, error to imagine that Demobilisation commences when the smoke of the boats conveying troops appears on the horizon just outside the territorial limits of Australia.
>
> *AWM 4/30/1/1 Pt. 1, 'Report by the Director of Education AIF as to the Manner in which the AIF Education Service is Affected by Repatriation and Demobilisation,' n.d.*

This statement is as true today as when it was written towards the end of the First World War. Australia had been transporting men and materiel to Egypt and Europe since late 1914, but the work of sending the AIF home was not a case of simply taking a well-oiled system of shipping men and materiel overseas and turning it in reverse. In fact, in some ways the end of the war saw as much global upheaval as the conflict itself, and this would delay the return of many Australians for months. Fortunately for those Australians whose thoughts turned to home as the guns fell silent on 11 November 1918, AIF authorities were well aware of the difficulties ahead, and had long been preparing for the complicated process of sending troops home. Pre-Armistice preparations were heavily predicated on the requirements of the Australian nation, and fears over reintegrating a large glut of men into Australian society and employment. However, within weeks of the signing of the Armistice, the requirements of the men themselves were given more importance by the new head of repatriation, Lieutenant General Sir John Monash. This change in focus led to one of the smoothest demobilisation and repatriation processes of all of the dominion forces.

By late 1918, there were an estimated 87 000 Australian soldiers in France and Belgium, with a further 63 000 in the United Kingdom, many of those in hospitals or convalescent homes, and another 17 000 in Egypt, Syria and other minor theatres of war.[1] But more than just combatants, a considerable number of Australian men who had volunteered to go to England to work in munitions factories would be eligible for repatriation. Hundreds of nurses were serving abroad from France and Belgium to England, India and South Africa. Australian soldiers and munition workers were marrying English wives at an estimated rate of 200 per month – a number that was only expected to increase with the cessation of hostilities – and the wives were having children. In fact, estimates of the number of Australians requiring repatriation varied from 150 000 to 200 000 at various times.

But Australia was not alone in seeking to bring its citizens home. Every dominion of the British Empire had sent large contingents of men who had to be returned to Canada, South Africa, India and New Zealand. The French, too, had called on manpower from their old colonial networks, with nearly half a million men from west and north Africa sent to European fronts over the course of the war. The United States had as many as four million troops in Europe by 1918. There was a huge labour force from Asia and Africa that needed to be returned, and thousands of prisoners of war and refugees travelling home. After the war, French and Belgian roads and railways became so congested with traffic that travel was slow and difficult, even more so the closer the roads and railways were to significant ports. There was not enough shipping in the world to move the millions of people where they needed to go in a short time frame. This was the global situation that the Australian government and the AIF faced in their quest to get their men home as soon as possible.

There had been conversations around repatriation almost as long as there had been contingents being sent overseas. Three main aspects of the process of returning men to Australia were widely recognised, generally referred to as repatriation, demobilisation and rehabilitation: 'repatriation', referring specifically to the logistics of the return; 'demobilisation', the process of reducing the force through men leaving the military; and 'rehabilitation' or 'rehabituation', the process of individuals being reinstated in civil life. Australia is alone among the English-speaking nations in using the word 'repatriation' to refer to all three of these different aspects. From as early as 1916 it was obvious to many in both the upper echelons of the AIF and Australia's federal and state governments, that postwar repatriation was going to be an extremely complicated task. In their approaches to the problem of repatriation, the military and the government formed two sides of the same coin, as it were, with the military of necessity having more focus on the process of shifting the men home, and the government more on what would happen once they arrived. However, for some time the government's priorities were ascendant, and emphasis was placed firmly on the needs of the Australian nation, even in the limited military planning that could take place before the war ended.

In late 1917 it was deemed necessary to appoint an officer to coordinate the various suggestions for repatriation systems, and in February 1918 Major Guy Sherington was given the role of Staff Officer (Repatriation and Demobilisation). He began with a small but growing staff in London, and within six months had produced a 'Basic Definite Policy' on the repatriation process. Because there was no end in sight to the war (despite it only having a few months to run), Sherington struggled to get the fixed answers from government departments that would allow him to form more than a few basic policies. However, where he could not develop detailed policy, Sherington identified questions that needed to be answered by the Australian government in order to proceed. As far as possible, the Repatriation and Demobilisation Section formed a solid foundation for quick action once it was confirmed that the AIF would be going home.

On the most practical level, the Repatriation and Demobilisation Section had to negotiate the delicate shipping situation in order to win enough ships to send everyone home. The British Ministry of Shipping was responsible for the relevant lanes of transport to Australia, and in a series of Imperial Conferences gave Australian authorities a pre-Armistice undertaking of returning 200 000 AIF troops to Australia within nine months, that is, at a rate of 5000 per week.[2] This was a generous offer given the vastness of the undertaking about to befall the Ministry of Shipping, and Sherington impressed upon Prime Minister Billy Hughes and the commanding officer of AIF Headquarters in London, Brigadier General Dodds, that 'all other Dominions are endeavouring to force the hands of the Ministry of Shipping and secure more ships. For the present we also should do so'.[3] However, it was secretly felt by many in government that 5000 per week might prove to be too many returnees at once to be comfortably absorbed by the Australian nation. Despite their only having been absent from Australia for four or five years at most, the tens of thousands of men set to return in a block had the potential to cause serious damage to both the economy and existing rehabituation systems in Australia. Their use of shipping also threatened to seriously disrupt the amount of regular cargo space to and from

Bringing the AIF home: The organisation of repatriation 1918–19

Australia, as well as the normal process of immigration. Sherington was reluctant to do anything to lessen the undertaking, however, which is why he advised the government to keep the Ministry of Shipping to its word. Once shipping had been allocated to Australia, he wrote, 'we could if necessary put the break [sic] on the volume of troops returning and thus gain an increased cargo space in lieu of troop deck space relinquished'.[4] Throughout 1919 the process of securing shipping was one of constant negotiation. Ernest Scott, the author of the Australian official history volume devoted to the home front, noted drily that 'the Ministry of Shipping knew a surprising number of polite synonyms for "it can't be done at present"',[5] and having too much space made available to repatriating Australians never became the problem it was feared it would be. Much of this negotiation was done at regular Imperial Conferences with representatives of all of the dominions.

Even while Sherington was able to fend off the worries of the Australian government in order to protect the interests of its soldiers, in most cases he functioned within the concerns and policies of the government as his main priority. These domestic concerns largely framed the way the problem of returning the AIF was approached by the Repatriation and Demobilisation Section before the Armistice. In accordance with government preference, Sherington's office was a strong advocate of a systematic return by employment status. For many months, the intention was to organise repatriation with priority granted first to married soldiers (graded according to their length of service, their number of children and their future employment prospects), then to single soldiers with guaranteed employment, and third, other single soldiers in accordance to length of service.[6] It was strongly suggested that rather than return men by unit, each state should be given a weekly allotment of returnees to keep the process as even as possible. New South Wales, with the highest population, was unofficially advertised to receive 1050 men each week; Victoria,

810; Queensland, 420; Western Australia, 300; South Australia, 270; and Tasmania, 150. Australia's needs would further be put first in the order it was proposed that men of various trades return, so that primary producers would precede manufacturers and so on. The strangely specific example given was that 'a soldier employed at the Lithgow Iron Works rolling sheet iron should be returned to Australia before a soldier employed in manufacturing buckets from raw material which is secured from the Lithgow Iron Works'.[7]

For someone whose primary aim was to take an armed force from one continent to another, Major Sherington spent a lot of time pondering the impact of repatriation on domestic matters such as the Australian economy. Australia had a large war debt, and it was thought that, if done carefully, it would be possible to expand the economy with this newly returned workforce, juggling it with expected ongoing shortages of raw materials due to shipping problems, to successfully repay the war debt as soon as possible.[8] Sherington's 'Definite Basic Policy' openly stated it hoped to contribute to an overall plan that avoided 'displacing thousands of women who have entered the industrial life of Australia to make good the loss of production due to enlistment for service overseas' by taking their jobs and giving them to returned soldiers, and expanding the economy to repay the debt.[9] Given that so many factors on a grand scale constantly threatened to complicate proceedings, the fact that the Repatriation and Demobilisation Section was able to make headway in their plans at all was remarkable.

It should be noted that even as Sherington and his office had struggled through issues of global and national importance, they had at the same time been quite aware that the men would need to be occupied while awaiting a passage home. In June 1918, George Long, serving as an Anglican chaplain in the AIF, was appointed director of education and given a small staff to organise training courses for returning Australian soldiers. Long had been largely responsible for the founding of Trinity Grammar School in Melbourne at the turn of the century, and was a tireless advocate of education of all kinds. Understanding the potential disaster that tens of thousands of bored men presented, and despite his limited staff, Long produced a startling array of options to fulfil his obligations. Australian soldiers gained access to courses through British and European universities or other technical institutions. Men could be sent around Europe to gain experience in anything from new paediatric surgical techniques to the Danish wool trade. They could study the arts, law, medicine, engineering, agriculture, commerce, mechanics, artisanal trades, history, geography, mathematics, literature and physics. The educational program was strongly supported by both AIF authorities and the Australian government because not only did it provide something for the men to do, but it equipped them for their move back into civilian life, and gave them confidence in themselves for their return. By any measure, the Education Section was an enormous success. By early 1920, nearly 13 000 soldiers and nurses had completed courses, and thousands more had participated in part-time study or were working towards completing their course.

The other large-scale scheme used to keep men occupied was, of course, sport. Sports of all kinds had been a part of the life of the men of the AIF for the entirety of their enlistment, with competitions held between battalions, brigades and divisions in a variety of sports at different times. Even before the Armistice had been signed there had been moves made to hold an Army Boxing Championship Tournament between the various armed forces of Britain, the dominions and the United States. However, the Repatriation and Demobilisation Section did little to formalise sports competition in the manner of education until after the Armistice. At that point, the AIF dramatically increased the sports available to its men, with Major Sydney Middleton, a well-known international rugby footballer and Olympic oarsman in his pre-war life, appointed to begin organising sport up to corps level. In January 1919 the AIF Sports Control Board was formed, with Middleton as its secretary, to continue to organise, and fund, sporting activity of almost any kind as far as was possible. It was well known that 'almost anything that would take the place of drill would have been welcomed'.[10] Sports officers were soon appointed at every level from company to corps, and if there was enough interest in a particular sport, the Sports Section would facilitate a competition in it. Competitions were held between platoons, companies, battalions, brigades, divisions and corps. The Allied forces boasted many famous pre-war sportsmen in their ranks, and opportunities opened up to hold international competitions around Europe. Australian boxers competed against Canadians in Brussels; AIF rugby teams played the French in Paris. The Royal Henley Peace Regatta in July 1919 saw one of two AIF teams, with Syd Middleton a crewmember, win the King's Cup against teams from Oxford and Cambridge Universities, France, Canada, New Zealand and others. At all levels, men were occupied with playing or following competitions in rugby, golf, boxing, tennis, athletics, shooting, rowing, cricket and swimming, among many others.

The war ended with an Armistice on 11 November 1918. While it was not necessarily clear at the time how permanent this peace would be, the Australian Imperial Force was so badly depleted by months of hard fighting that it was disbanding battalions. It was at this point that the focus of the Repatriation and Demobilisation Section of the AIF changed. On 20 November 1918, nine days after the Armistice was signed, the commanding officer of the Australian Corps, Lieutenant General Sir John Monash, took up a position in direct liaison with the Ministry for Defence with the intent to organise the repatriation of the AIF. Almost immediately the focus of those planning the process changed. Monash asked his officers to:

try to envisage the psychology of the man in the ranks today. He now has a confused and uncertain outlook. No one has yet spoken to him with any sense of definiteness. He asks 'what is going to happen? Are we going to Germany? If not, why don't they send us home?' etc. There is a general feeling of uncertainty and unrest among the men, and, every day that passes while that feeling of uncertainty and unrest continues, the men are slowly, from the psychological point of view, slipping from our grasp.[11]

Monash was a shrewd judge of men and turned his focus onto those under his command in order to make the extended process of repatriation go as smoothly as possible. He said, 'we have to begin by creating a morale throughout the AIF, a morale, which for want of a better word, I will call the "reconstruction morale" … that is to say, an attitude of mind on the part of every man as regards his future duties to himself, to his family and to his country'.[12] Whereas the welfare of the men going home had been a secondary, if important, consideration in repatriation plans, it was now to become the absolute priority. This was supported by Prime Minister Hughes, who refused to hear anxious talk of too many men returning at once. Instead, he fully backed 'repatriation at the maximum rate'.[13] Monash adopted an open policy, saying it was the responsibility of both he and his officers to tell the troops 'all we possibly can as to the elements of the problems, as to the probable course that events will take, and as to what we hope in the course of time to be able to do for them'.[14] Whereas Sherington had had the needs of the Australian nation at the forefront of his planning, Monash only saw the more immediate problem of tens of thousands of potentially unhappy Australian soldiers cooling their heels waiting for a passage home.

Both the education and sports efforts of the AIF were mirrored by similar schemes in the British and Canadian armies, among almost all others. They were extremely successful at keeping men occupied, fit and mentally content to at least some degree, and were strongly supported and expanded by John Monash. Nevertheless, rioting and unrest among the hundreds of thousands of young men awaiting repatriation all over Europe was a constant threat in the months following the end of the war. In March 1919, Canadian troops at Kinmel Park in Bodelwyddan, North Wales, rioted over delays in repatriation and sub-standard conditions in their staging camp there. The Canadians suffered at least another 12 instances of serious unrest over general issues of dissatisfaction while awaiting repatriation in 1918 and 1919, which resulted in a number of men being killed, wounded and convicted of mutiny. British and French forces, too, dealt with unrest despite widespread efforts to keep their men busy during the repatriation process. The primary difference with the AIF seems to stem from the open communication advocated by John Monash on his appointment to liaison between the AIF and the Australian government, his focus on the welfare of his men, and his ability to create the perception that above all else the process was 'fair'.

One of Monash's most famous innovations was his insistence that men be returned to Australia on a 'first come, first go' basis. Anzac 'originals' – those who had served on Gallipoli and had survived the Western Front – were already on their way home for Australia leave. Australian soldiers who had been unable to spend their leave at home simply because of the distance were, after up to four years' service, being sent back to Australia for an extended period of leave. Also known as 'Anzac leave' or 'home leave', Australia leave was expected to be temporary, with the soldier returning to the war after a period of months. But with the war over, of course they would be able to stay in Australia. Even though circumstances had changed, and the temporary Australia leave program would be replaced with permanent repatriation, Monash had no intention of disrupting the expectations of those who thought of themselves to be the next eligible for home leave.

A few thousand Australians took the opportunity to be discharged from the military in the United Kingdom – among them Syd Middleton – although the Australian government was reluctant to allow them to do so. But the vast majority waited their turn for weeks and months in the United Kingdom, Belgium, France, Egypt and Palestine. Changing the process to sending these men home by occupation or marital status ran the very real risk of sparking complaints of 'unfairness' that in turn would lead to unrest. Monash kept everybody awaiting repatriation well appraised of the difficulties involved in the process of returning them home, and in return his men rewarded him with a relative lack of insubordination. Monash's 'reconstruction morale' ideal was created among the young men to enough of a degree that they remained manageable throughout the months of their long wait to return home. They engaged with the locals near their camps, attended cinemas and theatres, travelled throughout Britain if they wanted to, studied their courses, played sport, and often enough, complained mightily about the entire process, as soldiers are wont to do. But on the whole, they had enough faith in a system that was set up to serve them as well as possible, and fine-tuned to their needs, problems and sense of fairness, to maintain order, and wait their turn.

By February 1920, there were no more than 3243 serving members of the AIF in the United Kingdom, with a few more scattered around Europe. Just 3000 soldiers, wives and dependants were still awaiting repatriation. Finally, accurate numbers could be determined, with records showing that 149 969 men had embarked on the six-week voyage to Australia, with another 1104 nurses and 16 626 wives and dependants repatriated.[15] To emphasise the difficulty this posed for the Ministry of Shipping, the movement of this many men, women and children took 176 voyages, which they were forced to share between 137 different ships. Of course, in Australia 'repatriation' means more than moving people from one place to another. In parallel with this military operation of repatriation, Australian authorities were working to set in place 'domestic repatriation' policies, procedures and institutions – the work of 'rehabituation' or 'rehabilitation'. The work of these departments would continue for decades, as indeed it does for new generations of veterans as the Department of Veterans' Affairs.

It is hard to overestimate the difficulty of bringing the AIF back to Australia from where it had been fighting in Europe and the Middle East. This was a process involving the movement of tens of thousands of young men, their bags, their weapons and their dependants. It had the potential to disrupt the entire Australian economy if done poorly. It had to be negotiated through a world torn asunder by war, along railways and shipping lines that simply did not have enough space for the vast numbers of people hoping to use them. Everywhere were people longing to return to the relative normality of their pre-war lives, from refugees to farmers to ex-servicemen and women, with Australian soldiers asked to wait patiently among the impatient hordes for their turn. And while initial preparations for repatriation were focused clearly on the needs of the Australian nation, those in charge of the process following the Armistice in 1918, notably John Monash, could see that the needs of the men would be of far more importance in the short term. Measures such as the education and sports sections of the Repatriation Department abroad helped impatient young men to pass the months and prepare for their return. But among the most important shifts in focus following the Armistice was Monash's policy of openness and honesty with his charges. By scrupulously observing the soldiers' need to see 'fairness' in the system, and by being frank about the difficulties being faced, the Australians suffered far less insubordination and unrest than other nations, and managed to negotiate the difficulties of repatriation particularly successfully. For tens of thousands of young men who had experienced the horrors of war, this was as good a preparation for the difficult years to come as they could hope for.

5

THE VETERAN CHALLENGE: REPATRIATION BENEFITS FOR AUSTRALIAN SOLDIERS

Martin Crotty

As the guns fell silent on the Western Front in November 1918, the Allied powers and their soldiers and sailors could regard with relief and satisfaction the winning of a major challenge. For all the blundering and wastage, for all the carnage and tragedy, at an horrific cost and yet a little earlier than many had anticipated, victory had been won. It had taken four years and cost millions of lives, but the Great War was over. Germany and its allies were defeated.

But the First World War had no tidy end, no moment when the switch could be flicked back to the 'normality' of mid-1914. Peace negotiations were long, messy and often bitter. War continued between the Tsarist and Red armies in Russia, revolutions spread through the defeated powers, and new states struggled into existence – often violently. The Armistice of November 1918 and the Treaty of Versailles, signed in June 1919, concluded the major armed stoush in Europe, but spawned others.

Even countries that emerged victorious faced major problems and challenges. War economies struggled to revert to peacetime operations, and many entered recessions in the early 1920s. Civil rights that had been suspended for the duration were largely restored, but it was a haphazard and at times incomplete process. Wartime hatreds and hostilities towards former enemies lessened but did not disappear entirely, as did the wartime divisions within combatant nations. Governments faced mountains of debt, a new and uncertain international environment, and fresh problems at home.

Veterans and reintegration

Not the least of the post-war challenges was how to bring home and reintegrate the millions who had been welcomed, cajoled or forced into uniform. Governments were well aware of the many precedents of returned soldiers behaving in an unruly fashion, and their potential to make trouble. These were, after all, young men who had been instructed in how to use weapons, who had become accustomed to violence, and indeed taught that it was a legitimate means to an end. In the Australian case, there were still around 150 000 soldiers overseas when the Armistice was signed.[1] Among Australia's veteran population were hundreds who had been blinded, thousands who had lost a leg or an arm, tens of thousands who suffered the effects of gunshot wounds, and tens of thousands more suffering a range of other war-induced physical ailments.[2] Less quantifiable, but perhaps even more numerous, were those suffering a degree of psychological injury, ranging from debilitating 'shell shock' to milder forms of moral and mental damage. Even if most of those who returned were, superficially at least, relatively 'normal', tens of thousands were not. Most Australian soldiers were forever shaped and marked, and in many cases profoundly damaged, by their war experiences.

If the nations attempting to reintegrate veterans faced enormous challenges, so too did the veterans themselves. It was at the point of demobilisation that the men who had actually fought the wars assumed a degree of commonality. Their war experiences had all been different, often dramatically so. Some had fought at sea, others at high altitude in what were then cutting-edge aircraft. Some had fought in the heat and sand of Arabia, and others in the mud of the Western Front – and a great many had barely fought at all, serving instead in logistics, training and intelligence. Most were privates; some were officers. Some had fought for years, others for weeks. Their war experiences were diverse and variegated, and no two were exactly the same.

And yet, when the war ended and the time came for demobilisation, Australian servicemen – like soldiers, sailors and airmen the world over – all faced essentially the same questions. What would they do for work? How, if they needed it, would they receive more training and education? Where would they live? Who would tend to their wounds and their mental scarring? How would they make up the lost time, time spent in the services when they would otherwise have been advancing their education and careers, and starting families? How would they resume these and all of the other peacetime activities that they had put on hold?

This was a difficult set of challenges for veterans, regardless of which nation or empire they had fought for. Soldiers returned to societies that were weary if not exhausted and, in some cases, totally devastated by their war efforts. They had to dust off old skills, look up old acquaintances, contact former employers, adjust their manners and habits, and make their way in a peacetime world that was far removed from life in the armed forces. The mass citizen armies that fought the First World War ensured that they had plenty of fellow travellers, and that they could potentially organise into powerful collectives. But fellow veterans also competed for jobs, housing and other scarce resources.

Many Australian veterans struggled with the challenge, and lived much-diminished lives afterwards. They suffered from increased mortality, higher than average rates of unemployment, post-traumatic stress disorder (PTSD) or 'nerves' as it was then known, war-related wounds and other ailments that required ongoing attention, from haunting dreams and restlessness to an inability to settle. These veterans are not honoured for having sacrificed their lives – for the good reason that they did not. They are not recalled on memorials or rolls of honour as part of Australia's toll of 60 000 dead. But they – and in many cases their families – were nonetheless among the casualties of war.[3]

While damaged veterans have long-appeared in representations of the war – such as Leonard Mann's novel *Flesh in Armour* (1932), George Johnston's *My Brother Jack* (1964) and Roger McDonald's *1915* (1979) – they have become noticeably more visible over the past four decades. Returned soldiers are now more likely to be portrayed as victims who are troubled by their war service, than as proud warriors who have been enlarged by it. Indeed, as historian Christina Twomey has shown, the idea of the traumatised veteran has since become central to Anzac mythology.[4] The damaged veteran has also been the subject of much historical research. Marina Larsson, for example, has examined the burden borne by veterans' families, and Elizabeth Nelson has written about inter-war domestic violence.[5]

Australian treatment in an international context

While the trope of the traumatised veteran has powerful cultural cachet, it is important to consider the experience of returned soldiers in light of the evidence. When considered in an international context, it becomes clear that if Australian veterans had a difficult time settling back into peacetime, it was not for a lack of trying on the part of their government and compatriots. While no amount of government assistance or community appreciation could completely accommodate all the challenges that soldiers faced upon demobilisation, the Australian national government arguably offered its veterans more support than any other country.

Australian ideas about service provision and care for veterans evolved rapidly. It was initially assumed that the private and charitable sectors would provide most of the services returned soldiers required, but as enlistment numbers and the length of deployment increased, it was clear that the state would have to accept the burden. The Commonwealth government accepted the primary role in all fields except soldier settlement (a joint Commonwealth and state enterprise) and established the Repatriation Department in 1918. At the behest of veterans and their representative organisation, the Returned Sailors' and Soldiers' Imperial League of Australia (RSSILA, forerunner of the RSL), this evolved into a Repatriation Commission, which began operation in 1920. The 'Repat' attended to the administration of most of the schemes affecting returned soldiers. In its day-to-day activities it operated at arm's length from government, and some of the Repatriation Commissioners were men appointed from a list provided by the RSSILA.[6]

By late 1919, as the rush of Australian veterans returning home was ending, the pattern of benefits available to returned soldiers and their dependants was taking its essential shape, although additions were made during the inter-war period. Through the Repatriation Commission, the War Service Homes Commission and other agencies, the Australian government offered a wide range of benefits as compensation and reward for the sacrifices and achievements of Australian soldiers. Veterans could receive housing in the form of war service homes; they could purchase the homes at discounted prices, sign up to home loans at discounted interest rates and receive grants to furnish their homes. In terms of work, the government offered an extensive system of vocational training, grants for tools and starting businesses, and preference in appointments to (and promotions in) the public service. Health care was available for war-related maladies free of charge through repatriation hospitals, while those who suffered from ongoing ailments that could not be cured received pensions – as did those who were dependent on disabled soldiers, and those dependent on soldiers who were killed. Veterans received further material reward in the form of a war gratuity, payable at one shilling and sixpence per day for overseas service, and one shilling a day for the time that they were in Australia. For those who enlisted early this could amount to a considerable sum of money. Crucially, returned soldiers received ritual recognition and praise, especially on Anzac Day when they were hailed as heroes who had given birth to the Australian nation. They were also recognised on war memorials, rolls of honour, and through the badges and medals that displayed their claim to superior civic status.[7]

'Repat' benefits were far more generous than those available to people in civilian life who faced similar challenges after, for example, industrial accidents. Historian Stephen Garton has gone so far as to call this a system of 'welfare apartheid' – one system of benefits and compensation for veterans, and another, inferior one, for everyone else. War pensions were completely non-means tested and liberal in terms of eligibility, with no time-limit imposed on claims. From the early 1930s, generous appeal mechanisms for both eligibility and pension rate were introduced. It is a reflection of the system's relative munificence that the number of pensioners increased significantly during the inter-war period. By 1938 the cost of the repatriation system amounted to just under one-fifth of the entire Commonwealth government's budget.[8]

The Australian repatriation system was much more generous than those available in comparable countries. The Australian pension rate for a 100 per cent disability was, with allowances for a standard family, close to the average wage. It was substantially less in places like Britain where, even though the base rate was higher, there was little to no allowance for the cost of supporting dependants. British veterans had a much tougher time getting pensions, dependants even more so, and they were forced to rely on charity to a much greater extent than Australians. Canadian and New Zealand veterans appear to have been better treated than their British counterparts, but not so generously as Australians, while American veterans were considerably worse off, with meagre benefits for the disabled, and almost nothing for everyone else.[9]

Explaining veteran success

Why did Australian veterans do better than comparable groups? Fellow historian Mark Edele and I considered this question at some length several years ago. We looked at the different outcomes for Soviet and Australian veterans after the two world wars (the Soviet veterans received almost nothing until decades later), and distilled a number of factors that shaped positive veteran outcomes. We surmised that those who had volunteered had a stronger claim to benefits than those who had been conscripted, for the moral claim upon men to enlist should, one would expect, be matched with the moral claim to reward services voluntarily given. We proposed that victors would normally be better rewarded as they had achieved the desired goal, and that veterans would be more likely to be generously compensated the more their suffering and sacrifice exceeded that of those who did not serve. Outside the circumstances of the conflict, we suggested that unified veterans' movements, a democratic political system where veterans could exercise power at the ballot box, fear of unruly or even revolutionary veterans, and the availability of financial and other resources were the major elements of the matrix of factors that determined whether or not veterans were well rewarded and compensated.

We argued that all of these factors ran in favour of Australian veterans after the First World War. They were volunteers who had won – who had given birth to the nation according to official and much popular rhetoric – whereas civilians on the home front had

The veteran challenge: Repatriation benefits for Australian soldiers

faced no substantial danger and had sacrificed relatively little. Prime Minister Billy Hughes needed the returned soldiers as a voting bloc to support his shaky Nationalist government, and the diggers were unruly enough, often enough, to suggest that they might resort to violence if they did not get what they sought. Further, they had a powerful veterans' organisation in the form of the RSSILA.

The terms upon which Australian returned men could stake their claims for monetary and other compensation were vastly different from, for example, the veterans of Russian Tsarist armies. The Russians were conscripts who had been defeated, the civilian population had suffered terribly, and upon its withdrawal from the First World War, the country was engaged in bloody civil war for several years. At the end of the civil war, Tsarist Army veterans were seeking benefits from a totalitarian government they had not fought for, which owed them nothing, and which had virtually nothing to give them in any case. Russian and Australian veterans of the First World War received vastly different responses to their claims upon the state because they ventured those claims in almost exactly opposite circumstances.[10]

When Mark Edele and I brought in a co-author, Neil Diamant, for a book on global veteran outcomes, and widened our research to look at a range of other cases following the two world wars, we found some interesting outcomes.[11] Firstly, Australian veterans after the First World War retained their position, in our opinion, as the best looked-after veterans in the age of total war, although they are possibly equalled by American veterans following the Second World War, who had the benefits of what became known as the GI Bill of Rights.[12]

However, we also found plenty of cases of veterans being well looked after despite many among our matrix of factors running against them. Take the case of German veterans. They fought on the losing side in both world wars and had an appalling track record of immoral behaviour in the Second World War, especially. Their comparative sacrifice was diminished by the suffering of German civilians, and they had to appeal to regimes other than those that sent them to war after both 1918 and 1945. And yet Germans were better catered for than British veterans, who received comparatively miserable treatment after both world wars, despite being on the winning side. Germans also did better than American veterans after the First World War and Russian veterans after the Second World War, both of whom received next to nothing for many years.[13]

What we eventually concluded was that nothing mattered so much as the ability of the returned soldiery to exert influence and pressure on post-war governments, and the government's willingness and readiness to respond. Volunteer status, winning, the relativities of soldier versus civilian sacrifice, and moral debt were useful when the returned soldiers metaphorically or literally sat down with governments to hammer out a deal, but they were peripheral. Political connection and power trumped all else.

It was the constant lobbying and pressuring of the American Legion and the Veterans of Foreign Wars which eventually resulted in the GI Bill in the United States. It was the inability of Russian veterans to organise and the totalitarian nature of the Soviet government that meant that they got very little. The Weimar Republic's well-justified fear of German veterans resulted in generous benefits. British veterans felt cheated by the insipid lobbying of the British Legion, which was slow to organise and too wedded to the sources of power to press the case for veterans forcefully.[14]

It was, ultimately, the work of the RSSILA that secured the best possible outcomes for Australian veterans. The RSSILA was an impressive organisation. It was founded earlier than any of its overseas counterparts, in mid-1916. It secured mass membership, so that at the time of the most crucial negotiations with the government, it had almost half of the returned soldiers in its ranks. It formulated clear and generally defensible demands, and lobbied for them insistently. It was well connected to government, but never captured by it. In crucial negotiations in late 1919, the RSSILA tantalised Hughes with hints of political support, but never compromised itself and never delivered that support. And it threatened and occasionally employed violence. More than any other veterans' organisation, the RSSILA operated intelligently, ruthlessly and persistently, and as a consequence it secured a repatriation deal for Australian veterans that was better than that of any other combatant nation in the First World War.[15]

Conclusion

None of this is to deny that veterans often found it difficult to return to civilian life, for governments could never answer all of the challenges that a veteran faced after demobilisation. But three crucial realities need to be borne in mind.

Firstly, the Australian government and Australian community did thank, honour, reward and compensate Australia's returned soldiers – to an extent unmatched by any other belligerent country at the time. Doubtless more could have been done, but any suggestion that Australian veterans returned home to an uncaring nation should be rejected.

Secondly, most veterans benefited greatly from this. Most transitioned relatively peacefully back into civilian life, and that they did is a testament both to them and to the Australia that welcomed them home. For every damaged and dysfunctional veteran, there were many more who found a way to cope. Some may have suffered in only minor ways, and many more probably enhanced their skills, confidence and maturity through their wartime experiences.

And thirdly, we need to acknowledge that nothing could be done for many veterans. There was a feckless and ill-disciplined element in the returned soldier population, as there was in the Australian Imperial Force, as has been well established.[16] But for all the others, for all of those who could never settle despite their best efforts, or could never be rehabilitated physically and mentally, or who lashed out in uncharacteristic and inexplicable violence, or who drank themselves into stupors to dull their minds, or who committed suicide – they are the historical proof that war's damage can never really, no matter what efforts are made, be made good. So many of the survivors lived diminished or truncated lives despite their own best efforts and despite the best efforts of the government and the country that sent them to war. Some things were just beyond repair.

6

AUSTRALIAN NAVAL ACTIVITIES IN THE PACIFIC AT THE END OF THE GREAT WAR

David Sutton

The missions of HMAS *Fantome* and HMAS *Encounter*, both carried out at the end of the First World War, provide snapshots of an Australia seeking to simultaneously assert itself in its region and remain a steadfast agent of the British Empire.

HMAS *Fantome*

In early October 1918, two companies of Australian servicemen pushed forward to take up a commanding position overlooking their military target, a small village nestled in remote countryside. The Australians, armed with rifles and two belt-fed Maxim machine-guns, saw their well-armed enemy surround the town on the ridges opposite. Just before 10.30 am Captain John Francis Robins ordered the Australians to open fire. It was a crushing Australian victory.

This scene could describe any number of small engagements in France and Belgium during the Great War. It occurred, however, on 6 October 1918, one day after the battle of Montbrehain, Australia's last infantry battle on the Western Front. It took place not in France, but in the New Hebrides, today's Vanuatu, against native tribesmen on the island of Malekula.[1]

The Australian companies were from the Royal Australian Navy (RAN) sloop HMAS *Fantome*, which since 1917 had been conducting patrol duties in the western Pacific. *Fantome*'s mission began in late September 1918 when the French High Commissioner reported to the British consul in Noumea that a French planter named Meglia had been murdered on a remote island of the New Hebrides. It was apparently a revenge killing by an aggrieved chief who had sworn to kill three white men (though the cause of his grief remains unknown), and the murder was enough for the colonial authorities to decide that '[e]xemplary punishment [was] necessary [in the] interests of Europeans frequenting [the] Island'.[2] British and French colonial claims over the New Hebrides had been something of a heated subject in Australian politics for decades, and it was only in the lead-up to the Great War that the two European powers began to see each other as colonial allies rather than rivals in the Pacific. By 1918, the New Hebrides fell under an ill-defined arrangement of joint British and French rule.[3]

In the early hours of 6 October, a landing party of 65 officers and ratings of the *Fantome*, six French settlers and 18 armed native guides landed on the west coast of Malekula, and proceeded to climb up into the high country towards the village of Malua. This was no easy task – Malua sits on a 100-metre-high plateau that rises sharply from the coast, and they had to scale it while carrying two 30-kilogram Maxim guns and their ammunition.

By mid-morning they occupied a spur overlooking the village and sent forward a French settler, accompanied by two native guides, to negotiate. Their hope was to persuade the locals to hand over Meglia's killers. Soon after arriving it became apparent that the heights opposite were teeming with 'armed bushmen', not from the village but from the island's interior.[4] These 'clamorous visitors' threatened that any Maluans who surrendered to the Australian-led landing party would be fired upon.[5]

Australian naval activities in the Pacific at the end of the Great War

With negotiation seemingly impossible, the Australians opened fire; the bushmen returned it 'almost simultaneously'. Captain Robins later reported that 'the expedition met with strong fire opposition and was for a considerable time under hostile fire'. After about an hour of sporadic violent exchanges, in which the Australian Maxim machine-gun fire was described as 'most efficient', at least four Malekulans were dead. Robins reported that they had been 'well-punished for the murder', so after pausing for lunch, the landing party returned to ship.[6]

The Australian action on Malekula was well received at the time by the colonial authorities and the public at large. The British Resident Commissioner described it as 'a most successful expedition … carried out but with little bloodshed, and the loss of life in the native side was chiefly due to the defiant attitude which they foolishly assumed'.[7] The French High Commissioner expressed his sincere thanks for the ability of the Australians 'to chastise the assassins of our unfortunate compatriot Meglia … The success has been complete and we estimate that the punishment that you have just inflicted on the natives of Malua is sufficiently exemplary that they will long remember'.[8] Australian newspapers reported the story in detail, described the action as 'excellent', and noted that the expedition 'had done much good towards maintaining order and the future safety of the whites, and of the better conducted native population'.[9] The available sources do not shed light on Malekulan reactions to the attack.

An Australian Department of Veterans' Affairs educational aid describes the *Fantome*'s mission as having 'more in common with pre-war colonial adventures than the slaughter in Europe and the Middle East'.[10] Indeed, the mission shows that Australia was willing and able to use deadly force to maintain control of European colonial holdings in the Pacific; United States President Woodrow Wilson's concept of a peoples' right to national self-determination obviously did not apply to all. By assisting to maintain joint colonial ownership with another European power, the mission was simultaneously transnational and national – Australia played its role in protecting what Marilyn Lake and Henry Reynolds have described as the 'imagined community of white men' across the globe, and presented itself as a regional force to be reckoned with in the post-war world.[11] As Stuart Bedford has argued, such displays of force were equally about impressing settlers and the wider public in neighbouring colonies as they were about subduing native populations.[12]

HMAS *Encounter*

A month later another Australian ship, HMAS *Encounter*, set out for the Pacific. This new mission was equally far removed from the carnage of the trenches, but in its own way sheds light on Australia's position at the end of the Great War. On 20 November 1918, just weeks after the guns on the Western Front fell silent, the New Zealand government sent a desperate appeal to Australia. The New Zealand–administered territory of Western Samoa, seized from the Germans in 1914, had contracted the dreaded Spanish flu. This devastating virus had spread across the globe with alarming speed. It is unknown exactly where it had originated, though most sources indicate it began somewhere in America, and the massive movement of troops during the war created the perfect conditions for it to spread far and wide. An estimated 20 million people died in the Great War; at least 50 million died in the influenza epidemic that followed.[13] One Australian First World War veteran later wrote of the epidemic: 'The flue [sic] went on and on like the War, thousands of life [sic] was soon ended'.

The influenza came to the Pacific islands in early November 1918 when the former New Zealand troopship SS *Talune* made a round trip from Auckland to Fiji, Samoa, Nauru and Tonga.[15]

Australian naval activities in the Pacific at the end of the Great War

Within weeks of *Talune*'s arrival in Apia, four out of every five Samoans were infected. At the time New Zealand was dealing with its own deadly flu outbreak, so it instead asked the Australian government to provide the necessary aid. Just two days after New Zealand had made its request, the Australian Navy Department sent the cruiser HMAS *Encounter* from Melbourne to Sydney, where it was provisioned with medical and other supplies, and two days later, on 24 November, it was despatched to the Pacific.[16]

The team sent to assist the relief effort consisted of the regular ship's company, three naval sick berth ratings, a New Zealand serviceman familiar with Samoa, and a medical component headed by Surgeon Lieutenant F Temple Grey of the RAN. Assisting him were 40 officers and medical orderlies of the Australian Army Medical Corps (AAMC), among whom were several young medical students who had only just graduated, proudly donned their khaki uniforms, and had been 'straining every effort to get away to the front ever since'. The end of the war denied them their wish to join the 'ranks of the nobility' by fighting in France; instead they would witness the mass deaths that came in the aftermath of the Great War.[17]

Encounter was originally intended to assist only in Samoa, but as it re-coaled at Suva, Fiji, the ship's commander, Captain Hugh Thring, found that Fiji was in the grips of its own flu outbreak. The local governor turned down offers of assistance, but informed Thring of an even worse epidemic on Tonga, where 95 per cent of the population was estimated to be infected. Despite his orders concerning only Samoa, Thring left a small team to travel to Tonga. Unfortunately, engine troubles on their intended transport and a flu outbreak on the other RAN ship present, HMAS *Fantome* (fresh from its punitive patrol to the New Hebrides), meant that the Tongan relief party was temporarily stranded in Fiji.[18]

Encounter arrived at its main target, Apia, on 3 December. The medical teams immediately set to work, and many of

Encounter's crew volunteered their services to assist on land. They landed tonnes of sorely needed medical supplies in rough conditions, and four medical relief teams spread across the islands of Upolu and Savai'i. One medical section remained on *Encounter* and sailed to Tonga, where they were finally able to provide much-needed help after the failed attempt from Fiji.

Overall, the epidemic in the Pacific was devastating. A 1919 New Zealand commission estimated that deaths in Samoa alone were upwards of 8500, or more than 20 per cent of the population. In Fiji, approximately 9000 died (5 per cent of the population), with another 1500 in Tonga (6 per cent).[19]

The medical assistance that the Australians – aided by locals, white settlers and a New Zealand garrison – were able to provide undoubtedly saved many lives. They brought desperately needed supplies and medicine, and boosted the overwhelmed and ailing medical staff already present. *Encounter*'s relief operation to the Pacific was Australia's first overseas disaster relief mission, and by all accounts it was carried out in the spirit of genuine concern for the people affected. Australia responded to the developing crisis with impressive rapidity, and the fact that crew members volunteered to go ashore at Apia to assist the specialist medical staff, despite the significant risk of infection, speaks to their willingness to help out those in need.

It must be remembered, however, that the mission was also about maintaining order for the British Empire in its recently acquired colonial holdings, and an element of colonial paternalism pervades many of the available sources. Private Jack Brayley of the AAMC wrote home from Safune on the north coast of Savai'i that he was 'having as good a time as can be expected, considering there are only about 12 white men on the island'. He added the 'island is noted for heat and rain (when it isn't one, it's the other), flies, mosquitoes, sandflies, dogs, cocoanuts, and niggers'.[20]

Newspaper reports made a distinction between the rates of infection among the native, 'half-caste' and European populations, and reported that the task of combating the disease was one of 'no small proportions, because of the reported disregard of most of the natives for the fundamentals of health'.[21] The official historian of Australia's overseas emergency relief operations, Steven Bullard, points out that the frequent references to 'lazy' or 'helpless' natives, seemingly incapable of looking after themselves, ignore the fact that the severity of the outbreak was largely caused by 'the failure of advanced Western methods to prevent and treat the disease, which was itself introduced by the colonisers into a population with limited immunity'.[22]

Similar to the mission conducted by *Fantome*, *Encounter*'s disaster relief was both transnational and national in its ambitions. Australia acted on behalf of a Commonwealth partner, New Zealand, in a spirit of genuine concern for the people affected by the flu, regardless of their nationality, and in doing so it made a statement about its position as a regional power. It is unlikely Australia would have been able to respond to the crisis without systems and structures streamlined by years of war, and through improved naval and medical capabilities, Australia was able to present itself as a benevolent guardian of the Pacific colonies. It was an opportunity too good to refuse.

Australia enters the 'blood stream of the world'

The destruction of the German Empire during the Great War caused a redrawing of the world map. By annexing German colonies such as New Guinea and Samoa on behalf of the British Empire in 1914, Australia and New Zealand became effective colonial masters of large swathes of the south Pacific. The annexations were formalised at Versailles in 1919, and until then the two countries helped to govern the far-flung and newly acquired Pacific corners of the empire while the Mother Country was otherwise engaged in Europe.

One of the great legacies of the First World War, therefore, was that it presented Australia with an opportunity to fulfil long-held strategic – and in many ways, colonial – aspirations in the Pacific. There had been calls for Australian colonies to establish a defensive 'frontier' in the Pacific islands well before Federation.[23] By the mid-19th century the colonies had developed what historian Humphrey McQueen described as their own Monroe Doctrine in the Pacific, in which any seizure of Pacific islands by anyone other than Britain was to be vigorously opposed.[24] In 1883, in one of pre-Federation Australia's first attempts to flex its imperial muscles in the region, the colony of Queensland annexed Papua lest it fall into German hands. This was in an attempt to cajole Britain into taking possible colonial acquisition by rival European powers in the region more seriously, but London's swift nullification of the annexation showed that Britain would not yet be dictated to by its far-flung Pacific colonies.[25]

By the end of the Great War, many Australians maintained their close ties to the British Empire, but saw their imperial and national role as having been granted new vigour by the blood price bought in the trenches of the Western Front.[26] Acting Prime Minister William Watt declared in the Australian parliament that '[t]his war has brought Australia into the blood stream of the world, and we can never get out of it as long as nations are nations'. Australia's politicians at the time flatly rejected the notion that Pacific islands be returned to Germany, and instead embraced the idea that they should fall under Australia's control (on behalf of the British). During parliamentary debates in the days after the Armistice, Australian politicians on both sides repeatedly reassured each other that they 'did not enter the war for plunder', that 'this Parliament is not out to grab territory'. At the same time, however, they argued that it was vital for Australia to seize the opportunity to establish the long-coveted defensive frontier in the newly 'unoccupied' Pacific islands. Australia, they said, 'should hold these captured German Possessions in fief and in trust for the payment of some of the losses to which Australia has had to submit in consequence of the war'.[27]

Politicians of the time justified their ambitions in the Pacific not only in terms of defence strategy but also in terms of benevolent British rule. Little over a month after the Australians of *Fantome* had killed at least four natives on Malekula, acting Prime Minister William Watt argued:

> If there was no other reason, civilized humanity would be justified in expelling Germany from countries where she had subjected the aboriginal people to the grossest cruelty. It may be said, without any exaggeration, that in no island country over which the German flag has flown during the last thirty years is there anything in the hearts of the people but hatred of their German masters.[28]

This rhetoric was part of a long-established British imperial notion that their empire was better than all European imperial rivals. According to this view, those other empires brought exploitation and suffering; Britain brought prosperity, civilisation and cricket.

Fantome's expedition was not Australia's first punitive expedition to the New Hebrides, but it showed a willingness to use deadly force in maintaining European colonial control. By contrast, *Encounter*'s expedition was something entirely new, an international disaster relief mission ostensibly carried out in the spirit of genuine altruism. The RAN and AAMC were able to respond to the disaster so quickly because by 1918, Australia's military organisational structures were well oiled and efficient machines. In each case, Australia was above all acting as an agent of the British Empire, but for better or worse, one more willing to assert itself in its region in the post-war world.

7

PLANS FOR PEACE, FEARS OF WAR: DEFENDING AUSTRALIA IN 1919

Honae Cuffe

The First World War upended Australian politics and society alike, leaving political parties frayed, some 60 000 dead and a public calling for peace and recovery. Yet even before the war had ended, there were those in Australian political and defence circles looking to the next great conflict. This time they feared it would be a war in Australia's immediate region with then ally Japan. At the 1919 Paris Peace Conference (also known as the Versailles Peace Conference), Australia's defiant spokesman Prime Minister William Hughes addressed these fears. At times he was openly hostile towards the Japanese delegation, and he demanded that Australia control Germany's former territories in the South Pacific on the basis of national security. Much of the existing scholarship dealing with the Paris Peace Conference tends to foreground Hughes' cantankerous nature, his strident nationalism and desire to assert Australia's distinct voice at its first international conference. This approach has contributed to a fetishising of the individual, with Hughes' mission in Paris seen largely as a personal one.[1]

This chapter addresses the imbalance with a focus on the peacemaking process, exploring how Hughes and his contemporaries perceived peacemaking and the effect that wartime experiences – namely Japanese naval advancements and the occupation of Pacific territories – had on approaches and expectations at Paris.

For Australia, peacemaking was not simply about negotiating the defeat terms of the Central Powers, it was also seen as an opportunity to pre-emptively protect Australia against Japanese aggression. With this fundamental link between peacemaking and defence in mind, this chapter considers the outcomes of the Paris Peace Conference and concurrent defence planning as part of a campaign for Australia's post-war security.

A suspect ally

Australia's isolation – both as a remote outpost of the British Empire and an outsider among its Asian neighbours – together with its immense, exposed coastline and pre-existing suspicion of Japanese expansionism, tested relations between the two nations during the First World War. Japan had entered the war in August 1914 on the consensus that the Imperial Japanese Navy (IJN) would escort Allied flotillas in the Indian and Pacific Oceans and capture German territories in the East and South China Seas. Japan, however, had entered the war with hopes to broaden its Pacific empire. The IJN quickly extended operations, capturing Germany's North Pacific territories (the Marshall, Mariana and Caroline Islands) by the end of 1914. Australia had initially been charged with taking over German New Guinea and was instructed by the British to send an expedition to the North Pacific to relieve Japan of occupation duties. The Japanese government protested this plan, and Britain, which could ill-afford a confrontation between a dominion and an ally, accepted a compromise. Japan would not seize anything north of the equator and the empire would not seize anything south.[2]

The division at the equator did little to lull Australia's concerns. The Australian government saw in Japan's territorial advances both an attempt to make inroads in a region that was traditionally Britain's sphere of influence and the accumulation of strategic points from which to launch a policy of aggressive southward expansion, with possible designs on Australia. Accordingly, the Australian government sought out intelligence on Japanese naval movements and attitudes towards Australia and the Pacific. The RAN paid close attention to Japan's naval movements, and the British Ambassador in Tokyo, upon Australia's express request, forwarded clippings from the local press that made reference to Australia and the Pacific territories. In March 1916, Major EL Piesse, formerly a staff officer in the Australian Army Intelligence Corps, was appointed as Director of Military Intelligence to oversee the organisation and assessment of this information. In May 1918, he was transferred to the newly established Pacific Division in the Prime Minister's Department, where he served as the principal adviser on Far Eastern intelligence, Japan's intentions in the Pacific and the strategic significance of Germany's former Pacific territories. In this role, Piesse produced some alarming reports that acknowledged the potential for the North Pacific territories occupied by Japan to become hubs from which to secure new areas for markets and immigration.[3]

Australia saw the Great War as 'a war for security', as described by John Latham, a naval intelligence officer during the First World War and assistant secretary to the British Empire Delegation to Paris. Defence and peacemaking were intertwined, with Australian policymakers believing 'Australia's sacrifices entitle her at least to such security as the Peace Conference can give'.[4] During the war, those in Australian political and defence circles had been candid about this expectation. They pressed the British government for its policy on the post-war arrangements for Germany's former Pacific territories, making clear that Australia expected to be granted direct control of New Guinea and the adjacent islands and desired Britain's full support in this endeavour. In mid-1918, Hughes made a short layover in the United States on his way to London for a meeting of the Imperial War Cabinet. In a series of meetings and speeches, he placed the control of the Pacific territories at the centre of his campaign for Australia's post-war security. According to Hughes, the potential for islands 'within striking distance' of Australia to be possessed by an unfriendly power 'means that our country must always sleep with the sword half drawn'. If Australia's security was to be guaranteed, it needed local hegemony; it needed, Hughes declared, 'an Australian Monroe Doctrine in the Southern Pacific'. Hughes presented peacemaking as an opportunity for pre-emptive action against future 'predatory designs' on the region, calling on the US 'to stand by [Australia] around the peace tables' and support the nation's claim to Germany's former South Pacific territories.[5] Hughes was seemingly discussing Germany's predatory nature; however, as historian Peter Spartalis observed, in view of Australia's long-standing fear of Japan and fixation on the nation's wartime activities, the implication that Japan was a similarly predatory power is clear. It was against this backdrop that Australia approached peacemaking in Paris.[6]

The Paris Peace Conference and the mandate system

The Paris Peace Conference opened on 18 January 1919 and negotiations lasted nearly six months. Australia attended as a division of the British Empire delegation and was represented by Hughes and his Deputy Prime Minister and Minister for the Navy, Joseph Cook, who were joined by their advisers, Solicitor-General Robert Garran, Hughes' personal secretary Percy Dean and Latham. Areas of interest to the Australia delegation included securing war reparations from Germany and the embryonic League of Nations, specifically reservations that the organisation would impinge on domestic jurisdiction over immigration and trade. The League was proposed by US President Woodrow Wilson and inspired by his

Fourteen Points. The Australian delegation feared that these moral principles for international peace would interfere with domestic affairs, forcing the nation to adopt unreasonable tariffs and threatening the nation's restrictive immigration policy that denied entry to non-Europeans.[7] But it was the issue of Germany's former Pacific territories that proved the most contentious. The so-called 'battle for the colonies' began on 24 January. Hughes, with a large map of the Pacific in hand, addressed the Council of Ten. He was adamant that Australia should annex the South Pacific territories on the basis of national security. Despite this rationale and Hughes' attempts to corral US support the previous year, President Wilson could not be convinced to support annexation. Wilson, an idealistic anti-imperialist, favoured a mandate system that operated on the basis of trusteeship and progress towards self-government, to be administered by the League. With Hughes redoubling his commitment to annexation and Wilson threatening to leave Paris, the question of the Pacific territories threatened to derail the conference.[8]

Hughes' 'intolerable bluntness', in the words of historian JR Poynter, coupled with his long-standing suspicion of Japan, has contributed to an idea of national security being his own personal mission in Paris.[9] True, the portfolio of Minister for External Affairs was suspended in 1916–21, with Hughes' adopting the responsibilities by default and his personal views invariably shaping policy-making. Hughes may have been alone in his methods, but he was not alone in his objectives. Like Hughes, Latham saw the control of the South Pacific territories as inseparable from Australian security. However, he feared that Hughes' tactless, hard-line approach in Paris was alienating Australia from the United States and antagonising Japan, a powerful ally and potential adversary respectively. On 29 January, Latham, along with his British and Canadian counterparts in Paris, proposed a compromise. Rather than one broad mandate, they proposed three classes (A, B and C) with differing levels of autonomy. The C-class category, in which the Pacific territories were included, was considered the furthest from self-government and 'best administered under the laws of the Mandatory as integral portions of its territory'.[10]

While Hughes initially accepted the mandate system in principle on 30 January, it was not until May that an agreement was made on the system and distribution of territories. Defence loomed large in the reasons for this delay. Article 19 of the League Covenant prohibited the building of fortifications and garrisoning on mandates. This stipulation concerned Hughes and he called for the 'unfettered control' of matters of defence, security and immigration. He argued that Australia's wartime efforts to capture the arc of islands to its north – the nation's so-called 'natural bastions' – demonstrated the nation's merit and right to control these territories. '[Australia] now demands to be placed in the position of such complete control of these territories as will give her real security.'[11] Latham presented a different view. In a report titled 'Mandatory System and the German Pacific Islands', Latham assessed the strategic value of the Pacific territories in the event of Japanese aggression towards Australia. He argued that Article 19 would actually 'affect Japan more seriously than it would affect Australia'.[12] If the mandates were able to be fortified, Australia would be at a strategic disadvantage with Japan's much larger and more powerful military brought closer to Australian shores. In the event of war,

> Australia would face Japan at closer quarters than ever before and would largely lose the great protection which distance now gives. The defensive position of Australia against Japan would be markedly impaired while the offensive position of Japan would be greatly improved.[13]

Moreover, while the mandates themselves could not be fortified, the territories around them could. Britain's string of colonies throughout the Asia-Pacific area could, in theory, be built up to deter Japanese aggression and expansionism and, if necessary, forces based there could move in to defend the mandate territories and Australia. Latham accordingly encouraged Australia to accept the mandate system in spite of the limitations on fortifications and garrisoning. That Latham's strategic appraisal of the mandate system had Japanese aggression specifically in mind is indicative of Australia's view to the next great conflict and the importance of peacemaking in securing concessions that would hopefully pre-empt this.

It was both the strategic logic presented by Latham and the decision to treat the C-class mandates as geographical contiguities, subject to the laws of the mandate power (allowing Australia to extend the *Immigration Restriction Act* to its mandated territories) that convinced Hughes, albeit gradually, to accept the mandate system as an acceptable alternative to annexation. Australia was granted full mandatory control of New Guinea and Nauru under the joint British Empire mandate.[14]

Imperial defence planning for the Pacific

Australia saw the security of the South Pacific as inexorably linked with imperial defence planning. In a report prepared for the British Empire delegation to the Peace Conference, Latham described the future of the Pacific territories as not only an Australian concern but an empire one. He argued that if they were in the hands of an enemy, other British colonies, trade routes and lines of communication nearby would all be compromised. Latham went on to recommend that Australia's naval frontier be expanded via a system of bases extending from Singapore to Tonga, with a squadron of the British Royal Navy aiding in their construction and defence.[15] The key point here is that Latham was seeking to convince Britain of the strategic value of the Pacific and the need to commit resources there.

This was not the first instance of Australian policymakers exploring post-war defence options and seeking a commitment from the British. In September 1917, Cook requested that the British Admiralty reassess the maritime defence needs of Australia and the Pacific, suggesting that a major imperial naval base was needed either in Australia or a nearby British territory. Plans were made to send an Admiralty officer to Australia to investigate, although in view of the wartime context, the British indicated that no action would be taken until after the war had ended. In December 1918, the Australian government was informed that the Admiral of the Fleet, Lord John Jellicoe, would visit to review the situation in the Pacific. Cook's original request that the Admiralty review Pacific naval base requirements had been justified on the vague basis of 'the experience of the war'. Future correspondence indicates that these experiences were Japan's naval advancements and new Pacific territories.[16]

In May 1919, immediately prior to Jellicoe's visit, acting Prime Minister William Watt dispatched a report outlining Australia's concerns and the questions he hoped would be addressed during the Admiralty review. Along with plans for greater empire defence cooperation, projected shipbuilding programs and questions concerning the supply of strategic materials, the unmistakable overtone of this document is fear of war in the Pacific. Watt requested that Jellicoe provide an assessment of the 'naval strategical problems affecting Australian waters and the Pacific'. This included probable routes of attack on Australia, 'with special reference to occupation by a foreign power of Islands north of the Equator' and Britain's strategy in the event of war with any of the Pacific powers.[17] While it was never explicitly stated, there is no doubt that the Pacific threat Watt had in mind was Japan. Interestingly, this report and Jellicoe's visit coincided with the finalising of the mandate system in Paris and Latham's emphasis on using imperial defence to protect Australia's new Pacific territories. The fundamental motivation underlining Australian peacemaking and defence planning, both in Paris and at home, was control of the South Pacific.

Jellicoe's report mirrored Australia's concerns. He isolated the Pacific as the most likely area for future conflict and judged Australia to be 'powerless against a strong naval and military power without the assistance of the British fleet'. He advised that a Far Eastern Fleet and major naval base be established in the Pacific in the next five years, with Singapore the recommended location. This strategy was expected to protect both the North Pacific and Indian Oceans and allow two zones of conflict to be operational, Europe and the Pacific.[18]

Jellicoe's plan formed the basis of the Singapore Naval Strategy, the primary strategy for the protection of Britain's imperial interests in the Pacific. The original plan rested on two pillars: a large fleet of capital ships stationed permanently in the Pacific and a new base at Singapore able to support this fleet. However, Britain's immense war debt and public demand for financing social services rather than defence industries meant that these recommendations went beyond what the country could reasonably afford. Instead, a base would be built but only fully garrisoned when required and the recommended five-year construction timeline was pushed back to eight years (a deadline that would not be met). While Australia continued to rely on the Singapore Strategy, it did not do so uncritically. As I have argued elsewhere, the inter-war period, particularly the latter half of the 1930s, was marked by Australian policymakers questioning the strategy and pursuit of defence and diplomatic initiatives in addition to reliance on Singapore.[19] The shortcomings of the Singapore Strategy aside, the strategic thinking by key Australian policy-makers that underpinned its conceptualisation remains significant.

Conclusion

Throughout the First World War, there were those in Australian political and defence circles looking to Japan and fearing the next great conflict. As this chapter has demonstrated, this insecurity and suspicion fundamentally shaped how Australia approached peacemaking. It was not simply about dealing with a defeated enemy, it was also seen as an opportunity to pre-emptively build up defences against the next one. The Australian delegation accordingly approached the Paris Peace Conference with the intention of securing concessions that would ensure post-war security, the cornerstone of which was the control of the South Pacific. The link between peacemaking and defence was not limited to events in Paris, with key Australian policymakers seeking to couple the concessions won at Paris with imperial defence planning. The objective here – although not fully realised – was to build up a broader strategy for post-war defence. All this is not to suggest that Hughes' prickly demeanour and nationalist convictions did not play a role at Paris. However, in stepping back from the individual, this chapter aims to provide deeper insight into Australian policy thinking on peace and defence in 1919 and how this thinking was ultimately shaped by the experiences of the Great War.

The experiences and sacrifices of the First World War sharpened Australia's sense of nationhood and national interests. Australian leaders became more willing to articulate these interests and interrogate what role the nation could play in the empire and the new world order that was taking shape.[20] Where Australia's wartime contribution had ostensibly proven the nation's worth, the peacemaking process was the opportunity to translate this into an equivalent voice in international affairs. When reflecting on the themes of aftermath and commemoration, Australia's plans for peace and fears of war highlight both the domestic and international significance of the Great War and expand our understanding of the broad appeal of the national mythology that surrounds the war.

SOCIAL, POLITICAL AND PERSONAL LEGACIES

8

ANZACS AND AUSTRALASIANS

Marilyn Lake

The children unborn shall acclaim
The standard the Anzacs unfurled,
When they made Australasia's fame
The wonder and pride of the world.

Edgar Wallace, 'Anzacs', The Anzac Book[1]

There is a little remarked-upon paradox at the heart of the Anzac legend. A nationalist myth has built on and commemorated a transnational formation – the Australian and New Zealand Army Corps. In a discursive sleight-of-hand, Anzac has been appropriated as the basis for a stridently Australianist commemoration in which the landing of Anzac forces at Gallipoli was transformed into a uniquely Australian affair, a 'national foundation legend', in the words of Steve Gower, a former Director of the Australian War Memorial.[2] 'A nation was born on that day of death',[3] So the story ran. Allegedly an account of the past, the Anzac story represses history, even as it reifies it.[4] But the return of the repressed is always imminent in the invocation of the name itself.

When presenting public talks on the mythology of Anzac during the past several years, I was often asked, 'What about the New Zealanders?' It was a question, I must confess, to which I didn't pay sufficient heed. But while working on my book,

Progressive New World, I came to recognise that the Anzac legend's disavowal of its transnational origins reflects a larger historical amnesia in our country, that of the history and idea of 'Australasia' itself, which had indeed once been 'the wonder and pride of the world'.[5]

In the years before the First World War, Australians and New Zealanders – white settlers in the self-governing British colonies of the southwest Pacific – shared an Anglo-Saxon identity, democratic aspirations and expansionist ambitions. Increasingly, however, 'Australasia' had come to denote a progressive new world, whose definitive 'socialistic tendencies' became a beacon for advanced democrats everywhere – in Europe, the United Kingdom and the United States.[6] For Australians and New Zealanders, progressive labour laws, enshrining an ideal of economic equality and opportunity, were a particular source of pride and common identity.

The former New Zealand Labour Minister W Pember Reeves' two-volume 1902 publication *State Experiments in Australia and New Zealand* gave memorable contemporary expression to this shared sense of communal pride in labour experiments.[7] 'Arbitration became one of the best known expressions of Australasian identities', Philippa Mein Smith and Donald Denoon have written in their general history of Australia, New Zealand and the Pacific, 'claimed simultaneously as distinctively New Zealand and Australian. It was indeed distinctive in that no other settler society adopted it'.[8]

Numerous investigators arrived from overseas in the last years of the 19th and early years of the 20th centuries to see these Australasian 'experiment stations' for themselves. Harvard philosopher Josiah Royce visited Melbourne and Sydney, in 1888, when he became a close friend and confidante of Liberal leader Alfred Deakin and an attentive reader of *The Age*'s weekly journal, *The Leader*, to which he subsequently subscribed. While in Sydney, he decided he must also visit New Zealand, breaking his return journey in Auckland, rather than the Sandwich Islands (Hawaii). There he gathered up more periodicals and political publications to read on his voyage across the Pacific. As he wrote to Deakin, soon after he left Australia, he had decided to try to obtain 'more ideas of your political life in the colonies in general by remaining within range of your newspapers' and he wanted especially to understand 'the State Socialism of the political tendencies in all Australasian life'.[9] This would become the main subject of the articles he published in the following year in the *Atlantic Monthly* called 'Reflections after a Wandering Life in Australasia'.[10]

Chicago-based journalist Henry Demarest Lloyd arrived in Australia and New Zealand a decade later, first visiting Catherine Spence, in Adelaide, to whom he delivered a letter of introduction from their mutual friend, the labour economist John Commons. In his subsequent writings, Lloyd hailed the 'democratic efflorescence of Australasia' and the 'renaissance of democracy' in these southern lands.[11] He was especially impressed by the industrial arbitration system in New Zealand, 'a white man's country if ever there was one', he enthused, praising the fact that all political efforts – including immigration restriction – were dedicated to upholding a high standard of living for the white working man. Australia and New Zealand were as one in this determination, as pointed out by Reeves, who was lauded by Lloyd as an originating genius: 'in the front ranks of the geniuses who have proved themselves able to affect human destiny for good'.[12]

Another aspect of the much-heralded democratic advance in these lands was the world-historic achievement by New Zealand and Australian women of political rights. In 1902, when Vida Goldstein represented 'Australasian' women at the first international suffrage conference in Washington DC, American delegate Ellen Wright Garrison wrote in her autograph book: 'To Australasia all the world gives ear'. Modern progressives, women as well as men, were all admirers, Garrison assured her international visitor, of the southern lands' path of 'bold adventure and experiment'.[13] Goldstein was 'a "light-bringer" from the Southern Seas'.[14]

This history has unfortunately been largely forgotten. Nationalist and masculinist historical narratives have systematically denied or minimised the significance of transnational and regional communities – including feminist ones – to the fashioning of progressive political identities.[15] The 'narrative contract' between history and the nation – in historian Sudipta Kaviraj's felicitous phrase – has served to exclude or diminish transnational identifications and modes of self-definition.[16]

Yet Anzac soldiers, in their self-conscious egalitarianism, democratic insouciance, irreverence and sense of white superiority, gave military and literary expression – in *The Anzac Book*, for example – to their sense of themselves as embodiments of the fraternal 'white men's countries' of Australasia.[17] The subjects of cartoons in the *The Anzac Book* were named as 'Perspiring Australasian' or 'Slowly Freezing Australasian' and they sought to distinguish themselves, above all, from class-bound, snobbish, hierarchical, Old World British-accented officers.[18]

It is unfortunate that in forgetting the Australasian constitution of Anzac, we also disregard the world-historic democratic achievement that defined this progressive new world of the southwest Pacific at its founding. There is a further paradox here: that the commemoration of the Anzac spirit has actually served to expunge its radical, historical underpinnings – manhood suffrage, minimum wages, industrial arbitration, state-owned railways and utilities, women's rights, old age and invalid pensions – from historical and popular memory. 'Australasia's fame' – in Edgar Wallace's words – would now seem indeed to be lost to the world.[19] Years of continuing and costly Australian commemoration of Anzac have ironically only served to exacerbate this failure of historical memory.

What did the construct of 'Australasia' – which 'Anzac' both embodied and commemorated – signify? It was more than geographical shorthand. Most pre-war contemporary observers, locals and visitors, noted the strong political values that bound the Australian colonies and New Zealand into a distinctive New World political community, their democratic and socialistic tendencies setting them apart from other communities in the English-speaking world. 'No English community elsewhere', noted Royce in his 'Reflections on Australasia', 'has sought to govern itself in just the way here exemplified. Here are pure democracies with what an American must unhesitatingly call strong socialistic tendencies'.[20] Shortly afterwards, another US researcher, Helen Page Bates, a PhD candidate at Wisconsin working with economist Richard Ely, also emphasised the novelty of Australasia's political values and orientation. There, she observed, governments began to take to themselves many new and extensive functions never previously exercised by the state. There was no 'imitation of any other nation'. Roads, railroads, telegraph and postal services were all under state control.[21] Bates' mentor, Professor Ely, also came south to see these experiment stations for himself during the war – at a time when their progressive character was under attack.

One of the most influential of US investigators, Victor S Clark, arrived at the behest of the US Labor Bureau in 1903. After extensive research in both Australia and New Zealand, Clark published *The Labor Movement in Australasia: A study in social democracy* and a number of reports and journal articles. The two countries were the 'most interesting legislative experiment stations in the world', he noted, 'and they experiment so actively because their political institutions were extremely democratic'.[22] In a lively correspondence with Edward Tregear, the provocative secretary of the New Zealand Department of Labour, Clark came to appreciate the distinctive political commitments that bound Australasia into a distinctive union and defined its opposition to the values of Old World Britain.

In Tregear's view, Australasians engaged with democratic self-government to build a new world ruled by different values. In Old World Britain, he wrote, people had been 'instructed to reverence rank, wealth, landed-proprietorship, state religion and vested interests'. In Britain (and the United States), they had been instructed in economic doctrines and 'taught to respect old trade-jargons about "freedom of contract", "supply and demand", "liberty of the subject" – phrases subtly concocted for the repression of all upward industrial effort and for the support of financial privilege'. In New World Australasia, on the other hand, the people, empowered by manhood and womanhood suffrage, could 'dare to think for themselves' and devise new policies for the people's benefit and betterment.[23]

This was the world that the Anzacs represented on the world stage. In defining their achievements, however, historically minded commentators – such as Ernest Scott and other British newspaper men – and conservative military and political leaders preferred to attribute the soldiers' valour to their British imperial heritage or to define their military service as a distinctly national achievement. Thus, the English press correspondent Ellis Ashmead Bartlett reported in 1915: '[t]hese raw colonial troops, in these desperate hours, proved worthy to fight side by side with the heroes of the battles of Mons, the Aisne, Ypres and Neuve-Chapelle'.[24] 'The Australian and New Zealand troops have indeed proved themselves worthy sons of empire', declared King George V the following year. At the end of the war, more nationalist encomiums kicked in. The Australian General Brudenell White opined: '[u]p to the time of this war we were merely an offshoot of the British race ... Now we are a nation' and the official Australian war correspondent, CEW Bean, confirmed: 'Australia rides safely in harbor to-day, a new nation'.[25] Thus, death and destruction on an unprecedented scale – almost one in five Australian soldiers was killed – were transformed in nationalist discourse into a life-giving creative force. The Australian soldiers gave birth to a nation.

Yet paradoxically even as the nation was said to be coming to life, the war also saw the rebirth of empire. Ties with the Old World – once repudiated – were deliberately reinvigorated and strengthened through a range of economic, cultural and political initiatives undertaken by the British and Australian governments.[26] State socialism, once praised as a modern progressive force – and as 'Australian as being mates' – was now ostracised as foreign and as threatening as Bolshevism.[27]

Australian participation in the imperial war in Europe strengthened imperial orientations at home and sidelined the once potent regional ideal of democratic Australasia. Symbolic institutions such as arbitration courts and the living wage came under concerted ideological attack during and after the war. The esteemed president of the Commonwealth Court of Conciliation and Arbitration, HB Higgins, was forced by the machinations of Prime Minister WM Hughes to resign his position on the court.

A significant British move to consolidate imperial interests in Australia came with the trip made by Sir Henry Rider Haggard in 1916 with the aim of opening Australian lands to the settlement of British ex-servicemen after the war. Haggard was delegated by the Royal Colonial Institute in London to meet with state and federal government authorities in Australia, and his visit signalled a British intention to reinvigorate its imperial strategy. In a memorandum to the Australian Premiers' Conference in May 1916, Haggard wrote:

> The Royal Colonial Institute and its sympathisers are of the opinion that the state of the Empire, with reference to its white population and otherwise, and the dangers by which undoubtedly it will be confronted in the future, demand

that its citizens should as far as possible dwell within its limits.[28]

British imperial solidarity was necessary to safeguard the post-war world.

At the same time, a struggle broke out among Australian returned soldiers about the meaning of the legacy of Anzac – between loyalists urging imperial solidarity and radical democrats calling for economic justice.[29] The Returned Sailors' and Soldiers' Imperial League of Australia (RSSILA) – forerunner of the RSL – was formed in 1916 with conservative politician Lieutenant Colonel WK Bolton at its helm. The following year in Melbourne – still the federal capital – the Returned Sailors' and Soldiers' Australian Democratic League was formed to challenge the RSSILA in its claim to represent all returned soldiers, but the mobilisation of such radical Labor-aligned groups only served to further alarm conservative political leaders, such as Prime Minister Hughes and prominent businessmen, such as WL Baillieu. After intensive lobbying, the RSSILA was granted official status by the Nationalist government in 1918, ensuring their version of Anzac gained political ascendancy.

In recent years the federal government and its agencies have heavily promoted the myth of Anzac as a founding national legend. Schoolchildren have been inculcated with the story of the birth of a nation on the shores of Gallipoli. Military history has thus assumed a central place in Australian historical memory.[30] At the same time the world-historic democratic achievements that once drew visitors from around the globe to Australasia – manhood and womanhood suffrage, industrial arbitration and the living wage, mothers' pensions and children's courts – have sunk into historical oblivion. Yet the invocation of the spirit of Anzac should always remind us that the Australian and New Zealand Army Corps emerged from and embodied the progressive democratic new world of Australasia. A shared institutional commitment to economic justice and equal opportunity distinguished these communities of the southwest Pacific from the social and political order of the British empire, which would, however, devour them.

9

AUSTRALIAN POLITICS IN THE WAKE OF THE FIRST WORLD WAR

Frank Bongiorno

The First World War had a remarkable impact on Australian politics, splitting the Australian Labor Party (ALP), reconstituting the Liberal Party as the Nationalists, and inaugurating the Country Party as a major force. The war weakened a Labor Party that in 1914 had seemed poised to dominate federal politics, and it disturbed a two-party system then only a decade old. The system, however, absorbed these shocks, resulting in a modified two-party structure at the federal level and in most states (Victoria was an exception), rather than reversion to the 'three elevens' bemoaned by Alfred Deakin in 1904. Meanwhile, a Labor Party that performed poorly in national politics between the wars did better at the state level, both in winning government and implementing policy. The ALP proved a resilient political organisation, regaining power just in time to be devastated by the Depression, and being again poised for power as the next global crisis unfolded in the early 1940s.

The First World War has also been seen as instrumental in undermining the optimistic and progressive political culture of the Federation era. In radical nationalist accounts, pre-war experimentation and openness gave way to post-war timidity and conservatism.[1] The inter-war years are commonly dismissed as a time of policy stagnation or national stasis sitting between the livelier periods of nation-building during the early Commonwealth (1901–14), and the Second World War and post-war reconstruction (1939–49).[2] The First World War stoked enmities based on antagonisms of class and religion, polarised political actors according to their attitudes to empire and nation, and introduced a new fissure between those who had served and those who had remained behind. This chapter, however, challenges the familiar notion that war strangled the taste for experimentation and innovation. The inter-war years were less barren than they have been presented by many historians.

Anzacs in politics

The immediate aftermath of the war was especially turbulent, as thousands returned to a country buffeted by industrial strife, economic uncertainty and the deadly Spanish influenza. In Melbourne in July 1919, there were wild riots of returned soldiers, who stormed the offices of the Nationalist state government.[3] In Fremantle, returned soldiers were among the wharfies who confronted police and strike-breakers, a boatload of the 'scabs' provocatively accompanied by the Nationalist premier of the day, Hal Colebatch. One wharfie was killed.[4] The Returned Sailors' and Soldiers' Imperial League of Australia (RSSILA) has sometimes been given the credit or blame for directing the political energies of Australia's returned soldiers away from confrontation with government towards more conservative channels. The reputation of returned Australian soldiers for fascist-style politics possibly comes, in large part, from *Kangaroo* (1923), written by the English novelist DH Lawrence during a short visit to Australia. But it also owes something to the biggest and best-known of the post-war digger street violence, the Brisbane red flag riots in March 1919, during which returned soldiers protested violently against socialists and Russian migrants.[5]

Recent historical research has complicated the image of the conservative digger. The historian Robert Bollard has pointed to the strains of left-wing radicalism and industrial militancy among returned men.[6] Much of the First AIF comprised working-class men – most commonly younger men who had grown up in the shadow of the 1890s depression, the big strikes and the rise of the Labor Party. They were shaped by the development of a working-class consciousness that found expression in the digger culture that they had made during their travels, with its strains of larrikinism, mateship and entitlement. Historian Nathan Wise has shown how, as soldiers, these men displayed the culture of the union movement to which they had belonged in civilian life.[7]

The politics of the RSSILA itself were also more complex than they have sometimes been painted. An early president, William Bolton, also a Nationalist senator, aroused anger after urging members of the organisation to abstain from strikes.[8] But he would soon be replaced by a much more consensual figure, Gilbert Dyett, a Gallipoli veteran who had opposed conscription and supported voluntary recruitment during the war. The historian Martin Crotty has shown that Dyett, a long-serving and influential national president, avoided political partisanship and revealed himself an astute negotiator, gaining many concessions for his members from the government.[9]

There remained, of course, plenty of scope within state branches and local sub-branches for conservative politicking. But even if Anzac mythology sat much more comfortably with imperial loyalism than radical socialism, conservatives did not have a mortgage over the soldier vote. All parties ran candidates with war service even if the best known, who tended to be senior officers, inevitably represented the Nationalists or the Country Party. The 1919 federal election saw an influx of AIF commanders into the federal Senate as Nationalists, including the legendary Harold 'Pompey' Elliott, who would die by his own hand in 1931.[10] Another soldier-politician was the young and elegant Stanley Melbourne Bruce, who entered the

House of Representatives at a by-election in 1918, offering himself to the Nationalist delegates at the preselection 'as a plain soldier and business man' and 'no politician'.[11] Bruce had been educated at Cambridge and wounded at Gallipoli while serving in a British regiment. The rise to national leadership of this quintessential Anglo-Australian would be rapid and, by early 1923, complete.

The military presence was strong in the ranks of the Nationalists at both state and federal levels. Figures such as Major-General Sir Charles Rosenthal – a Nationalist member of the New South Wales parliament widely considered the original for 'Kangaroo', the fascist leader in Lawrence's novel – secured the intimate association of military service with conservative politics.[12] The conscription controversy had created difficulties for many soldier-politicians with Labor affiliations or sympathies, and for those who aspired to parliamentary careers. Campbell Carmichael had been a minister in the pre-war New South Wales state Labor governments, subsequently gaining a reputation as an energetic and successful recruiter as well as joining up himself and serving on the Western Front. While remaining a Labor parliamentarian, he had managed to avoid taking a conspicuous stand over conscription, which he favoured, but he was drifting away from a party that no longer had its heart in even voluntary recruitment.[13] In 1919 Carmichael led a People's Party of Soldiers and Citizens, which, as well as taking up the grievances of returned soldiers, advocated producer and consumer cooperatives, profit-sharing and class cooperation.[14] Although himself the representative of a city electorate, his party was cooperating with primary-producing organisations in October 1919 and threw in its lot with the New South Wales Progressives, who would later become the Country Party.[15] But at a Sydney meeting during the 1919 federal election campaign, Carmichael endorsed the Nationalists and Hughes, whom he declared 'one of the strongest fighters for the good of Australia and for the British Empire ever known in history'.[16] Carmichael was still implacably opposed to the Nationalist premier of New South Wales, William Holman, and it may well have been mainly for this reason that the People's Party of Soldiers and Citizens ran candidates at the 1920 state election, though they failed to pick up a seat.[17]

By this time, it was clear that soldiers would not form a coherent voting bloc or viable political party. The war, however, had brought about profound changes to Australian politics. Questions of loyalty were prominent; the loyalty in question was that to the British Empire, conceived as a Protestant cause. The war and postwar years saw an upsurge of religious sectarianism. The Democratic Party, a Catholic organisation, had contested the 1920 New South Wales state election, but like the Soldiers' Party, it failed to break through then, or at a subsequent election in 1922, which saw a peak of sectarian rancour. More striking was the way denominational differences and conflicts in Australian society coincided with party loyalties. The process by which Catholics and Protestants increasingly lined up on different sides of politics began well before the war, but the divisions of the later war years both hastened and magnified it, in ways that would shape Australian politics for generations. After the 1920 New South Wales election, which resulted in the formation of a Labor government, 25 out of 43 Labor Party caucus members were Catholic. Half of those who joined the cabinet from 1920 to 1922 – 7 out of 14 – were also Catholic. The Fuller Nationalist Government that succeeded it, by way of contrast, did not contain a single Catholic.[18]

Farmers flex their muscles

The earth was beginning to move under the feet of Billy Hughes, who had managed to hold on to the prime ministership after Labor split in 1916 by joining his anti-conscriptionist followers to the opposition. While there had been a war to win, his former opponents were willing to support him, even as they recognised and bemoaned his faults and failures. Hughes, whose nickname of 'The Little Digger' spoke to a supposedly special bond with the returned man, supported high tariffs, public enterprise and government economic intervention. To put it mildly, these policies were not universally loved on the right of Australian politics. But Hughes' problems were compounded by the emergence of a new force. Since colonial times, Australian parliaments had contained members from rural electorates who were seen, as a group, to be the voice of country interests. These had sometimes called themselves 'country parties', but they were not really political parties so much as loosely organised groupings or factions. But, bearing ideas about the moral virtue of country life and the superior value of landed enterprise, and hostile to pampered city elites, the Country Party emerged out of the First World War as a force in its own right. By disrupting trade, increasing costs, undermining labour supply, dislocating finance and drawing governments into a more direct role in marketing, the war had increased the incentives for farming organisations to intervene more directly in political affairs. At the 1919 federal election, it won 11 seats in a house of 75 – just shy of the number needed for the balance of power between the Nationalist government and Labor opposition.[19]

The Country Party did not admire Australia's ever higher and wider tariff walls, which increased the costs of farmers. Its second federal leader, Earle Page, a doctor from northern New South Wales, adopted an increasingly aggressive posture towards the Hughes government, coming within a vote of defeating its budget in 1921. But his best chance came after the 1922 election, at which the Country Party won the balance of power. Hughes' removal was part of the price Page exacted for entering a coalition, but the good doctor also gladly received the deputy prime ministership and five ministries out of the 11 available. Bruce became Prime Minister, and Page replaced him as Treasurer. With the formation of the Bruce–Page government in early 1923, the coalition tradition was inaugurated. With a few stumbles along the way, it has endured to this day.

The Country Party's appearance was arguably the most significant development in Australian politics between the wars and to a great extent a product of the Great War itself. Its habit of forming coalitions modified without destroying an essentially two-party system at the federal level. Policy calculation also changed, as government survival came to depend fundamentally on keeping the Country Party satisfied. That party's emergence also registered a revised understanding of rural political representation. A country member might once have been rarely seen in his electorate, and he was indeed sometimes a city man. But the defeat of distance by the telegraph and train had already before the war produced a kind of country parliamentarian much more embedded in the civic life of his local community. The motor car and the emergence of the Country Party completed the job.

Political innovation

The rise of the Country Party, with its backward glance to pioneering days sitting uneasily with its push to secure for the bush the benefits of modernity, has bolstered the idea that Australia entered a conservative phase between the wars. It is true that there was less initiative in some areas than before 1914. There was less federal activity in social security for ordinary citizens, but this was partly because the government faced a considerable challenge in meeting the needs of returned soldiers and their families and it provided fairly generously. State government was also active in this field, such as in offering opportunities for soldier settlement on the land.[20] At the same time, the federal government became more active in the field of health, setting up the first federal department in 1921, an initiative that gained some momentum from the uncoordinated response of state governments to the Spanish flu.[21]

In electoral politics, there was continuing innovation. The alternative vote, a variety of preferential voting, was adopted from 1918 for House of Representatives elections. While it had been debated since the very earliest years of the Commonwealth and used in some states, it was now a convenient device for ensuring that in three-cornered contests involving Nationalist and Country Party candidates, the Labor Party would be less able to slip in between them. It has endured and was followed, in 1924, by another lasting innovation resulting from a private Senator's bill: compulsory voting in federal elections. Following on from its introduction in Queensland state elections in 1915, federal compulsory voting was a response to poor turnouts at recent polls. After the Commonwealth's move, all states had introduced it for lower-house elections by 1942.[22] In 1921, Queensland, under a Labor government, became the first Australian state to abolish its upper house. (The following year, the same government became the first to get rid of hanging.) But not every innovation endured. In a short-lived electoral experiment, New South Wales combined multi-member constituencies and proportional representation for lower-house elections between 1918 and 1926

The earliest women parliamentarians were also elected in the 1920s. Women's contributions to the war effort through voluntary work, their status as mothers of the brave Anzacs, and their prominence in the debates over conscription, all probably enhanced their political status. Certainly, the biographies of the few women who entered the state parliaments in the 1920s point to the war's role in engaging their interests, focusing their efforts, and providing administrative and platform experience. The war presented opportunities for patriotic and philanthropic activity and, in a few cases, it provided the impetus to parliamentary service whose flavour suggested a continuing preoccupation with health and welfare, especially of women and children.

Federal franchise law had from 1902 empowered women to vote as well as to stand for parliament. But with the exception of South Australia, which granted women the right to sit, along with the vote, in 1894, the states continued to prohibit female candidates. Queensland was the first to move to allow women to sit as well as vote, in 1915, and all states had followed by 1923, when Victoria – also the laggard on the franchise before the war – finally granted women the right to stand for parliament. No influx of women into the nation's parliaments followed, however: political parties showed a distinct disinclination to offer women winnable seats, or to let them keep those that they won. Edith Cowan took a seat in the Western Australian assembly as a Nationalist in 1921, becoming the first woman to enter an Australian legislature. But she lasted only a term, defeated by a Nationalist man at the following election (and despite Cowan herself also having Nationalist endorsement). The first Labor woman parliamentarian, May Holman, was also a Western Australian. She won the Labor seat held by her father on his death in 1925. The first New South Wales female parliamentarian, Millicent Preston Stanley, was elected in 1925 as a Nationalist. Like Cowan, she lasted just a term.

The period also saw a political awakening among Indigenous people. Several organisations emerged that were 'Aboriginal' in the sense that they were run by Aboriginal people themselves – often of a mixed racial background – and they expressed a distinctively Aboriginal point of view. The man who is now perhaps the best known of these activists, William Cooper, called this 'thinking black', but it is arguable that several organisations had this notion as their guiding idea.[23] Like later Aboriginal groups, these emphasised land rights, but in their case, the grievances often related to recent dispossession. In the early years of the century and into the interwar years, agricultural land on government reserves had been taken from established Aboriginal families and leased or sold to white settlers. Aboriginal people also opposed the theft of their children by the increasingly aggressive Aboriginal Protection Board. Paternalistic governments isolated Indigenous people on dismal reserves that enforced a strict discipline, while trying to get lighter-skinned Aboriginal people off reserve land entirely.[24]

White sympathisers did play a role in organisations such as the Australian Aboriginal Progressive Association, led by Aboriginal man Fred Maynard. But it is the political activism of Indigenous people themselves that emerges strongly. The campaigning by the veteran, Cooper, and the Australian Aborigines' League in Melbourne in the 1930s is of great interest to the political historian, not least for the stress they placed on the need for special Aboriginal parliamentary representation.[25] Here, too, was a call for political innovation, although one that met with a predictably unfavourable response from the white men who dominated the political system.

Right and left

The era's reputation for conservatism or stagnation rests to some extent on the record and image of the Bruce–Page government. It is easy, of course, to ridicule Bruce, a man who seemed more English than any real Englishman. But Bruce regarded himself as a modern man, one who would bring the methods of business to the business of government. He was attached to the ideal of efficiency more than to the free market. Accordingly, he called for a scientific tariff which, although vague, implied that industry protection should not be provided willy-nilly.[26] His government, in fact, redefined protection to help farmers compete successfully on world markets. There was nothing especially scientific about this: it had much to do with his dependence on the Country Party. So, his government introduced export bounties and incentives, worked towards more efficient marketing, and encouraged migration from Britain, all with the aim of promoting 'development', which was understood as a predominantly rural phenomenon. 'Protection all round' – a product of the shift towards government assistance for farmers during the war, as well as the development of manufacturing responding to the wartime disruption of international trade – would survive until the 1980s.[27]

The Bruce–Page government was innovative in other respects. It improved the budget process.[28] It granted funds to state governments to support road construction. It established a Loan Council that would in 1927 assume exclusive control of federal and state government borrowing. Yet, even as measures such as these augmented the federal government's financial clout, there remained scope for state government initiative in social and economic policy. The Theodore Labor government introduced an unemployment insurance scheme for Queensland in 1923, the Lang Labor government a widow's pension in New South Wales in 1926 (legislated 1925). Both Ted Theodore, the former bush union official, and Jack Lang, the former Sydney real estate agent and auctioneer, were masters of the game of rapidly shifting allegiances and winner-take-all factionalism. And while inter-war Labor politics had something of the character of a charnel house, governments were not bereft of constructive policy.

Labor did much better in state politics than federally. It governed in every state at one time or another in the 1920s; even in Victoria, where it was weakest, it formed minority governments. What any of these governments could do was often limited; obstructionist upper houses, dominated by the wealthy and – where they were elective – biased towards the countryside, were a problem everywhere except in Queensland. Yet, despite the moderation of all these premiers except Lang, the smell of extremism and even illegitimacy – the idea that it represented a mélange of Bolshevism and Sinn Féin republicanism – hung around the party in the 1920s. In the wake of conscription, the general strike of 1917 and the Russian Revolution, Labor seemed more militant, more aggressive, more disloyal than ever before, despite the obvious moderation of leaders such as Frank Tudor, Matthew Charlton and James Scullin.[29] Labor, after all, had buckled during the war in a manner that had betrayed the Anzac spirit – or so its critics held. Even as good and mild a Catholic as Scullin was attracted to more adventurous goals that might eventually – just how eventually, he never explained – lead to full-on socialism. The Communist Party of Australia emerged as a rival on the left. Indeed, in Sydney there were two parties in the early 1920s, each claiming to be the genuine article as certified in Moscow.[30]

For Labor moderates, the Communist presence meant Labor should exercise greater caution in clarifying how its own goals diverged from those of extremists. But others claimed Labor needed to respond positively to the leftward swing. In 1921, at its national conference, the ALP adopted as its objective 'the socialisation of industry, production, distribution and exchange'. Moderates, defeated over this matter, could take comfort from a subsequent resolution moved by the Victorian, Maurice Blackburn, which added the rider that the party did 'not seek to abolish private ownership even of any of the instruments of production where such instrument is utilised by its owner in a socially useful manner and without exploitation'.[31] Labor was vulnerable to the accusation that it had taken a dangerously radical turn, but accusations of disloyalty and extremism probably told more against the party federally than in any state, where the focus was more on bread-and-butter issues.

The waste land?

The years following the war had seen a challenge to the two-party system. Historians have underestimated the degree to which the Country Party upset this pattern because they have focused on the federal sphere, where coalition arrangements were established and, leaving aside the interregnum of 1932–34 when the United Australia Party ruled alone, endured in government with only occasional turbulence of any seriousness. But in Victoria, the Country Party contributed to a complex configuration of parties. Coalition government would not become the norm on the non-Labor side of politics in Victoria until the 1990s.

Partly as a result of the 'disruption' caused by the emergence of this new force, the period is not as bereft of innovation as has sometimes been suggested. It is true that the policy creativity of the early Commonwealth was not matched, yet it should have been surprising if it had been; consolidation was always more likely to follow the pre-war nation-building. All the same, the financial reforms to the federation of the Bruce–Page era were significant, and do represent a continuing process of institution-building. Similarly, while 'protection all round' has earned much opprobrium over the years, it was a reasonable solution to the political problem of balancing diverse interests and the economic one of developing a larger industrial sector. In this respect and others, the era after the First World War seems less of a political wasteland than it has been presented.

10

'THEY SHOULD AT LEAST BE GIVEN A VOICE': ABORIGINAL VETERANS AND THE RSSILA

Richard Trembath

About 1300 Aboriginal Australians served in the First AIF.[1] This was despite the *Defence Act 1903*, as amended in 1909, excluding from military service those who were 'not substantially of European origin or descent'. This provision was administered inconsistently, and with local variation, and, obviously, many Indigenous men entered the army. The horrific number of casualties, especially on the Western Front, resulted in a tweaking of military regulations in May 1917 which permitted the enlistment of so-called half-castes, though racial proprieties demanded that one parent had to be white and of European origin.

The Returned Sailors' and Soldiers' Imperial League of Australia (RSSILA) was formed in 1916 to represent the interests of Australian veterans. As the Returned and Services League of Australia (RSL) it continues in its advocacy, social and commemorative roles, though its influence has waned in recent years. It no longer has anywhere near the public recognition it once possessed. In the early 1990s, Bruce Ruxton, long-serving president of the Victorian RSL, was a fixture in the media, always good for a provocative statement if one was required. In 2019, few Australians, outside the RSL, could name or recognise any of its leaders. But, for much of the

20th century, the League had the ear of government and the muscle to push much of its program.

This chapter examines the sporadic efforts made on behalf of Aboriginal veterans by the RSSILA between 1918 and 1939.[2] These include formal interventions to correct perceived injustices, and informal relationships such as inviting Aboriginals to Anzac ceremonies and League social activities. For Indigenous soldiers overall, their reward for war service was to be omitted from the Anzac narrative, barred from the soldier settlement scheme, and to see the European descent clause remain on the statute books. At its best, at its very best, the RSSILA was lukewarm in its support for Indigenous veterans, but the steps it did take after 1918 presaged their more wholehearted efforts in the cause after the Second World War.

When Noah Riseman and I wrote *Defending Country* (2016) we identified several areas where the RSSILA intervened on behalf of Indigenous soldiers in the inter-war period. Our conclusion was that the League's 'occasional interest in Aboriginal veterans' welfare reflected wider trends in Australian society', especially apathy towards the social situation of Aboriginals. The areas we identified were access to repatriation benefits, publicising the Indigenous contribution to Australia's war, thus including non-white veterans in the Anzac legend from its inception, and welcoming Indigenous colleagues to League activities and facilities.[3]

The establishment in September 1917 of the Department of Repatriation, the ancestor of today's Veterans' Affairs, was a major step in broadening the Commonwealth role in welfare provision. In many ways, former soldiers were privileged members of the community in being eligible for disability payments, while their widows and children might also qualify for assistance. Aboriginal veterans were entitled to the same benefits as other returned men, though in some states pensions or gratuities were not paid directly to former soldiers or their families but were 'doled out' by government authorities when they saw fit. Aboriginal veterans in remote communities, or those who lacked the language skills to pursue claims, also faced difficulties in accessing benefits. A large-scale study into the health outcomes of Victorian Great War veterans shows that Aboriginals in that state did receive repatriation assistance, though other government agencies did little to help them.[4] In Tasmania, as opposed to the mainland states, Aboriginal veterans fared reasonably well in securing their entitlements, despite the previously noted social and geographical factors hindering the process.[5] The League's role in individual cases is very hard to determine, and further close study of repatriation files might be revealing.[6]

Newspapers from the inter-war period show that occasionally the RSSILA called for repatriation and other government assistance for Aboriginal veterans. For example, in April 1938 the City of Sydney sub-branch passed a resolution stating that 'all men of Aboriginal blood who served in the A.I.F. be granted full citizen's rights, and all social services be made available to them'. This was in response to the plight of an Aboriginal from Baryulgil in New South Wales, who had been wounded while serving in the 11th Battalion, but whose wife was being denied the maternity allowance on the grounds of her Aboriginality.[7]

In March 1939, the Conference of the Central Queensland District of the League passed a motion that tied the question of pensions to the restrictions placed on the movement and residence of Aboriginals in Queensland. This meeting asked that 'representations be made to the State Government with a view of aborigines who are returned soldiers being given their freedom from aboriginal settlements, if so desired, especially those receiving war pensions'.[8] Not long afterwards, Mr R Hay, a clergyman speaking at the League's Anzac Day ceremonies at the newly formed sub-branch at The Rock in southern New South Wales, also touched on the issue of pensions. In a short prayer Mr Hay noted that 'every returned man without a job and aborigine ex-servicemen without even the comfort of a pension, is a reproach to the government and to us'.[9] It is not surprising that government assistance to former soldiers was discussed more often at that time as veterans, especially those disabled by wounds or illness, aged and became increasingly incapacitated.

Now, we come to the soldier settlement scheme that was for Aboriginal veterans largely an unhappy experience. Soldier settlement was a major part of the post-war repatriation project, but Aboriginals were, for many reasons, excluded from it. In the mainland states we know of six Aboriginal applicants who managed to clear the bureaucratic hurdles and overt racism of the authorities and obtain rural blocks. Once again, in Tasmania, the story is better, with nine successful applicants who may have triumphed by not being regarded as 'Aboriginals' in a state that apparently no longer had Indigenous inhabitants. But deeming Aboriginals as unsuitable block-holders is only one part of this miserable story. In Victoria and New South Wales Aboriginal reserves were seized to provide blocks to returned soldiers. And in Victoria local branches of the RSSILA connived at this land grab by exerting pressure on the inaccurately named Board for the Protection of Aborigines to corral Indigenous people into one location in Gippsland and open the rest of their former homes up for subdivision and closer settlement.[10]

Despite the RSSILA's poor record regarding soldier settlement, some Aboriginal veterans participated in League activities, maintained friendship with white colleagues, and were part of a wider Anzac community at a local level. The story of Douglas Grant,[11] with its melancholy conclusion, has become better known in recent years, and we can glean other instances of mateship from the public record and family stories. In May 1934 the *Cootamundra Herald* reported on the funeral of one former

Aboriginal soldier who had served for three years in France with the 18th Battalion: 'Was there ever a more popular Aboriginal than the late John James Dunn, of Bethungra, who was killed by a car last Saturday night. The funeral in Cootamundra on Sunday was in itself a testimony to his esteem'. The Cootamundra RSSILA sent a wreath to Mr Dunn's service.[12]

Similarly, Walter McCready, an Aboriginal returned man from the 59th Battalion, a resident of Coranderrk, Victoria, who died in May 1935, was obviously respected for his war service. The president and secretary of the Healesville RSSILA both attended McCready's funeral. The irony here is that the Coranderrk Aboriginal reserve had been closed in 1924, despite the objections of some Victorian Aboriginal veterans, partly for the purposes of soldier settlement. It seems that mateship only went so far.[13] In Adelaide, on Anzac Day 1938, a newspaper reported that several Aboriginals from Point McLeay were 'prominent figures on the crowded steps of the R.S.S.I.L.A. rooms'. Two had been prisoners of war. The title of the article – 'All Cobbers Again' – is interesting. Wishful thinking perhaps or pious hope?[14]

Such instances of inclusion and collegiality should be treated carefully. As noted in *Defending Country*, local sub-branches of the League had considerable independence of action, and though former Aboriginal comrades might be visible at a public event like Anzac, this does not mean these same comrades were welcomed with open arms to regular League meetings. Tom Williams from the Salt Pan Creek camp in Sydney who was an active member of his local branch, and Douglas Grant who served as secretary at Lithgow, were probably exceptions to the rule. I would argue that for many Aboriginal veterans the League was somebody else's business. Yet, I would also contend that historian Philippa Scarlett is harsh in claiming that the purported wartime mateship between white and Aboriginal soldiers was transient. Not in all cases, I think.[15]

Sometimes, friendships or empathy might extend as far as white veterans calling for greater social justice for their Aboriginal counterparts. In 1930, for example, the Townsville branch of the RSSILA protested at the confinement of two 'half-caste returned soldiers' on Palm Island upon expiration of their prison terms for minor offences:

> The district secretary of the Townsville branch of the R.S.S.I.L.A. this morning characterised the confinement of these two men on an aboriginal settlement as amazing, and added that if they were good enough to fight for Australia in the Great War they were certainly good enough to mix with their fellow countrymen and enjoy the liberty for which they fought.[16]

Here, we see an argument that was first advanced by Aboriginal activists after the First World War. If you were up to fighting in the trenches, then you qualified for citizenship rights, however these were defined.

Four years later, the Belmore, New South Wales, branch of the RSSILA protested at the prison sentences imposed on eight Aboriginals from Northern Australia:

> The Belmore branch of the R.S.S.I.L.A. have, after discussion, adopted a resolution protesting against the methods adopted in the conviction and death sentence imposed on eight Northern Australia aborigines (since commuted to imprisoned for life.)
>
> The ex-soldiers also demand that an inquiry should be held and that the natives should have representation by a legal advisor of their own selection. The resolution points out the aborigines' lack of knowledge of the white man's laws,

and further points out that a long term of confinement is equivalent to a death sentence for the aborigines.[17]

The significance of this protest should not be overlooked. A small section of the League was protesting on behalf of Aboriginals who were not (presumably) returned men. And they were also displaying a sense of cultural niceties and difference that was not widely demonstrated throughout Australian society at that time.

By the early 1930s, the League was becoming more aware of Aboriginal veterans and their part in the First AIF. One way the New South Wales branch demonstrated this new interest was by attempting to count just how many Aboriginals had actually served, a process which, though incomplete, was still pursued vigorously. As a result, in November 1931 and January 1932, the branch published in its journal *Reveille* the names of those Indigenous soldiers it could identify in Queensland, New South Wales and Victoria.[18]

One of the most important markers of citizenship, perhaps the most important, is possession of the suffrage. In the inter-war period, many Indigenous Australians did not have the right to vote, excluded by repressive state legislation. As early as 1920 one regional conference of the RSSILA considered that denying this right to Aboriginal veterans was wrong. Their initiative was not followed by other sections of the League, yet their argument closely resembled that of Aboriginal activists at that time:

> The opinion has been expressed in some quarters that aboriginals who fought with the A.I.F. in the late war should be given the right to vote at State or Federal elections. It is concluded that if the aboriginals thought so much of their country by enlisting they should at least be given a voice in the election of men to run the affairs in that country. The Western District of the R.S.S.I.L.A ... at its conference in Toowoomba

> ... [carried] a motion ... that it be a recommendation to the authorities that aboriginals who fought with the A.I.F. be granted the privilege of voting.[19]

Finally, on the cusp of another global war, the League called on the Commonwealth government to grant citizenship rights to those Aboriginals who had served with the First AIF. As noted below, Canberra's response is best described as tepid, but now that the League had endorsed some circumscribed 'citizen rights' for Aboriginal soldiers, it kept returning to this issue:

> Soldiers' Notes
>
> Citizen Rights for Aboriginal Diggers Sought
>
> A suggestion by the R.S.S.I.L.A. to the Commonwealth Government that full citizen rights and their families, was replied to by the Prime Minister's Department.[20]

This suggestion from the RSSILA and the Commonwealth government's response received wide coverage in the Queensland press. The government's reply was a familiar one after the Second World War. The Commonwealth 'controlled' Aboriginals only in the Northern Territory and the Australian Capital Territory. Otherwise, it was up to the six states as to what privileges they did or did not grant to their Aboriginal populations. However, the federal Minister of the Interior 'recently announced that in the formulation of the aboriginal welfare policy for the Northern Territory, consideration would be given to the question of full citizenship rights to selected aborigines'.[21]

War, especially a protracted conflict, may promote social change or delay it, pending the outbreak of peace. Occasionally, things can go backwards. For example, when the Second World War began, the Australian government reverted to resisting Aboriginal enlistment in the armed forces, except in special circumstances. Again, this proved untenable as many Indigenous Australians did manage to enlist. In November 1941, the League renewed its call for Aboriginal veterans to be granted citizenship rights.[22] Then, as the Japanese conquered South-East Asia and European possessions in the Pacific, and many Australians sensed possible invasion, the Boulia, Queensland, sub-branch of the League resolved that it was 'a gross injustice' that Aboriginals should be barred from the army 'on account of their colour', especially given their service in the First World War. It was not the time 'to allow petty prejudices to interfere with the defence of Australia'. Other sections of the League shared this sentiment.[23]

The crisis of 1942 meant the shelving of the European descent clause, though the colour bar in the armed forces was not formally lifted until 1949–51. The threat to Australia's north resulted in the formation of two specifically Indigenous formations, the Torres Strait Light Infantry Battalion and the Northern Territory Special Reconnaissance Unit. These initiatives, plus the publicity given to Lieutenant Reg Saunders, generally hailed as the first Indigenous commissioned officer, should have seen the final removal of impediments to Indigenous participation in the defence forces. Not quite. After the war, the Chifley government tried to restrict Aboriginal membership of the sizeable Australian component of the British Commonwealth Occupation Force (BCOF) in Japan to a minimum, ostensibly so the racial susceptibilities of their Japanese 'hosts' would not be upset. It was a policy shot through with confusion and contradiction and many Aboriginals ended up serving in BCOF.[24]

SOCIAL, POLITICAL AND PERSONAL LEGACIES

In April 1946, the Victorian branch of the League urged their federal executive to take action regarding the exclusion of Aboriginal veterans from civil society. They noted the 'high service rendered by Australian Aborigines' in the forces for which 'their subsequent treatment as civilians' seemed poor reward. The Victorians, perhaps influenced by Reg Saunders coming from that state, requested the executive to ask the Commonwealth government to lift some of 'the regulations restricting the social life of Aborigine ex-servicemen'.[25]

This was well meaning but rather general and probably referred to permitting Aboriginal servicemen (not all Aboriginals) to drink in pubs and purchase alcohol legally, an important privilege in its own right. Later in 1946, the League's 31st Annual National Conference passed a more specific resolution calling on the government 'to grant the franchise to Aboriginal ex-servicemen'.[26] This push by the League was sustained and ultimately successful, although it took three years of effort. The Victorian branch continued to play a leading role in arguing that service in the forces was proof that one had qualified as an Australian, to some degree anyway. It is evident that support for extension of voting rights to Aboriginal veterans was strong among the League rank and file, stronger than it had been before the Second World War. Some of the rhetoric is reminiscent of the rights-based language that gradually became more frequent in political discourse after 1945 and the formation of international organisations such as the United Nations. For example, William F Wannan from the Caulfield Central sub-branch of the Victorian RSL, wrote to the *Argus* newspaper in March 1947 that a recent meeting there had unanimously agreed that the franchise be extended to Aboriginal ex-servicemen:

> It is to be hoped that other sub-branches of our league, as well as every progressive organisation throughout the country, will take up this cause. We cannot regard ourselves as an

enlightened or democratic community while a section of our citizens, which played so proud and worthy a part in our war effort at home and abroad, is denied those rights which are an essential part of democracy.[27]

The Chifley Labor government, otherwise known for its vigorous legislative activity, did not move quickly in implementing what the League desired, but in its last year the *Commonwealth Electoral Act 1949* automatically granted the federal vote to Aboriginal servicemen. However, in Queensland and Western Australia, Aboriginals remained largely excluded from voting in state elections.[28]

Without the specific circumstances of the Second World War, especially greater public awareness of Aboriginal participation at home and overseas, the 1949 Act would never have been. Without League pressure the Act would never have been. And without the slow growth of empathy in some sections of the League in the interwar period that organisation might not have supported even limited electoral reform for the Aboriginals with whom they had served.

The history of the League remains sadly underwritten, and what history there is, is generally souvenir in nature rather than critical. As far as the problematic relationship between the League and Indigenous Australians is concerned, closer study of state level and local organisations is necessary, overdue in fact. One question could be, why, until late in the 20th century, did the League wax and wane in its acknowledgment of how Indigenous Australians had served in Australia's wars?

11

ANZAC TRAUMA AND FRONTIER VIOLENCE? RE-EXAMINING THE CONISTON MASSACRE

Thomas J Rogers

The personal impact of front-line service in the Great War has long been a topic of debate.[1] Since the late 20th century, historians have considered how soldiers' wartime experiences might have affected their lives on return to Australia. There is, however, a danger in assuming that all criminal or irrational behaviour committed by returned men was a direct result of their service. This chapter considers the case of the perpetrator of the 1928 Coniston Massacre, the former soldier turned police constable William George Murray. In the wake of the killings, an official inquiry found that 31 Central Australian Aboriginal people had been killed, but the true figure was probably much higher. That same inquiry cleared Murray and his followers of all wrongdoing, accepting his claim that they had killed people in self-defence.

In some retellings of the events, Murray's war service is presented as the key to understanding the violence. Murray's wartime experiences might have inured him to death and killing, and military drill might have provided him with mechanisms for coping with stress and trauma. However, it is too simplistic to assume that his life was solely defined by any trauma resulting from the years 1914–18. Instead, it is more productive to consider Murray's involvement in two very different conflicts that shaped the Australian

20th century: the Great War and frontier violence. This chapter makes two interpretive interventions. Against the claim that Murray had no police training, I contend that his time on the frontier was the equivalent of training on the job. To those who claim Murray went 'military' during the massacre, I disagree and say he went 'frontier'. Examining the two conflicts in which he participated allows us a clearer insight into both, and suggests ways forward in the study of their impact on Australian society.

A soldier on the frontier?

Over the last three decades, historians have re-examined the stories of Great War soldiers returning to Australia. In addition to physical wounds, historians have been concerned with the psychological effects of war service. This has followed greater public awareness of lasting wartime trauma. It is possible, however, to conclude erroneously that all returned soldiers brought back invisible wounds that determined their post-war experiences and actions.[2] We cannot simply assume that Murray perpetrated a massacre of Aboriginal people as a result of his war experiences. Beyond simple speculation, there is little evidence that Murray's war service led to his committing a frontier massacre a decade after returning. Instead, as we shall see, his time as a frontier policeman steeped him in a frontier attitude that allowed him to justify the mass killing of Aboriginal people. His actions were not shaped by the war, but by much longer and deeper patterns of Australian violence. He was a participant in two conflicts that were very different in aims, scope, and nature, but each in its own way has left indelible imprints on modern Australia.

Much is made of the lack of police training that Murray – and many other police in the Northern Territory – received before going on duty. Instead, commentators make note of his AIF background and battle experience. Almost as a throwaway line, the authors of the most comprehensive scholarly account of the killings argue that 'when confronted in Warlpiri country Murray went into "military mode", simply falling back on his war experience and acting as if he was in a war, a state with which he had much experience'. The authors then describe Murray's tactics. When Murray's men first encountered a group of Aboriginal people, 'at Murray's order, [they] formed an extended line – in the tradition of the Light Horse – with Murray in the centre'.[3] Another historian describes how 'in true military style Murray moved into the camp ordering them to disarm'.[4] These descriptions of Murray's tactics are not necessarily wrong, but they do not give the whole picture. In any case, settlers commonly used tactics such as these in much earlier frontier massacres, suggesting that Murray's actions fitted into a longer history of colonial conflict.

Sidney Downer, a mid-20th-century historian of the Northern Territory police, suggested a different interpretation of the Coniston killings. He concluded that Murray had 'successfully conducted the final war between white men and [A]borigines in Central Australia'.[5] Setting aside the apparent approbation with which Downer reported this, his frank characterisation of the events is a useful historical interpretation. What happened at Coniston was only the bloodiest stage of a conflict for the country and its resources. One of the punitive party later described the events in words that could also be used to describe the overall objective. He said, '[i]t was either the native go down or we go down'.[6]

Murray's Great War service

Murray enlisted in the AIF less than a month after the British declaration of war in August 1914. He joined the 4th Light Horse Regiment, because he had nine years' experience in a Victorian mounted infantry militia unit. With this unit he left Australia in October as part of the first convoy bound for the European and Middle Eastern theatres.

The Australians arrived in Egypt in December, and commenced training in camps near Cairo. Horses were unsuitable for the mountainous terrain of Gallipoli, so the squadrons of Murray's unit were broken up and the dismounted troopers reinforced the infantry on the peninsula from May 1915. In August, Murray was wounded in his left shoulder and was evacuated to a British hospital on the island of Malta, and then to a hospital in Egypt. He returned to Gallipoli in October. By this time, British commanders were already planning an evacuation of the peninsula, and Murray returned to Egypt in December.

In Egypt, the AIF was reorganised and greatly increased in size. In order to take advantage of their mobility, the light horse regiments were deployed to the Sinai–Palestine campaigns. Murray did not join them. He was a member of one of the few light horse squadrons that were sent to the Western Front. In France, his squadron joined other Australian, New Zealand and British mounted troops to form the II Anzac Corps Mounted Regiment. In the stagnant trench warfare of 1916 and 1917, mounted soldiers could not be used to their full tactical potential, so Murray served in a variety of detachments in rear areas and in the front lines. In the front-line trenches, the men of the unit fought dismounted as regular infantry. When not at the front, their roles included traffic control and policing, manning anti-aircraft guns, and guarding prisoners. Murray was slightly wounded in his right arm near Fleurbaix in August 1916, but remained on duty.

By September 1917, Murray had been promoted to the rank of sergeant. He was detached to the School of Instruction and as a result did not follow his unit into the Third Battle of Ypres later in the year. Murray returned to his unit in March 1918, two days before German forces began their last-ditch effort to win the war, now known as the German Spring Offensive. This offensive ushered in a war of movement, in which his unit's mobility at last became an advantage.

Along with other Australians who had served in the war from the beginning, Murray was granted time at home, known as Anzac leave, in October 1918. He returned to Australia and was discharged in March 1919. Later that year, he joined the Northern Territory police, and began a series of postings before becoming constable in charge at Barrow Creek in 1926. This was the position he held at the time of the Coniston killings.[7]

Murray's experiences on Gallipoli and the Western Front do not offer any unique insights into his actions at Coniston. His proficiency with a rifle and military discipline were fostered in his pre-war militia service, and as we shall see, his attitudes to Aboriginal people and how to police them stem from a much older Australian frontier tradition.

The Coniston killings

The exact sequence of events in the Coniston story has never been settled with certainty. What follows is a brief version of events drawn from the inquiry into the killings, Aboriginal oral history from decades after the events, and the few scholarly secondary sources that exist.

By 1928, Central Australia had been in the grip of drought for four years. Dingo trapper Frederick Brooks sought and received permission from his friend Randal Stafford, the squatter of Coniston cattle station, to go trapping on the land. Stafford warned that he and the Aboriginal woman he lived with, Alice, had received death threats from local traditional-living Aboriginal men. Nonetheless, Brooks and the two Aboriginal boys who trapped with him set up camp on Yurrkuru, a soakage west of Coniston station. There, it appears that Brooks arranged with Warlpiri man Bullfrog Japanangka for the latter's wife to do his laundry in return for food and tobacco. However, Brooks did not uphold his end of the bargain and was murdered by Bullfrog and another man in early August 1928.[8]

A second incident involving a white man occurred around the same time. In late August 1928, William 'Nugget' Morton, of nearby Broadmeadow station, was attacked by a large party of Aboriginal men in retaliation for his sexual abuse of local women. Though badly wounded, Morton managed to kill one of his attackers and survive the attack. Responding to the Brooks murder, in late 1928 Mounted Constable Murray arrived from Barrow Creek. Ostensibly seeking to arrest the murderers, he led a punitive expedition north along the Lander River. This heavily armed party comprised both white and Aboriginal men. Murray also led a similar expedition with Morton, again ostensibly to arrest his attackers.[9]

The first act of mass killing occurred when Murray and the party rode into a camp of Aboriginal people near Yurrkuru. He later said that his party killed five people there in self-defence and claimed they were all involved in Brooks' murder. This pattern of attack was repeated over the following weeks, and Murray later testified that his party had killed 17 Aboriginal people. On expedition with 'Nugget' Morton, Murray claimed that a further 14 people were killed while resisting arrest. Similarly, all those killed were said to have participated in the attempt on Morton's life. These figures gave rise to the officially accepted death toll of 31.[10]

Shocking as the massacre was, it is best understood as the most dramatic stage in the overarching struggle for control of the country. Aboriginal memories and retellings of the killings provide context in a way that white written records do not. In the 1970s, Warlpiri woman and Bullfrog's granddaughter, Rosie Nungarrayi, recalled the tactics used by Murray and his party: '[t]he whitefellas followed the tracks at soakages. They rode up with two men on the side and another in the middle – just like they were rounding up bullocks'. She also described Murray's party returning to seek out more people: '[b]ack over the tracks, looking for people who had come back after the shooting. Even then he shot more people'.[11] Nungarrayi's recollections, and those of other Central Australian Aboriginal people, show that Murray targeted local Aboriginal people as a group. This was not deliberative police work, as Murray presented it. The killings had an ongoing effect and presence in the region. Some years after the massacre, Aboriginal stockman Walter Smith visited the Lander River and saw what he thought were wild watermelons. They were skulls. 'A man felt sorry,' he recalled. 'There must have been two hundred of them – big ones, little ones, men, women, kids, everyone.' Smith's recollections suggest that the officially accepted death toll of 31 was too low.

The effects linger to this day. Francis Jupurrurla Kelly, a Warlpiri Elder and a co-director of the powerful 2012 film *Coniston*, told an audience in Sydney, 'We never [just] lost our people, we lost our Countries too'.[12] These remarks by Nungarrayi, Smith and Kelly respectively highlight the tactics, the aftermath, and the broader strategic outcomes of the killings. The massacre that began at Yurrkuru was not an isolated, random outburst of violence carried out by a war-ravaged madman. It was the bloodiest act of a struggle for country and resources.

A frontier attitude

Police on the 19th-century South Australian frontier, which included the Northern Territory, operated in 'a special zone of police/Aboriginal warfare'.[13] In this zone, police superiors occasionally recommended actions that would have been unlawful or ambiguous in a normal policing context. Remote subordinates decided when and how to suspend ordinary rules of behaviour, especially when it came to arresting or firing on traditional-living Aboriginal people. Police officers and settlers alike articulated a frontier attitude from the middle of the 19th century. At its core was the recognition that Aboriginal people and settlers were engaged in a struggle over control of the land, its resources and its usage. During his decade of police work in Central Australia, Murray would have been steeped in this frontier attitude.

Peter Egerton Warburton, the South Australian commissioner of police, exemplified the attitude in 1855 when he recommended that 'savages' who killed settlers should be summarily executed.[14] Two decades later, in June 1875, the South Australian public was outraged when Aboriginal men speared the white telegraph stationmaster at Roper River.[15] Paul Foelsche, Sub-Inspector of the Northern Territory Mounted Police, ordered his men to capture all members of the attacking party, 'either dead or alive'. He ended his orders ominously: 'I cannot give you orders to shoot all natives you come across but circumstances may occur for which I cannot provide definite instructions'.[16] Warburton and Foelsche informed their subordinate officers that extra-judicial killing was sometimes acceptable. Settlers likewise argued that legal niceties should not always be observed. In 1890, the *Northern Territory Times* summarised the frontier attitude with the following line: 'it is quite clear that the [A]boriginal question ... can only be settled to the satisfaction of the white man by a liberal use of powder and ball'.[17] At around the same time, a government official in the Territory received a letter from a settler in the Gulf Country who had survived a spearing. The settler related how the encounter had changed his attitude towards Aboriginal people, and he reported simply: 'I now shoot at sight. Killed to date thirty-seven'.[18] This settler openly admitted to his crimes to a government official with no fear of legal retribution.

The frontier attitude was alive and well among the men of Murray's 1928 punitive party. One of the white members, the prospector Jack Saxby, told the inquiry that he had been set upon by a number of men with spears at the second camp the party had attacked. Dismounting from his horse, he fired four or five shots with his rifle, telling the inquiry: 'I do not know whether I hit them or not. I certainly tried'. Regarding his previous experiences in the Territory, he told the inquiry that he always carried a revolver, and he made no secret of having 'had occasion to shoot at blacks before this trouble. I have had to shoot to kill'.[19] When giving evidence at the inquiry, other members of the party also described a violent and uncertain frontier, and sought to justify the killings.

Randal Stafford, Coniston's squatter, accompanied the party on its first raid on the camp at Yurrkuru before returning to the homestead. During the raid, he was posted to the far end of the camp to catch anyone who might flee from the arresting constable. He was not happy to see the bodies when he re-joined the party, but he reasoned: '[i]f I had been in the place of Constable Murray I would have shot too. I wouldn't let them get me first'. Coniston station employee Billy Briscoe gave evidence that he did not murder anyone, but he justified the killings by observing that '[i]t was absolutely essential for the natives to be shot to save our own lives'. Referring to the second punitive party, Morton used very similar phrasing. He told the inquiry, 'It was absolutely essential for the preservation of the lives of Constable Murray and myself for these natives to be killed and we did not kill one black more than was necessary to get off with our lives'.[20] The frontier zone that Saxby, Stafford, Briscoe and Morton presented to the inquiry was a borderland of violence.

The members of both expeditions – the first to find Brooks' murderers, and the second to find Morton's attackers – were aware that they could be accused of having indiscriminately carried out reprisal attacks on local Aboriginal groups. Indeed, the chairman of the inquiry raised the possibility, putting to Murray that '[i]t has been suggested that these were reprisals or punitive expeditions to clean up the blacks so that they would never return'. Murray replied: '[t]hat never entered my head or that of any of my party so far as I know. My last instructions were not to shoot unless it was absolutely necessary. We had opportunities to shoot perhaps hundreds'.[21]

Saxby also rejected the possibility of the raid being a reprisal. 'This was not a party got up for the purpose of wiping out the blacks before the blacks would wipe out the settlers', he told the inquiry, adding that '[w]e could have killed 100 if our object was for reprisal'.[22] The similarity of their evidence, combined with Walter Smith's estimation that he saw 200 skulls, suggests that the expedition members killed many more people than the 31 to which they admitted. Furthermore, Bullfrog Japanangka, the man who killed Brooks, was never arrested and lived openly in Yuendumu until his death in 1959. This extraordinary fact suggests that pacification of the local population, not police work, was the overarching objective of the punitive expeditions.

The French political theorist Jacques Sémelin argues that a massacre is committed for a rational political purpose. Despite how shocked we might be on learning about a massacre, it is possible to identify what the perpetrators wanted to accomplish. Sémelin also noted the propensity for killing to descend into the irrational, with madness often ascribed to the killers.[23] Discussion of the Coniston Massacre often includes the inference that Murray was broken: that only a man so damaged by the horrors of industrial warfare could behave this way. Francis Jupurrurla Kelly expressed this view when he said,

> he was a madman that Murray, Sergeant Murray, because he was fighting at Gallipoli in that time and he came along and he was a little bit sick in his head, you know from war, gone crazy. Shooting innocent people and children.[24]

The filmmaker's words cut through to a truth about the killings that more distanced academic observers often miss, no doubt because re-enactment was central to his film project. A killing spree must involve some sort of madness. But we must not allow that to obscure our understanding of the settler objective of clearing the country of traditional-living Aboriginal people. As Kelly also pointed out: 'After that massacre, [Aboriginal] people got pushed away. Station owners got their land, and the miners got their gold, and we shifted onto government settlements'.[25] The Coniston Massacre was a calculated act in a long tradition of frontier killings, not a moment of madness.

Murray as a participant in two conflicts

It is possible that Murray's AIF experiences shaped his actions in Central Australia. However, it is far more likely that his nine years as a frontier policeman steeped him in local attitudes that had been around for nearly a century. It was these attitudes, expressed by 19th-century police officials and 20th-century settlers alike, that led him and his party to view his bailiwick as a zone of conflict and struggle for resources. If we fail to consider the frontier attitude, the Great War threatens to frame our understanding of warfare. The terrain, circumstances and objectives were very different in Europe and Australia. Almost no similarities existed between the two conflicts, yet in different ways, each profoundly shaped Australia's 20th century. The fascinating aspect of Murray's case is that the two conflicts he participated in have a markedly imbalanced representation in present-day understanding. The Great War has become a much-mythologised conflict, whereas frontier conflicts feature very little in public discourse, education or commemoration. With a clear-eyed view of the aftermath of the First World War and frontier violence, however, we can come to a better historical understanding of both conflicts.

12

REMEMBERING THE RESILIENT

Joan Beaumont

On 5 February 1931, Harold 'Pompey' Elliott, who had commanded the 15th Brigade of the AIF during the First World War, returned from his city office to his home in the Melbourne suburb of Camberwell. He handed his sister-in-law, Belle, the insurance policies for his children and some share certificates, saying she might need the money.[1] Later that night, Elliott was found in the kitchen, his head in the oven. The air was full of gas and he was semi-conscious. Some days later, he was admitted to the Alfred Hospital, in the hope that this might prevent his making another suicide attempt. Elliott stayed there almost a month, and then came home; but on 22 March he was readmitted to a private hospital in Malvern. The staff there were supposedly on 'suicide alert', but Elliott somehow kept hold of his shaving gear. At 4.25 the following morning, he was found with a razor blade embedded in a deep gash near his left elbow. He had died of blood loss.

Later that year, in December 1931, Charles Hawker, a South Australian who had fought with the British Army on the Western Front, stood for the federal parliamentary seat of Wakefield, which he had first won in the 1929 electoral landslide that brought down the government of SM Bruce.[2] Once re-elected, Hawker was appointed Minister for Markets and Repatriation (a portfolio renamed Commerce in 1932). He later resigned from the ministry over the issue of whether parliamentarians' salaries should be reduced (he thought they should) but remained prominent in federal politics. His war wounds had left Hawker with only one eye, nerve damage in one arm and partial paralysis from the waist down, but he travelled widely across remote areas of Australia, Europe, Russia, China and Japan, to keep informed on rural, national and international developments. By the late 1930s, Hawker was considered to be a potential successor to Prime Minister Joe Lyons. However, he was killed as a passenger in a plane crash in late 1938, near Mount Dandenong in Victoria.

On 18 November 1933, a third veteran of the First World War, and recipient of the Victoria Cross, Hugo Throssell, rewrote his will while his wife, the renowned author and radical activist, Katharine Susannah Prichard, was travelling in Moscow.[3] The following morning, at first light, Throssell removed his Webley revolver from its harness and loaded it with a single bullet. Still in his pyjamas, he sat in a chair on the back veranda of his home in rural Western Australia and shot himself in the temple.

Two of these three narratives are well known. The deaths of Elliott and Throssell attracted considerable publicity at the time they occurred, since both men were celebrities during the First World War and well-known public figures in the post-war era. Ninety years later, both men continue to figure prominently in the national narratives of war, as represented in the Australian War Memorial. Hawker, by contrast, is relatively little known, except perhaps in his home state of South Australia where an electorate is named after him (though this is no guarantee of fame). Yet Hawker's post-war life spoke to remarkable resilience. Why, then, has his story of post-war adjustment, which by many criteria seems to have been extraordinarily successful, attracted less attention than the succumbing of Elliott and Throssell to what we would now call post-traumatic stress? Furthermore – and this is a far more intractable question – why was it that the man who, in a physical sense at least, was left with the most traumatic legacy of war, proved ultimately to be the more resilient?

Life histories

The search for answers to these questions must begin with the life histories of these three men. Elliott had a somewhat impoverished and troubled childhood, living on a selection near Charlton, Victoria, where the family struggled to make a livelihood from the harsh Australian environment. His father was frequently absent, having an insatiable wanderlust, and when Elliott was only eight years old, his older brother became criminally insane, possibly because of a personality change that resulted from a fractured skull. The family's financial position was transformed when Elliott's father struck it lucky on the Western Australian gold fields, but then, tragically, one of Harold's sisters suicided after a bout of severe influenza. Harold ultimately became a brilliant, prize-winning student at the University of Melbourne, was a champion athlete, and graduated as a lawyer. He served in the militia and with the 4th Victorian (Imperial) Contingent in the South African war of 1899–02 and was mentioned in dispatches and awarded the Distinguished Conduct Medal.

Elliott was 36 years old when he volunteered for the First World War. Wounded on the first day of the landing at Gallipoli, he soon recovered to take charge of a battalion during the August 1915 offensive. On the Western Front he commanded the 15th Brigade from 1916 to 1918, including at the catastrophic battle of Fromelles in July 1916. So distraught was he at the pointless loss of life in this diversionary action, that he greeted the survivors with tears streaming down his face. In later actions, Elliott gained the reputation for being a brilliant, if idiosyncratic, commander, able to respond rapidly to changing tactical situations, and to deploy his troops effectively. Willing to take considerable – even foolhardy – personal risks while commanding at the front, he became a household name among the troops and the population at home. However, Elliott also gained a reputation among his superiors for poor judgment, undiplomatic candour about British troops and a lack of emotional control. Hence, in May 1918, he was not given command of a division when the leadership of the Australian Corps was reorganised. This 'supersession', as he called it, was an injustice which 'colored all [his] post war life'.[4]

On his return to Australia, Elliott became a prominent advocate for returned soldiers: providing free legal advice; raising funds for, and unveiling, war memorials; working to establish Anzac Day as a semi-sacred annual rite; and taking a leadership role in the RSSILA. His legal practice was re-established without difficulty, and he became President of the Law Institute of Victoria in 1927. He also stood successfully as a Nationalist senator for Victoria in 1919; and in 1927 finally gained the divisional command (3rd Division) that had eluded him in 1918.

Throssell, in contrast to Elliott, had a secure childhood, his father, George, being a short-lived premier of Western Australia and a prosperous landowner and merchant. Though forbidding and remote, George was also an indulgent father, and his children lacked nothing material. Hugo was adored by his five sisters and gentle mother. He was 29 when he volunteered in Western Australia for the 10th Light Horse. He first served at Gallipoli where he was in the fourth line of the disastrous charge at the Nek. Some weeks later, Throssell won the VC when he led his men in a frenetic hand-to-hand exchange of bombs with the Ottomans at Hill 60. This action, in which he was wounded, made him, like Elliott, a national celebrity. While recuperating in Australia in 1916, he made a triumphal tour to promote recruiting. As his son, Ric, later recalled: he made '[a] stirring figure in polished riding boots, breeches, Sam Browne and the emu feather-tufted slouch hat, the modest purple tab of the Victoria Cross on the left breast of his tunic'. He 'only had to appear for enlistments to improve'.[5] Prichard, too, later recalled, that 'If we dined in town, I could hear the whispers going round: "Throssell, V.C." and crowds collected to cheer us as we passed'.[6] Returning to the battlefront in 1917, Throssell saw out the war in the Palestine campaign. Being wounded at Gaza in April 1917 and catching malaria in the Jordan valley, he spent much of the last year of the war in hospital.[7]

After the war, Throssell had sufficient private means to settle on a property outside Perth and to raise capital for speculative land purchases. By virtue of his VC, he enjoyed a privileged status within the community of ex-servicemen. However, this asset was compromised when Throssell announced at a Victory Parade in July 1919 that his experience of the horrors of the war had made him a socialist. At a time of rampant anti-Bolshevik sentiment, this meant that Throssell, like Prichard, came under the surveillance of ASIO. As the Australian economy slipped into depression in the late 1920s, Throssell's debts mounted. Much of the property he had bought with borrowings from the banks remained unsold; and his tenants were unable to meet their rental payments. In April 1931, he was retrenched from his position at the Discharged Soldiers' Settlement Board, supposedly because of budget cuts. Throssell then invested in a series of increasingly wild speculative ventures: oil exploration in the state's northwest; prospecting for alluvial gold near Coolgardie; and staging a major rodeo-style event – only to find that he could not recoup his costs because regulations forbade charging an entry fee on Sundays. When he committed suicide shortly after, on the back of his will he wrote 'I have never recovered from my 1914–18 experiences, and, with this in view, I appeal to the State to see that my wife and child get the usual war pension'.[8] They did, but it was of little consolation. Prichard, who read the news of her husband's death in a British newspaper, wrote years later:

> I went overseas ... on the understanding that Jim [Hugo] would do nothing while I was away to make me regret leaving him. It was a terrible mistake ... I had absolute faith in him and don't know how I survived the days when I realized I would never see him again. The end of our lives together is still inexplicable to me.[9]

Throssell's son, then a child of 11, was likewise bereft:

> It was not possible that a man I loved so much could have wanted to die. He couldn't have. He could do everything. He couldn't have wanted to leave me by myself. ... How could he have wanted to leave us? We were so happy, the three of us.[10]

Hawker was considerably younger than Elliott and Throssell – only 20 years of age – when he volunteered for the war.[11] A scion of a wealthy South Australian pastoralist and Merino stud breeder, he had an idyllic life in a family that had sufficient wealth to travel and fund his education at Geelong Grammar. Hawker was studying at Cambridge when war broke out. Deeply infused with imperial sentiment, he joined a British regiment, the 6th Battalion Somerset Light Infantry. The first injury that he suffered was at Loos, in September 1915; it was here that he lost his left eye and suffered nerve damage in his left arm. By most standards, his war service would have ended then. However, after 14 operations, Hawker insisted on being sent back to the front. He suffered his second, more grievous wound at Poelcappelle in late 1917. Although his paralysis suggested that he would never walk again, after further surgery, and with relentless personal determination, Hawker managed to walk with leg irons and sticks. Before returning to Australia he went back to Cambridge in a wheelchair and graduated with a high second-class honours. Back home, he took courses in forestry and botany, assumed an active role in managing family properties in the mid-north of South Australia, learned to drive a specially adapted car, and took on leadership roles in the RSSILA. Ultimately, as mentioned, he had a successful political career as a member of successive Nationalist/United Australia Party governments.

Resilience

It is difficult for the historian to explain the seeming differences in these men's ability to cope after the First World War. The term 'resilience' is now regularly appropriated in popular discourse and across a wide range of disciplines, and eludes easy definition and measurement.[12] In the natural sciences, where the term originated, 'resilience' describes 'the capacity of a material or system to return to equilibrium after a displacement': that is, the process whereby a substance will 'bounce back' to its original shape.[13] However, in the social sciences 'resilience' has come to be understood more as a complex process of adaptation and change, especially after personal loss and trauma. In this sense it is often applied to both social systems and individuals. So far as individuals are concerned, then, resilience has been defined as the means by which 'effectiveness in the environment is achieved, sustained or recovered despite adversity' or 'the fact of maintaining adaptive functioning in spite of serious risk hazards'.[14]

The question that continues to challenge scholars across disciplines is what mix of personal attributes and societal variables enables some individuals to maintain this adaptive functioning, while others exposed to similar stimuli do not. And what explains why certain individuals, who might seem to have the qualities required for resilience, ultimately prove more vulnerable than others? Beyond this, how do we measure 'success', given that much of the discourse about resilience is subjective in its assumptions about preferred outcomes?

Within a vast field there is some consensus that resilience can be jeopardised by a standard field of 'risk factors'.[15] There is an often-observed correlation in children, for example, between persistent delinquent behaviour and 'a multi-problem milieu such as parental criminality, poor parental supervision, cruel, passive, or neglectful attitudes, erratic or harsh discipline, mutual conflict, large family size, and socioeconomic disadvantages'.[16] Yet none of this is inevitable or predetermined, and the degree to which risk factors impact upon a particular individual is highly variable. Moreover, the impact of stressful or risk situations can clearly be moderated by protective factors: that is, variables that enable individuals to adapt more successfully to trauma than they might otherwise have done.[17] Among these, it has been argued, are the temperament and personal attributes of individuals: their cognitive skills and their reflectiveness when confronted with new situations; and their capacity to remain positive in relation to others. Then, there is family environment – the warmth, sense of cohesion and support that this provides – and systems of social support – caring agencies and community organisations, including religious institutions.[18] Indeed, religion has been suggested as having the potential to moderate the relationship between stress and depression and trait anxiety.[19]

Beyond this, it has been argued that individuals seem able to be resilient if their life experience has some sense of coherence: that is, if the stimuli confronting them make cognitive sense 'as information that is ordered, consistent, structured and clear—and, hence, regarding the future, as predictable'. Moreover, resilience can be facilitated if experiences are manageable, in that individuals are able to mobilise resources, either by having direct control over them or by accessing them by various means. Finally, coherence is achievable when an experience is meaningful: that is, when 'life makes sense emotionally ... [and] at least some of the problems and demands posed by living are worth investing energy in, are worthy of commitment and engagement, and are challenges that are welcome rather than burdens that they would much rather do without'.[20]

Elliott, Throssell and Hawker: Trauma and resilience

Returning now to Elliott, Throssell and Hawker: self-evidently, their traumatic experience of war constituted a grave risk factor for each man. Each of the three endured several years of warfare, including exposure to enemy fire, direct participation in armed combat, and witnessing the death and wounding of fellow soldiers and civilians. Each was wounded several times, while Elliott and Throssell carried an additional burden of personal bereavement, in that both lost brothers during the war. For Elliott this was the third sibling to die across his lifetime. Throssell memorably found his brother, Ric, among the wounded after the infamous charge by the 10th Light Horse at the Nek in August 1915, by whistling a tune that was secret to them. But at the second battle of Gaza, in April 1917, where Hugo was wounded in the thigh and foot, Ric was killed. As his namesake nephew would later write:

> There could be no more adventure in [the war for Hugo] when Ric was killed ... The strange joy of battle that sustained him at the Nek and Hill 60 and inspired the men who fought with him died after the Gaza action. There were no more 'great charges' in his diary; no inspiring anecdotes.[21]

Elliott, for his part, learned of the death of his brother at the height of the third battle of Ypres, at the very time that he also received the devastating news of the failure of his business partner in Australia. He wrote to his wife, Kate, on 2 October 1917:

> Poor old Geordie [his brother], I saw him dead so white and rigid and still and his loved ones left behind him. And we have buried him so far from home amongst strangers to him. ... I cannot tell you what I went through that night. After I knew that Geordie had died I would have gladly welcomed a shell to end me.[22]

Given the paucity of medical records, we lack precise information as to how the physical and emotional traumas of war affected each man's mental health after the war. Throssell's Department of Repatriation file details his physical problems after the war: recurrent attacks of malaria, headaches, shortness of breath and, inability to do sustained hard work.[23] At various points during the 1920s, medical officers also noted that Throssell was 'restless and nervy', 'depressed', and subject to 'mental excitability' and sleeplessness. Soon after the war he was granted a 50 per cent pension, which was later reduced to 30 per cent, and then raised in 1923 to 40 per cent. His suicide in 1933 was deemed by Repatriation officials to be 'war-related'.

Elliott's medical file is relatively sparse and records that his general health was considered 'good' at the time of his demobilisation in 1919.[24] Elliott himself, however, admitted privately that he had mental health issues in the immediate aftermath of war. In correspondence with his family in early 1919, he said that he was suffering 'fearful fits of depression' and 'fits of the blues', while feeling 'listless and helpless – nervous breakdown due to war strain'.[25] Elliott's later behaviour suggests a man whose emotional state became increasingly fragile in the decade after the war. He could not resist raising the matter of his 'supersession' in federal parliament; and in the late 1920s he continued to harass, by mail and in public, those whom he held responsible for his lack of promotion. Some of his former commanders became 'deeply concerned' at his inability to let this grievance go. As General Sir John Monash wrote to him in September 1929:

> I have myself felt that the affection and confidence of the men of the AIF was worth a great deal more to me than any empty honors. This same affection and confidence you have enjoyed in rich measure ... After all, you commanded a celebrated Brigade during the period of its greatest successes ... Is it not a great thing to have lived to play such a role in the greatest war in History? Then why worry as to the verdict of posterity upon so brilliant and soldierly a career?[26]

When Elliott finally suicided in 1931, he was judged by Repatriation to have been be depressed and 'temporarily insane' – though his death was also judged to be war-related.[27]

Hawker, in contrast, seems to have retained robust mental health after the war. No detailed official record of his health seems to be extant, but the National Library of Australia holds the correspondence between many of Hawker's acquaintances and his sister (and biographer) in the early 1960s.[28] Although these witnesses were unlikely to have voiced criticism, it is striking how, without exception, they were in awe of Hawker's ability to remain positive, good-humoured and gregarious in the face of often excruciating and chronic pain.[29] Hawker's carer in the early post-war years, Corporal W Hughes, later recalled that when having his back massaged, Hawker would 'never swear like a trooper. He knew how to bear pain ... with a smile too, though you knew he was suffering [he] used to mutter; "Nil desperandum"'.[30] There seems to have been only one occasion when Hawker manifested any sign of depression; this was when he had to lie in hospital on a water mattress for seven months, so sensitive was his body to movement in his vicinity. But even then, according to one account, he spent his time learning Greek![31] Hawker himself conceded that he considered suicide when he was 'first hit' in 1917. Lying on the battlefield, knowing he was partially paralysed, for hours before being brought in by stretcher-bearers, he considered taking a packet of morphia tablets that he always carried.[32]

However subjective such a conclusion may be, it seems that Hawker was blessed with a temperament that acted as a 'protective factor'. His battles with injuries did not retard his development, but seem rather to have operated as 'catalytic agents of resistance, or of more constructive responses'.[33] He became a quintessential over-achiever, developing his upper body strength so that he could swim, ride horses (mounting the saddle without help), climb ladders to boats unassisted, drive a specially adapted car, change flat tyres, and so on. Fiercely independent, and spurning sympathy, he would rather fall than accept help from others. Typically, he judged whether his mobility was improving by counting the number of times he fell when climbing the hill behind his property, North Bungaree, using two walking sticks![34]

What, then, of the other 'protective factors', beyond temperament, that might have assisted these men's adjustment to post-war life? All seem to have had strong support from their families, at least in the first years after the war. Elliott's disrupted childhood and personal losses were presumably countered to some degree by the warmth of his own extended family. At the heart of this was his beloved wife, Kate, his 'sunshine lady', and his two children to whom he gave 'boundless love and support'.[35] Throssell's marriage to Prichard was initially very passionate: they had 'a strong physical connection' and their early days together were remembered by Prichard as 'halcyon', full of 'gay camaraderie'. They adored their only son, Ric.[36] However, the marriage became strained during the Depression years as Prichard despaired of Throssell's increasingly risky financial ventures.[37] Hawker, in contrast, never married. He told Hughes, that he was determined 'to allow nothing with women to go on too far because he was not going to be a burden on any woman or take advantage of her natural sympathy'.[38] However, he had a supportive family, including a father who followed his career with interest and a sister whose devotion to him was such that she wrote his biography in order that a new generation of Australians could have their hearts 'quickened by his story of courage'.[39]

Beyond their families, each of Elliott, Throssell and Hawker had well-developed systems of social support. As we have seen, all were prominent in veterans' advocacy and professional and political organisations. We do not know how much, in Throssall's case, this was compromised by his stand in 1919 on socialism. Prichard believed that this was the reason he lost his role as soldiers' representative on the Discharged Soldiers' Settlement Board.[40] Politics and also leadership roles brought their stresses as well as their rewards. As the Great Depression set in, Elliott was distressed that he could do little to help returned soldiers thrown out of work; and was maddened by the deflationary policies adopted by the Labor government of James Scullin, including its decision to abolish the compulsory military training scheme in 1929. Hawker, meanwhile, had his own battles over government policy, that led to his resignation from the ministry.

It is impossible to do more than speculate about another protective factor: namely, the degree to which life seemed coherent, purposeful and invested with meaning. This variable is intrinsically beyond measurement. Suffice to say that Elliott's biographer notes only that Elliott was 'favourably disposed to the doctrines and rituals of the Presbyterian church'.[41] Hawker, in contrast, was known to have had a strong Christian faith. One of his cousins recalls him having 'a great sense of God'. He would sing hymns with children 'all the way home from an expedition. He sang at the top of his voice "Onward Christian Soldiers" and other hymns'.[42] Perhaps Throssell's socialism might have provided a comparable teleological framing of his life, but it seems more likely that it was passion for Prichard that originally inspired this commitment. It may be an overstatement to say, as does one of Throssell's biographers, that Prichard 'went to work on him … strongly influencing his possibly weakened mind'; but his infamous Victory Day speech was written with her assistance and Throssell remained on the margins of Prichard's activism in the 1920s.[43] We can only speculate as to whether Throssell experienced cognitive dissonance as he tried to reconcile her passionate anti-war stance (a result of her brother's death) and his own status as a decorated war hero.

As for the capacity to mobilise the resources to make life manageable, here we need to distinguish between different phases in the post-war decade. Initially, all three men seem to have benefited from reasonable financial security, which facilitated their transition to civilian life. Hawker particularly benefited from having the financial means to access expert medical interventions in London, and to recruit a full-time carer and chauffeur who accompanied him back to Australia. However, when economic recession hit Australia in the late 1920s and early 1930s, Hawker suffered significant financial loss with wool prices collapsing and the sheep stock of his properties dropping from 37 000 to 9000 over the five years of drought and Depression.[44] In 1933 he had another financial reverse when fire destroyed much stock and fencing on his property. Throssell's losses at this time, as we have seen, were ruinous. Elliott's financial position, in contrast, seems to have been secure, although, according to one of his advisers, this was not how he saw it.[45]

More significant perhaps than their financial situation was the way in which both Throssell's and Elliott's health deteriorated in 1930–31. In 1931 Throssell started to have considerable pain in his right eye because of a small fragment of metal embedded in his cornea. He suffered regular headaches, and then, when organising his rodeo in 1933, broke two bones in his foot when it was crushed by a horse. In his last years, Elliott was plagued with nightmares, ghastly flashbacks and tormenting memories of the many young men who had died under his command. This led him, in July 1930, to launch a very public and trenchant critique of the ineptitude of those responsible for the battle of Fromelles. His blood pressure rose, he suffered from diabetes and then experienced a severe head injury while horse riding. Was he also, one wonders, haunted by the memories of the earlier trauma of his sister's suicide?

Ultimately then, these three case studies confirm the complexities associated with any discussion of resilience. Clearly, it is a state that cannot be predicted against any template of variables, however useful the insights of psycho-social categories such as risk and protective factors might be in framing our analysis. Rather the journey of adaptation to trauma, and the creation of a new 'normal' in the post-war years, was highly individualised, shaped not only by socio-economic influences but also by inherently unquantifiable variables. Moreover, these three case studies suggest that resilience was not a fixed state. Although Elliott and Throssell killed themselves in the early 1930s, both had more than a decade of what appears to have been productive life – at least if we judge them against some possible indicators of 'successful' adaptation to trauma, such as stability in personal relationships, the capacity to make a living, and the ability to maintain a family and perform community service. Whether they might have maintained that stability without the Great Depression is a key question. In his final suicide message, written no doubt with his family's entitlements to his pension in mind, Throssell blamed his war service, but it seems that he also saw suicide as the only means of escaping from his financial catastrophe. Prichard opted for a similar mix. She wrote to Repatriation in 1934:

> Nervously and physically, my husband's magnificent constitution was impaired as a result of war service ... but I resent the idea that his mind was ever in any way deranged. He feared that that it might become so. ... I consider that

his 'grateful country' made it impossible for my husband to live. He thought he had to die to provide for his wife and child.⁴⁶

Almost certainly, then, the war and the Depression need to be viewed as two interconnected stressors, with the economic crisis denying life, once again, of any element of predictability and manageability. It seems to have unleashed the psychological damage of the war in an arguably more intense form, since that trauma had not been resolved by psychiatric treatment. It is a conclusion that is given some weight by the fact that the highest rate of male suicide in the twentieth century – 28.1 deaths per 100 000 – was recorded in 1930, the first year of the Great Depression, not in the immediate aftermath of the First World War. Later research into PTSD also confirms that a second or later negative life event can impact severely on already traumatised individuals, making them less able to cope and 'more likely to develop chronic trauma symptoms'.⁴⁸

Remembering the resilient

Of the three men considered here, it is notable that Elliott and Throssell, but not Hawker, find a place in the national shrine of war memory, the Australian War Memorial. Elliott, who is described in the Memorial as 'one of the best-known characters of the AIF', is commemorated in the gallery devoted to the First World War in a portrait by WB McGuiness, a boot, complete with a bullet hole, that Pompey was wearing when wounded at Gallipoli, and the uniform in which he conducted the recapture of the French town of Villers-Bretonneux in 1918. His boot also features in educational materials developed by the War Memorial.⁴⁹ Throssell is profiled in the Hall of Valour devoted to winners of the Victoria Cross. His display includes his medals and Webley Mark IV service revolver –

although it is left ambiguous as to whether this was the actual weapon that he used to kill himself.

The prominence given to these two men in these Memorial galleries is not surprising. After all, this is a memorial and museum dedicated to Australians at war, and both men had distinguished military careers in the AIF. Elliott, moreover, is closely identified with two of the battles that have acquired especial prominence in recent Australian war commemoration, Fromelles and Villers-Bretonneux. Hawker, on the other hand, served with the British Army; he was wounded for much of the war and his reputation rested on his postwar political career, not his wartime military one.

More telling, however, is the prominence given to Throssell in a recent Memorial exhibition, 'After the War'. Here his portrait sits under the banner: 'What if your wounds are not visible?' A nearby display includes a poster advertising a public lecture by Throssell on the Light Horse, photographs from his marriage, a statement by the man who found Throssell after his suicide and Prichard's letter to Repatriation, cited above. The caption briefly summarises Throssell's wartime service, and then describes how he struggled 'with the memories of the war, the loss of his brother Eric ... and the horrors of fighting on Gallipoli and in Gaza'. It concludes by citing his suicide note. Notably, Throssell's financial struggles in the Great Depression are not mentioned. The possibility that his suicide note might have been written with the intent of securing his family's pensions is ignored. The nexus between his war trauma and his suicide is assumed to be direct.

This representation of Throssell's death, and the relative obscurity of Hawker, speak to the much-documented phenomenon in the collective memory of war: the dominance of the trope of victimhood and trauma. As historian Christina Twomey has put it, when post-traumatic stress was identified as a medical condition some three decades ago, the traumatised individual gained a new 'cultural prominence':

> [PTSD] in effect put in place 'the event' as the defining reason for the experience of trauma and transformed the sufferers of trauma from slightly suspect individuals to legitimate victims. In light of these changes to ideas about trauma and victimhood, the suffering of soldiers in war and the potential for them to be traumatised by it became a central trope in the public discussion of Anzac ... it is the suffering of veterans, their psychological fragility and the horrors they have witnessed that provide an important, if not an exclusive, framing device.[50]

There were, of course, many veterans of the First World War whose stories accord with this framing. As the work of Alistair Thomson, Marina Larsson, Bruce Scates, Melanie Oppenheimer and Kate Ariotti in particular has demonstrated, there were countless men whose post-war lives were blighted by the traumas, physical and mental, they suffered during the First World War.[51] Many were, to use Marina Larsson's term, 'shattered Anzacs'. Only two years after the war ended, some 90 000 ex-servicemen – or about a third of survivors – were receiving some level of war disability pension.[52] By 1938, the number of recipients had risen to 257 000: 77 000 of them were incapacitated soldiers and 180 000 were dependants. In the late 1930s, there were still 1600 men in hostels and homes for the permanently incapacitated and around 23 000 outpatients in repatriation hospitals each year.[53]

However, the life story of Hawker suggests that these statistics of disability and trauma should be complemented by a greater sensitivity to evidence of resilience. We need not see this as a matter of oppositions. As Elliott's and Throssell's lives show, even those who might be considered as ultimately victims of the war could manifest for years the capacity to adapt and live productive lives. The stories of soldier settlement documented by Bruce Scates and

Melanie Oppenheimer also reveal how men who were often profoundly damaged by the war could, at least for a time, respond to the huge challenges of farming often unproductive plots of land in the harsh Australian environment.[54] It is more, then, a matter of balance. The rich archives of the correspondence between veterans and the Department of Repatriation almost inevitably will lead historians of the future to focus on morbidity and mortality – questions that are, of course, of utmost importance in understanding the long-term legacy of the First World War. But, as Stephen Garton observed in 1996, the repatriation archive, by its very nature, is 'more likely to be a repository of complaint than compliment' – or one might add, resilience.[55] Hence, though the task of recovering the voices of the silent may be difficult, and notions of resilience imprecise, we need to acknowledge that for many survivors of the First World War this was a more appropriate framing of their post-war life than victimhood.

13

WILLIAM ROY HODGSON AND THE AFTERMATH OF THE FIRST WORLD WAR

Keir Reeves, Kathryn Avery and David McGinniss

Lieutenant William Roy Hodgson landed at Gallipoli on 25 April 1915. Three days later, while operating as a forward observing officer for his artillery brigade, Hodgson was reported dead as a result of Turkish sniper fire. Yet he survived to read his own obituary. Like Joan Beaumont's consideration of resilience (Chapter 12), this chapter represents another story that defies the idea of the shattered Anzac. Hodgson made the most of his lucky escape, forging a stellar post-war career as a senior public servant and diplomat. The crowning achievement of Hodgson's career came in 1947, when he sat as Australia's representative on the eight-nation drafting committee of one of the pillars of the post-Second World War world, the Universal Declaration of Human Rights (UDHR).

William Hodgson defies the dominant contemporary historical narrative of the returned soldier who was irrevocably damaged by his war experience. According to his own testimony, Hodgson's subsequent career achievements were enabled by his military service. He admitted in later life that: 'I always feel sorry for the man who is not a returned soldier … for he knows not what he has missed in life'.[1] Through an examination of Hodgson's life, this chapter seeks to balance the register of disturbed and traumatised veterans with

William Roy Hodgson and the aftermath of the First World War

the records of those whose war experience propelled them towards great achievements in their post-war lives. In the case of William Hodgson, he sought to assist in the creation of an international apparatus of conflict resolution that would prevent a catastrophe like the two worlds wars from happening again.

William Hodgson was born in Kingston on the central Victorian Goldfields in 1892, the son of a schoolmaster, Robert Hodgson, and his wife Margaret née Willson. He matriculated from the School of Mines in Ballarat (now Federation University Australia) in 1910.[2] In later years, Hodgson reminisced about the British imperialism that he was steeped in as a youth: 'the days when the old Empire was at its height … the days of jingoism and flag flapping, of the quoting of Kipling'. He recalled the local jubilation at British success during the Boer War: 'the big bonfires we had on Mafeking night [and] the map we had where each day we marked the progress of the march of Roberts to Pretoria'.[3]

In 1911 Hodgson was among the first intake at the Royal Military College at Duntroon. He graduated in 1914, just as the First World War broke out. As a lieutenant in the Fifth Battery, Second Artillery Brigade, Hodgson was among the men of the Anzac Corps who landed at Gallipoli on 25 April 1915. His 'great gallantry' in a position of 'great risk and responsibility' was reported in despatches.[4] After three days of fighting at Gallipoli, Hodgson was wounded in the hip by a Turkish sniper and presumed dead. He unexpectedly survived the wound, though he lived the rest of his life with one leg shorter than the other, and carried a noticeable limp. It was reported many years later at a conference in Europe that when Hodgson sought the support of a Turkish delegate, he 'pointed significantly to his leg, and cautioned the Turk against casting a vote in opposition to Australia'.[5]

Hodgson endured several operations in Egypt and England, before being invalided back to Australia in 1917. Like many returned soldiers, Hodgson relied on the Commonwealth Department of Repatriation for assistance in finding employment and also for ongoing medical support for his chronic conditions. A severe case of eczema on his face and hands that persisted throughout the 1920s had rendered him at the mercy of a seemingly unending regime of prescription drugs and medical appointments. From 1920 to 1927, Hodgson attended no fewer than one hundred medical appointments.[6]

Confined to administrative duties by his wounds, Hodgson was appointed to the Australian Military Forces General Staff at Army Headquarters in Melbourne in 1918. After serving in the training and administrative sections, he became head of military intelligence in 1925 and was promoted to major in 1926. During his spare time, Hodgson undertook an accounting course at Melbourne's Working Men's College (now RMIT University) and subsequently completed a law degree at the University of Melbourne.[7]

Hodgson resigned from the military in 1934 and moved into the Commonwealth public service. With his background in military intelligence, he attained the position of assistant secretary in the Department of External Affairs, which at the time was led by the secretary of the Prime Minister's Department. When the Department of External Affairs became a standalone department in 1935, Hodgson was elevated to the role of secretary at the age of 43; he held the post for the next decade. Hodgson's rise mirrored that of the increasing importance that the Commonwealth placed on international relations, triggered by Australia's reaction to Mussolini's invasion of Abyssinia.[8] Historian David Bird argued that Hodgson's elevation to such a senior position was due to his sympathy for a 'policy of conciliation' that aligned with Lyon's pro-appeasement stance. Therefore, as Bird claimed, Hodgson's rise 'may not have been as "accidental" as some in the department, like [fellow diplomat] Alan Watt, believed it was'.[9]

Two contrasting opinions emerged within the department as to Hodgson's suitability for the head position.[10] Historian Peter Edwards describes the view of Hodgson's supporters, including his former colleague, the diplomat and politician Paul Hasluck, that he was 'shrewd and tough' – approaching political matters with a methodical, clinical precision and discipline that only a military man could.[11] Hodgson had a keen interest in foreign affairs, particularly with respect to the Pacific and 'Far Eastern' regions in which he specialised while working in military intelligence during the 1920s. Correspondence ranging from speeches to cables and letters confirms that Hodgson had an intricate knowledge of a breadth of issues that affected Australian defence, international relations and the national interest. Other supporters included fellow Croix de Guerre recipient General Sir Harry Chauvel and Sir Brudenell White, former Commander of the AIF – both men had supported Hodgson's applications for External Affairs positions.[12]

By contrast, Hodgson's critics viewed him as ill-suited to lead External Affairs. According to Edwards, Hodgson was criticised on account of his educational background and previous experience. It was said that under his watch, External Affairs was treated as little more than a messenger service between departments; that it lacked any vision for steering foreign policy. Criticism was also made of Hodgson's reliance on those serving underneath him, such as John Hood, head of the department's political section.[13] There was also criticism of Hodgson's organisational skills. According to Hasluck, who incidentally regarded Hodgson as 'a much better man than most of his detractors', External Affairs records were 'among the worst organised and worst kept' among Commonwealth departments of the time.[14]

There was one matter about which both supporters and detractors agreed: Hodgson was consistently inflexible and uncompromising. According to historians Gordon Greenwood and Norman

Harper, 'Hoddy', as his supporters knew him, often lacked the essential diplomatic value of discretion. He was 'an army man at heart who chose "bold attack" over defensive measures and was never quite at home in the world of diplomacy'.[15] The authors cite a speech made by Hodgson to the United Nations Security Council on 23 December 1948 regarding the question of Indonesian independence as an example. Hodgson declared that certain recent Dutch actions against the Republican government in Indonesia were 'even worse than what Hitler did to the Netherlands in 1940'. While Hodgson might have been under instructions by his superiors to make a strong statement, the form of words was provocative and insensitive.[16]

Hodgson was integral to the inner workings of the Australian political machinery in large part because he had direct access to the Prime Minister. For example, he played a vital role in drafting memoranda as an adviser to the Australian delegation at the 1937 Imperial Conference.[17] In light of the deteriorating international situation, particularly the decline in Australian–Japanese relations following the 1936 trade diversion policy, the Australian delegation sought assurances regarding British Far Eastern policy. The aims were three-fold. First, to seek answers from the British chiefs-of-staff about the capacity of the Royal Navy to send a fleet to the Singapore Naval Base should hostilities break out in the Pacific. The Australians worried that a European war would tie up Britain's naval resources, thus encouraging Japan to sweep further southward towards Australia. Second, the Australians aimed to discourage Britain from standing in the way of a German 'Anschluss' of Austria that would see Italy and Germany 'at once divided'.[18] The delegation also proposed, through a memorandum drafted by Hodgson along with Stanley Bruce, Richard Casey and Alfred Stirling, to form a multilateral pact of non-aggression for countries bordering the Pacific, whereby all parties would agree to respect each other's sovereignty. The aim was to secure support from the United States through a system of collective security at the same time as recognising the Japanese puppet state in Manchuria (Manchukuo) as a means to confine Japanese expansion to northern China, and not southward towards Australia.[19] The conference was a failure for Australian policy. The British delegation could not guarantee the timely arrival of a fleet to Singapore in the event of a European war; the Pacific Pact proposal lacked support from the outset, and the appeasement of Germany was essentially quashed.[20]

While the League of Nations failed to prevent the outbreak of the Second World War, the belief in the need for a universal governmental body survived. Hodgson was no exception to this belief. In a speech to the South African Veterans' Association in 1945, he demonstrated an unwavering commitment to the ideals upon which the League rested, particularly in relation to international lawmaking. He hoped that a new world order would rise up from the miseries of yet another global war, one that was supported by popular consensus. For Hodgson, the failure of the League came down to a lack of collective will rather than the League machinery itself. It was not enough for diplomats to gather around a table for discussion without support from the people:

> It is wrong to say that the League of Nations failed. It was grand in conception and noble in principle. It was the nations that failed the League. There was not the will behind it to make it work ... and it had no will just because of one thing – the common people had little or no faith in it, did not stand behind their Governments, did not force their Governments to support it. We must this time all play our part in getting behind this new world organisation.[21]

Having come close to death on the battlefield, Hodgson believed that achieving security and 'peace for all' through a collective framework was 'the only true and lasting memorial to those who paid the supreme sacrifice' – something he would continue to fight for.[22]

Hodgson at the United Nations

Following the end of the Second World War, Hodgson was appointed as Ambassador to France, and acting High Commissioner to Canada. He was an Australian delegate to the Paris Peace Conference in February 1947, and the next month took over from Hasluck as the head of Australia's delegation to the newly formed United Nations. Here he was a prolific and respected contributor to the formation of the post-war world order, serving as a member of the UN Human Rights Commission, the UN Security Council, the UN Committee on Admission of New Members, the UN Commission on Conventional Armaments, five subsidiary bodies of the Atomic Energy Committee, and chairmanship of the board to suggest candidates for the governorship of Trieste, all while he maintained his role as Ambassador to France.[23]

Hodgson believed that his war experience, combined with his academic qualifications, prepared him well for his new role at the United Nations: 'When I add [my degrees] to my military experience I am equipped to deal with most of the problems that arise at [the] UN. I can talk to the Military Staff Committee about principles of war, and I can understand the economists when they became technical'.[24] While he had become an enthusiastic advocate for human rights, Hodgson remained blunt and uncompromising in his personal interactions. He demonstrated 'an extremely critical attitude towards most foreign countries' and a 'peppery aggressive manner' that, according to the US State Department, seemed to be aggravated by the consumption of alcohol. Despite Hodgson's abrasive personal style, his talents were apparent to State Department officials, who noted that his 'blustering and provocative approach is said to hide a very thorough knowledge of the question under consideration'.[25]

In March 1947 Hodgson was invited to represent Australia on the eight-nation sub-committee to draft what would become the Universal Declaration of Human Rights.[26] 'The United Nations Bill of Human Rights is my baby', declared Hodgson. 'I have consistently labored to put teeth into the bill so that it will be more than pious resolution.'[27] Hodgson's colleagues on the drafting committee were the chair Eleanor Roosevelt, French jurist René Cassin (awarded the Nobel Prize for Peace in 1968 for his role in drafting the UDHR), Pen-Chun Chang from China, Charles Malik from Lebanon, Hernan Santa Cruz from Chile, Charles Dukes from the United Kingdom (replaced later by Geoffrey Wilson), and Alexander Bogomolov from the Soviet Union (replaced later by a relatively junior delegate, Valentin Tepliakov, then the more senior Vladimir Koretsky). This eminent group was supported by the Canadian John Humphrey, who was director of the UN Secretariat's Division for Human Rights.[28]

The drafting committee undertook a long and laborious process, involving heated arguments, abandoned drafts and delicate negotiations. Hodgson earned a reputation on the committee as a 'champion of small nations'.[29] Australia's role in this new global order was far from certain; its traditional reliance on Britain had been shaken by the experiences of two successive world wars, and particularly by Britain's inability to defend its positions in Asia. Hodgson saw the opportunity for Australia to emerge as a leader of smaller nations – a confident and assertive group that could form an influential alliance in the new global order, relatively separate from the 'great powers' – the United States, United Kingdom, France, China and the Soviet Union. Hodgson had earlier warned against over-reliance on the United States for post-war regional security.[30] He regularly railed against the great powers' use of their vetoes in the United Nations, to the extent that the USSR's representative to the UN, Andrei Gromyko, accused Hodgson of 'veto-phobia'.[31] There was a certain irony in Gromyko's observation, as he was popularly known as 'Mr Nyet' for his use of the Soviet veto option on the Security Council.

Hodgson, along with the External Affairs Minister, Herbert 'Doc' Evatt, who served as the third president of the United Nations General Assembly between 1948 and 1949, was especially concerned with how the new human rights system would be implemented, and proposed an International Court of Human Rights that would be resourced to prosecute breaches.[32] Hodgson sat on the Implementation Working Group of the drafting committee, and initially objected to the formulation of the UDHR if it was to be non-binding.[33] He argued that 'no International Bill of Rights would have any effect unless there was provision for enforcement'.[34] Australia's proposal for an International Court was 'widely commended' in the Implementation Working Group, wrote Hodgson, with even 'Governments previously in opposition, namely United States and United Kingdom' agreeing that the idea 'merited consideration and voted for its transmission'. Hodgson considered this to be 'a signal victory for [the] Australian proposal for [a] Court of Human Rights'.[35] However, despite his enthusiasm, the proposal did not receive majority support, and it was shelved.[36]

Notwithstanding reservations about his personality and diplomatic style, Hodgson served with distinction at the United Nations, earning praise from international colleagues. 'No greater service has been rendered the United Nations than that given by the Government of Australia', wrote the US Under-Secretary of State, Sumner Welles, 'and Colonel Hodgson's share in it when he was on the Council was considerable'.[37] Hodgson was invited to give guest lectures on the American university circuit, and in 1947 was awarded an Honorary Doctor of Laws by Bard College, where he delivered the commencement address.[38]

In 1949 Hodgson left the United Nations to serve as the British Commonwealth representative on the Allied Control Council for Japan. In 1953 he became High Commissioner to South Africa. Hodgson retired from the Australian diplomatic service in 1957, and died from cancer in Sydney within a year, at the age of 65.[39]

Conclusion

The globalist worldview that Hodgson professed during his diplomatic career was markedly different from the imperialist ideology of his upbringing. Hodgson, along with the External Affairs Minister for whom he worked, Herbert 'Doc' Evatt, represented a new form of Australian diplomacy – assertive, confident and committed to progressing an independent worldview. The internationalism of Evatt and Hodgson was informed by the two world wars and the decolonisation that was proceeding apace after 1945. Their embrace of internationalism and advocacy of the United Nations as an institution of peace echoed the response of far-sighted politicians, including Ben Chifley and Jawaharlal Nehru, to the post-war world.[40] However, the internationalist aspirations of Evatt and Hodgson were subsumed by the all-consuming logic of the Cold War – an event that played a key role in Evatt's political demise and the split of the Australian Labor Party in the 1950s. Ultimately, Hodgson's view of an overarching International Human Rights Court system proved impossible to implement in the polarised global political climate of the mid- and late 20th century.

The life of William Hodgson reminds us that the familiar narrative of the returned soldier who was irrevocably damaged by his war experience casts too narrow a beam over the First World War experience. In 1945, just before he was to embark upon his diplomatic role with the United Nations, Hodgson reflected on the First World War in an address to the South African Veterans' Association: 'The First World War gave us a great reservoir of fortitude [and] a capacity for facing adversity', he said. 'Many a humble little man hunched over an office chair, his hair thin and grey, is not really the person he appears to be. His eyes have looked on other sights, tragic and grim.'[41] Hodgson believed it was important to commemorate war and acknowledge its significance in nation-building, not based on 'a mere spirit of jingoism nor in a desire to lord our superiority, nor to celebrate the mere outward form of victory', but rather to acknowledge the humanity of its participants – their 'chivalry, courage, devotion to duty'.[42] The First World War was a catastrophic event that destroyed the lives of many it did not kill. But it equally produced men like Hodgson, whose experience left them determined to make the world a better place.

REPRESENTING THE GREAT WAR

14

'A SUITABLE MEMORIAL'? PAINTING, MEMORY AND THE GREAT WAR

Margaret Hutchison

No one could accuse the Australian government of failing to commemorate the centenary of the First World War. It allegedly spent around $600 million on centennial events between 2014 and 2018.[1] This orchestrated campaign of state commemoration contrasts with government attitudes during the war itself, when commemorative practices developed haphazardly, amid continual debates about which aspects of Australia's participation in the war should be remembered.

Australia's first official war art scheme was among these initial commemorative practices. It emerged in 1916 during a year of increased commemorative activity, sparked by events such as the celebration of the first Anzac Day.[2] Like much of the commemorative effort that would later lead to a national war records collection of artifacts, diaries and images – which still fills the Australian War Memorial in Canberra – the art scheme was managed by military officers and public servants working in London.

These men were focused on creating a collection of paintings and sketches that captured Australia's war effort on the Western Front and, to a lesser extent, in the Middle East. The decisions they made about which artists to employ and the subjects they should paint profoundly shaped the collection of Australian war art. With its emphasis on the military experiences of the infantry, the art program complemented and consolidated an emerging national memory of the war that was based on the fighting capacity of Australian soldiers.

Yet the decisions of the military officers and public servants who guided the official art scheme did not go uncontested. Artists and politicians in Australia challenged the vision of the war being preserved in a war art collection by those in London. Their competing proposals provide an insight into the process of memory making – a process that is always contested – and reminds us that what is remembered is always shadowed by what is forgotten.

Australia's first official war art scheme

The art program was the brainchild of Will Dyson, an expatriate cartoonist living and working in London, and Charles Bean, Australia's official war correspondent and later historian. Dyson was the first to voice the idea that art could be used to capture an Australian experience of the war. In August 1916 he wrote to Andrew Fisher, Australia's High Commissioner in London, proposing, 'that it would be of interest to the people of Australia of today and in the future to see sketches illustrating the relationship of the Australians to the war and interpreting the feelings and character of the Australian troops in France'.[3] His letter was the first formal suggestion that art might be used to interpret and preserve the Australian experience of the war, but Dyson was by no means the only person considering the use of visual forms.

Concurrently, Charles Bean was planning a role for art in a collection he envisioned would be housed in a future national war museum. He had become aware of the artistic talent within the AIF in his role as editor of *The Anzac Book*, which included numerous illustrations produced by soldiers serving at Gallipoli. Bean's ideas developed further when, during the battle of Pozières in 1916, he met Frank Crozier and saw his drawings of the fighting. Bean was deeply impressed by Crozier's numerous notes and sketches of the battle. He proposed to the Australian government that Crozier might be asked to paint several images from his observations of the battlefield, which he argued would be invaluable for a future national gallery.[4]

The two proposals from Dyson and Bean formed the basis of the scheme established by the Australian government in 1917. This program was managed under two separate sections: the first was overseen by the Australian High Commission in London and employed expatriate civilian artists. The second, managed by the Australian War Records Section, and also based in London, came under the Department of Defence and employed artists who were already serving in the AIF. Despite their lack of any professional artistic training, Henry Smart, Publicity Officer at the High Commission, managed the first section, while John Treloar, at that time Officer-in-Charge of the Australian War Records Section and later director of the Australian War Memorial, supervised the artists under the second. Bean acted in an advisory role as the AIF representative to both sections of the scheme.

Competing proposals

The schemes proposed successfully by Dyson and Bean were not the only ones pitched to the Australian government. Several competing plans from a range of individuals were put forward during the war, though most were sidelined or ignored. Many of these ideas came from prominent figures in the Australian art community. For instance, in early 1917 Baldwin Spencer, the eminent anthropologist and art connoisseur, and Bertram Mackennal, the renowned Australian sculptor, contacted Fisher and suggested that paintings should be made of significant battles in which Australian troops took part.⁵

Although conceived separately from Dyson's and Bean's proposals, Spencer and Mackennal's was remarkably similar. They argued that Australia should have a collection of battlefield paintings that would highlight Australian gallantry, prove invaluable to Australia's history and find a suitable home in Canberra. However, rather than employing talented artists from the ranks of the AIF as Bean had suggested in his proposal, Spencer and Mackennal recommended the use of eminent expatriate Australian artists, specifically Arthur Streeton.⁶

Streeton was a renowned landscape painter and a member of the Heidelberg School, who had made his name painting the sun-dappled hills around Melbourne. He had moved to Britain in 1897, one of a number of Australian artists who travelled to Europe and the United Kingdom to further their careers in this period. Streeton, like Spencer and Mackennal, was eager for Australian painters to be employed to capture the war effort on canvas.

Streeton was, in fact, so keen that he proposed his own scheme a few months after Spencer and Mackennal, which he developed in direct opposition to the art program Bean, Smart and Treloar were planning. His vision was more ambitious and notably emphasised the control of art experts. He contacted the men organising the Canadian art scheme, namely Lord Beaverbrook and Paul Konody, for information on the organisation of their art program and adopted their model for his own proposal. Streeton planned to commission between 40 and 50 of the best Australian and Allied artists. While he was presumably anxious to secure official funding, Streeton was adamant that he wanted the government to exercise 'no direction or control' over the art scheme.⁷ Instead, the program would be directed entirely by artists.

The tension between the official art scheme and Streeton's

proposal spilled over into the Australian press with the publication of a letter from Streeton in early 1917. He heavily criticised not only the government art scheme but also disparaged several Australian artists, including Septimus Power and Fred Leist, who had accepted positions as official war artists. The *Argus* reported that the incident had created 'some little ferment' in Australian art circles in London.[8]

The incident appears to have made little impression on the government, which initially took no specific action regarding either Spencer and Mackennal's or Streeton's proposals. However, in mid-1917 Fisher obtained permission for the expansion of the art scheme to include expatriate artists, though it is unclear whether this decision was influenced by Spencer, Mackennal and Streeton.

Focusing on the fighting front

All four proposals stressed the significance of images drawn from firsthand experience of the war. This was based on the idea that only artists who had personal contact with the troops and a direct understanding of the battlefield would paint the conflict compellingly. The emphasis on direct experience framed a male-dominated art scheme from the outset. Male artists were attached to divisions in the AIF or drawn from its ranks, but there were no comparable military structures with which women could associate.

Women were noticeably absent from the Australian war art scheme. Streeton planned to employ several female artists in his proposed art program, but there is little evidence that Bean or Treloar ever contemplated hiring women within or outside military structures during the war.[9] Their criterion appeared to be firstly that artists were Australian and secondly that they were available to travel to theatres of war.[10]

There were several female expatriate artists working in London and France during the war. These included Thea Proctor, Hilda Rix

Nicholas and Iso Rae, and even Dyson's wife Ruby Dyson. There were also painters who had joined the nursing services from whom Smart, Bean and Treloar might have selected artists, among them Bessie Davidson and Jessie Traill. But it was not until 1943, when Nora Heysen was commissioned during the Second World War, that a woman was employed as an official war artist for Australia.[11]

The exclusion of women from the proposals for an Australian art scheme, bar Streeton's, stood in contrast to other national war art programs. Both the Canadian and British schemes employed renowned female artists, though the number of women hired was considerably lower than that of men. Although the Canadians employed women artists on the home front, they took a rather gendered view of these artists, largely directing them to paint women's war work. The British scheme also employed female artists who worked under the Imperial War Museum's Women's Works Sub-Committee, formed to capture women's contributions to the war effort. These women painted military scenes as well as the home front.[12]

Contesting the art scheme

In Australia, artists and politicians alike were surprised that Bean and Treloar did not consider employing painters working at home. Several were vocal about this oversight. In mid-1918 artist Norman Lindsay and critic Bertram Stevens, among others, lobbied for the widely acclaimed landscape artist, Elioth Gruner, to be exempted from military service and commissioned as an official war artist to make paintings of the Australian home front. Lindsay argued that he personally placed Gruner next to Streeton in artistic ability. He claimed rather dramatically that it would be 'a reckless misuse of human economy to throw away a fine painter to make a poor soldier'. Lindsay added somewhat unkindly that this would be particularly irresponsible given that some of the official artists were 'very second-rate men and none are up to Gruner's standards'.[13] Even the acting Prime Minister, William Watt, became involved. He wrote to the Minister of Defence, George Pearce, arguing that Gruner's offer was a good opportunity to collect images of the war experience in Australia. Despite these efforts, however, Gruner was never offered an official commission.[14]

Smart, Bean and Treloar were not alone in ignoring artists at home. The Canadian program, which was much less nationally focused than its Australian counterpart, gave priority to the most talented artists of the time. For Beaverbrook and Konody this meant employing largely British artists.[15] In fact, Konody hired the best of all Allied artists, commissioning Belgian, British and Australian artists. He faced criticism over his selection of painters, including from the director of the National Gallery of Canada, Edmund Walker, who felt that if images were to be collected for Canadians, Canadian artists ought to be painting them. While Beaverbrook and Konody eventually hired Canadian artists, they continued to favour international painters. By 1921, the Canadian scheme had employed only 43 Canadian painters from a total of over one hundred official artists.

Alternative proposals

By mid-1918, it was clear that the men managing the scheme in London had no intention of including artists working in Australia or images of war activities at home. This continued to be a matter of concern to members of the art community in Australia. In June 1918 the Commonwealth Art Advisory Board began discussing in earnest the possibility of establishing a linked section or comparable scheme to commission war paintings in Australia.

Members of the board acknowledged that 'the chief interest of future generations of Australians will be centred in the wonderful achievements of their forefathers in the actual fighting on the battlefields of Gallipoli, France and Palestine'. But they warned that it was 'possible that the splendid work of various organisations behind the lines and at home may be overlooked and gradually forgotten'. William Trahair, a public servant in the Department of Defence, suggested that members of the board submit names of Australian artists who would be suitable to paint scenes of munitions factories, mills, training camps and troopships, as well as portraits of the individuals in charge of departments connected to Australia's war effort.[16]

Others in the art community were also developing ideas about including the war experience at home in the official art collection. In July 1918 the art critic Sydney Ure Smith suggested to government authorities that returned soldiers who were professional artists, such as Penleigh Boyd, 'could be useful painting war stuff locally'.[17] Although Ure Smith's proposal was referred to the Prime Minister's Department for consideration, it did not inspire a war art scheme within Australia, nor did it instigate the inclusion of the home front in the official art collection.

The Art Advisory Board again raised the issue of including the home front in the art program in October 1918. Its members drew up another list of suggestions for artworks dealing with war activities and the AIF in Australia. This second list was notably more focused on military activities than Traihair's initial suggestion – perhaps in the hope of gaining the support of those in London. The list included shipbuilding, military colleges, life at training camps, embarkation and disembarkation of troops, military equipment, military hospitals, undertakings of the Red Cross, processions, sketches of VC winners and other distinguished soldiers, and general events connected with military activities of visiting Allied troops.[18] However, despite these efforts, the art scheme based in London continued to focus on the fighting front, and a comparable program was never established for the home front.

Neglect of the home front

The Australian scheme stood alone in its disregard of the experience of the war at home. Overseen by Beaverbrook and Konody, the Canadian scheme deliberately documented the wartime experience on the British and Canadian home fronts. As early as November 1917, members of the Canadian war art committee sent British artists to Canada to paint scenes of the war effort on the home front. These subjects included munitions works, the declaration of war in Ottawa, the military camp at Valcartier and Halifax Harbour.[19]

But even these paintings of the Canadian home front were limited in their scope. As the Canadian art historian Maria Tippett has argued, there was a focus on central Canada in the images. The wheat production that allowed prairie farmers to keep their sons out of the trenches, the training camps in British Columbia and Alberta, the copper and nickel mines on the Canadian Shield, and the munition production in the provinces east and west of Ontario and Quebec were all missing from the official war paintings.[20]

The British were also concerned with commissioning images of the experience on the home front. The writer Arnold Bennet, who worked as the Director of Propaganda for France and was a member of the British War Memorials Committee responsible for overseeing the war art scheme, believed that the war effort at home was as significant and interesting as the battlefield. He drew up a list of subjects about which artists should be commissioned that fell into eight categories: 'Army, Navy, Air Force, Merchant Marine, Land, Munitions, Clerical & other Work by Women, and Public Manifestations'.[21] Consequently, the British collection includes numerous images of the war experience on the home front.

Despite their exclusion from Australia's official scheme, artists on the home front, usually women, produced paintings that depicted the nation's wartime experience. Grace Cossington Smith's painting, *The Sock Knitter* (1915), which portrays her sister, Madge, knitting socks for soldiers at the front, affords a glimpse into the experience of women at home. Aside from its subject matter, the style of the image is also significant; it is often regarded as the first entirely Post-Impressionist work produced in Australia. Cossington Smith captured other elements of the war experience at home. Her painting *Reinforcements: Troops Marching* (c. 1917), which shows civilians waving off troops as they leave for service, alludes to the bitter conscription debates that divided Australia during the war.[22] Hilda Rix Nicholas created poignant images of the cost of war, such as *A Mother of France* (1914). The artist's husband was killed very shortly after they were married in 1916, and her paintings and sketches are deeply personal images of grief.

Consequences of focusing on the fighting front

Proposals to extend the art scheme, to employ female artists or to include the home front were ignored by those men managing the commission and acquisition of official paintings in London. Instead, they selected ten official painters from the expatriate art community in London and tasked them with creating 25 images of the war. These men spent up to three months on the battlefield, living alongside Australian soldiers and sketching what they observed of life at the front. They included many of Australia's most renowned artists: George Bell, Charles Bryant, Will Dyson, Henry Fullwood, George Lambert, Fred Leist, John Longstaff, Septimus Power, James Quinn and Arthur Streeton. Five artists – George Benson, Frank Crozier, Will Longstaff, Louis McCubbin and James Scott – who were already serving in the AIF, were employed to sketch the war whenever they could be spared from military duties.

By the time of the Armistice in November 1918, the collection consisted of around three hundred small sketches and paintings of artists' observations of the war. This was a far smaller collection than other national schemes. The Canadians, for instance, had a collection of four hundred large canvases by the end of the war. But for Bean, the Australian images were 'a far more interesting set and a suitable memorial ... small pictures of what the artists actually saw at the front'.[23] The Australian collection was unified by a common theme, but it was made up of an eclectic array of subjects. Official artists produced images that ranged across a wide spectrum of genres, from soldiering life behind the lines, embarkation and disembarkation of troops and portraits of notable military personnel, to landscapes of the battlefields. Only one of the 15 official artists, George Lambert, had been stationed in the Middle East, and as a result the collection was dominated by artworks of the war on the Western Front.

With the cessation of hostilities, Bean, Treloar and Smart were able to pause and assess the collection. When commissioning artists after the war to produce larger, memorial-style canvases, they selected specific scenes they believed were missing. The fighting at Gallipoli was one such gap, and Lambert was tasked with retrospectively painting the peninsula, producing one of Australia's most iconic images of the war, *Anzac, the landing 1915* (1920–22).

The focus of these supplementary commissions remained almost exclusively on major military events during the war. Within this thematic framework, the experience of the infantry on the battlefield was highly favoured; the navy and Australian Flying Corps were notably underrepresented in the collection. For instance, of 53 images commissioned after November 1918, around 45 focused on the army, while the Flying Corps was represented by only two.[24]

Throughout the inter-war years, Bean and Treloar continued to add to and significantly expand the art collection. In contrast to the practice of the Canadians and British, the Australian art collection – made by, for and about Australians – focused almost exclusively on the exploits of the AIF in Europe. There were occasional instances of an effort to broaden the scope of the collection. Treloar acquired Rix Nicholas' *A Mother of France* in the 1920s and Will Longstaff's famous *Menin Gate at Midnight* (1927). But overall, Treloar and Bean remained committed to commissioning images of the conduct of the war in theatres in which Australians had fought.

As a result of its emphasis on military themes, the Australian official art collection represented a narrow vision of the nation's wartime endeavour. Experiences such as life in training camps, the embarkation of troops, women's wartime efforts and the bitter political disputes that divided the country were absent from the collection. An exploration of the competing proposals for the official war art scheme provides an insight into the politicised processes of memory-making during the war. These proposals show that the paintings we see in the galleries of the Australian War Memorial today are the product of a contest about who had the right to act as a witness to war and what aspects of the conflict were remembered. Where other official art schemes embraced a diversity of artists, and a broader range of subjects, including women's experiences and interpretations of the conflict as well as activities on the home front, the Australian art collection focused on the Australian soldier at war and ushered in a commemorative trend, at least at a federal level, of neglecting transnational contexts and privileging the national.

15

STAGING HISTORY IN BRISBANE'S ANZAC CENTENARY

Geoffrey AC Ginn

Right now we're in a fight that will shape how this nation sees itself for generations to come. When people will look back and ask: did the women sit back and let an entire generation be led into the flames? Or did they stand up and say the killing has got to stop? We're shaping history, Peg.

Michael Futcher, The Blood Votes: An Historical Drama, *Part 2 Scene 13 (fictional line delivered by Adela Pankhurst to Margaret Thorp)*

What is the meaning of the Great War for Australians today? And what do we think it meant for the men, women and children of 1914–18 who lived through the vast, unsettling conflict? As the chapters of this book show, these questions will always be challenging because the 'meaning' of history does not condense for us naturally or inevitably like dew in the morning. The creation and sharing of historical meaning are always contingent and contested, embedded in the moment and shaped by personal and impersonal factors such as culture, politics, gender, economics and age.

As Remembrance Day and Anzac Day took shape as solemn national occasions in the 1920s, they joined with Charles Bean's

Official History and the exhibits of the Australian War Memorial to construct a version of the war – a story, made up of its component plots, personalities and sub-stories – for consumption by the post-war Australian public.[1] Bean and his like mythologised the experiences of 1914–18 through what the folklorist Graham Seal has called 'cultural scripts', connecting the 'potent notions of community, nation and war' in written histories, memoirs, official rituals, memorials, commissioned artworks and the national war museum itself as it finally materialised in Canberra.[2] In essence, these scripts told of how the young nation 'answered the call' by dispatching a volunteer army to the front, and how 'our boys' fared as the devastating global struggle unfolded. The heroic elements of this mythic structure (extolling how Australian feats of arms captured the hillsides at Gallipoli, fought heroically under impossible conditions with mediocre British leadership, and beat a valiant retreat before returning to decisively break the stalemate in France) sustained a 'warrior cult' reading of the war from the Dardanelles to the Western Front. The shelves of any bookshop tell us that this narrative of Australia's war experience continues to command attention and shape popular memory.

The dominance of this version of the Great War, according to the historian Jennifer Wellington,

> removed the domestic experience of the war from the narrative of the conflict in Australia promoted after 1918 … activities like waiting for those abroad, and engaging in patriotic or domestic activities to support the distant war. This exclusion and the image of the war as overwhelmingly exotic and masculine enabled a strongly romantic, 'traditional' narration of the war as valour.[3]

This is not an abstract historical issue; significant political issues are at stake that go to potent, even existential, questions of national identity. 'The more our political parties seek to fortify the Anzac mythology as the unchallengeable centre of the Australian national imaginary', argues the essayist Ben Brooker,

> the more displaced become the alternative narratives that offer different, more desirable ways of knowing ourselves and where we have come from – ones that are grounded in the truth of our past, rather than the obscene fiction that to become a nation we had to make a blood sacrifice in somebody else's war.[4]

Certainly, the emphasis on valour and sacrifice, however we might think of such things, has obscured countless smaller stories. Most of them are less clamorous ones about how a generation endured the challenges and privations of a grim and demanding conflict, or more sobering ones about how societies at war splinter and fracture under this kind of pressure. As historian Joan Beaumont intimates in the title of her book *Broken Nation* and argues within its covers, far from 'making the nation' through the 'blood sacrifice' at Gallipoli, the experience of war had a devastating effect on the new Commonwealth.[5]

The recently concluded centenary commemoration provided a unique opportunity to weigh the Great War's place in the contemporary Australian imagination and to seek to influence its ongoing legacy. There was no shortage of resources for this task, because the extent of governmental enthusiasm, as measured in dollars spent on commemorative events, was astonishing. The former Australian Army officer and Lowy Institute fellow James Brown's provocative suggestion in 2014 that Australian governments would spend $325 million on the centenary, turned out to be overly cautious.

On the Honest History website, David Stephens and Ben Brooker recently put the figure somewhere over $600 million, with another $500 million proposed for the extension of the War Memorial.⁶ The splurge revived long-standing scepticism about 'Anzackery' (a term coined by the historian Geoffrey Serle in 1967) and the hitching of Anzac traditions to ideological projects of nationalism and militarism.⁷

While much of the official largesse was allocated to projects that bolstered conventional representations of Australian experience in the Great War, some funding was directed to endeavours that sought to rework the Anzac 'warrior myth', and inform a more critical and historically informed sense of the war years. Such aspects include the dreadful personal toll for those that endured the war, the impact on families and communities, the dilemmas posed by the scale and character of the conflict, and the thunderous debates about basic concepts like citizenship, loyalty, liberty and duty.

In this chapter, I consider two live theatre productions, both developed and staged in Brisbane in 2015–18, that took up this task in earnest: *The Blood Votes*, an original play dealing with the civil discord of the conscription debates of 1916–17, and *A Lost Story from the Great War*, an on-site heritage interpretation show using advanced sound and light special effects, an original script and 'in-character' performers. As theatre, both productions aimed to be dramatic and entertaining, rather than overt forms of memorialisation. But as educational commemorative events they also aimed to connect audiences in emotional, affective ways to Australia's Great War history and the experiences of the 'Anzac generation'.

The two projects began entirely independently of each other, on different scales with different funding support. But both arrived at a similar place: offering live, dramatic theatre, performed in situ at evocative heritage settings, to seize audiences with challenging accounts of the Australian experience during 1914–18. Each play was carefully scripted, drawing on factual historical information skilfully interwoven with fictional dialogue and action. The plays suggest how the combination of old-fashioned 'historical facts' with the creative reimagining permitted in theatre might connect audiences in news ways to the Great War. How did these two theatre shows go about encouraging these connections? And what do they suggest about the potential of immersive, affective history-making on stage?

A Lost Story of the Great War

The first of the two productions to be staged was developed by the Queensland National Parks and Wildlife Service from November 2015. *A Lost Story of the Great War* built on earlier educational programs for school groups and visitors to Fort Lytton National Park dating back to 2006, which were researched, written and performed primarily by a versatile Parks Ranger and seasoned performer in theatre education, Daley Donnelly. Other actors have assisted in script development and workshopping, notably Brisbane actor Zoe de Plevitz, who took on the dual roles of narrator and nurse. Performed monthly, the show takes visitors with hand-held lanterns around the fort's artillery emplacements overlooking the mouth of the Brisbane River, using interactive exhibition technology developed by Brisbane company Link Interactive.[8] The factual story of an Australian soldier unfolds through a sequence of dramatised episodes staged by the two actors, with character dialogue and narration synchronised to sound effects and visual projection.[9]

Using the biography of Ray Stanley, born in Brisbane in 1883, *A Lost Story* is structured to draw threads of connection between Stanley's pre-war service at Fort Lytton and his wartime experiences. His career links imperial defence preparations of the late-colonial period (suitably embodied by Fort Lytton itself, built in the early 1880s to defend Brisbane from the threat of naval attack) to the tragic human drama of active service in the Great War. Stanley trained as a submarine miner at Fort Lytton, before volunteering for the AIF and taking command of the 2nd Light Horse Signals Troop. His service took him to Egypt, Gallipoli and then with the 5th Division to Fromelles and the Somme in the autumn and winter of 1916–17. After being hospitalised in England with pneumonia, Stanley returned to France in 1917 with the rank of major, continuing to serve there through the final offensives from August to October 1918.

For its authors, the shift in persona suggested by wartime photographs – from Stanley as pre-war 'cheeky chappie' (in Donnelly's words) to sombre trench veteran, drained and exhausted – set the tone of *A Lost Story* as a theatrical piece. 'These men', Donnelly says, 'joined the war effort with humour and a sense of adventure, but what they experienced hollowed them out'. The show's dramatic sequence is organised accordingly: buoyant with imperialist rhetoric and optimism at the outset, we see the soldiers' initial bravado at Gallipoli darken into grim horror at the Western Front. Stanley provides the point of refraction, focusing the enormous historical catastrophe unfolding around him. The nadir comes when he is hospitalised with pneumonia and talks to a nurse who had also reached breaking point in France. In dramaturgical terms, this is the centrepiece of the play, the moment of deepest emotional pain, which helped the authors to orient the rest of the dramatic sequence. The scene and its dialogue are simple, direct, and affecting:

Stanley: You took ill?

Nurse: In a way. It was not being able to do anything to stop the pain. The wounds were so terrible. The many ways

> the human body can be opened up and torn apart and still keep breathing and still feel pain.
>
> Stanley: You've seen a lot.
>
> Nurse: I've seen too much. They call me Mother, or Mum, or … I'm not their mother. She's 12 000 miles away and she will never see her son again – and never like this … *(she weeps)*
>
> Pause.
>
> Stanley: They call me 'Mum' sometimes, too. *(Stanley and Nurse look at each other. They begin to laugh; laughter turns to tears.)*[10]

The primary intention underlying the fictionalised treatment of Stanley's experiences, according to Donnelly, was to bring home to audiences what the Western Front actually did to the volunteers who served there. Connecting visitors emotionally to history as experienced by real people in real historical circumstances was the objective, coupled with the basic educational challenge of supplying narrative to explain unfamiliar historical facts and developments. If the 'horror of the trenches' is familiar to the point of cliché, the questions typically asked by school students suggest little understanding of the volunteers and their motives: Why did they go? What were they fighting for? As a personal, authentic story, Stanley's archetypical journey provides one answer. 'It's the little personal details', Donnelly says, 'that are the way in for the audiences – without those, the larger picture is cerebral and unengaging for them'.

Older visitors might be more familiar with the war as history, but seem less aware of the pre-war imperial loyalism that groomed young Australian men like Ray Stanley for military service. Some appreciation of the pre-war context, it seems, comes with the show's brief account of Field Marshal Horatio Kitchener's visit to Fort Lytton in 1910. Against Elgar's *Pomp and Circumstance March No. 1* ('Land of Hope and Glory'), Kitchener's voice intones: 'it can never be said that a man is the worse for spending a few years, or even the best part of his life, in the service of his King and Country' (a phrase that Stanley repeats bitterly at the end of the show). The narrator chimes in with a key point: 'Kitchener recommended that the Australian Commonwealth engage in compulsory military training for all young men aged twelve to twenty-six'. At this point, shocked muttering and shaking of heads have been typical audience responses.[11] For the actors, these reactions confirm their sense that *A Lost Story* is hitting the mark as an effective mode of history education.

The Blood Votes: An Historical Drama

In similar vein to the producers of *A Lost Story*, a desire to find imaginative, evocative ways to communicate complex Great War experiences that are little understood today, motivated a group of history staff at the University of Queensland in 2015 to consider the public education opportunities of the Anzac centenary. Dismayed with the prevailing narrative of martial achievement and nation-building through 'blood sacrifice', the group, which included me, settled on developing a dramatic script dealing with the historical events of Australia's conscription debates.[12]

Why conscription? For a start, it is a compelling and intrinsically dramatic story that is little known outside the historical profession. With the war in Europe reaching a crisis point and volunteer recruitment on the wane, Labor Prime Minister Billy Hughes returned from Europe in mid-1916 and vehemently endorsed a system of conscription for overseas service. His views were expected to prevail, but were opposed by many in the community, including members of Hughes' own government, unionists in the labour movement, peace activists, sections of the Catholic Church and the Queensland Labor Premier, TJ Ryan. For the pro-conscriptionists of the Universal Service League and other patriotic associations, the crisis was at hand and the appropriate response was self-evident: duty trumped liberty, and a just war for civilisation could legitimately be fought by compulsion. The scene was set for a protracted, epoch-defining debate. Plebiscites on conscription were narrowly defeated in October 1916 and December 1917.

Another element that made the conscription controversy such a compelling choice for dramatisation, was the fact that Australia was the only combatant nation to sustain a broad public debate on the issue, at least in such explicit terms. Australians of all sorts – men and women, young and old, rich and poor, Catholic and Protestant, unionist and businessman – voiced their heartfelt views in public forums, newspaper articles and pamphlets. The Labor Party split over the issue and the nation fractured along lines of social class, religion, age, gender and ethnicity.

For these reasons, my colleagues at the University of Queensland and I were drawn to the conscription story because it represents such a dramatic moment in Australian history. Joan Beaumont writes that the debate over compulsion 'has never been rivalled in Australian political history for its bitterness, divisiveness and violence'. It was 'not simply a disagreement about the military need for conscription, but an irreconcilable conflict of views about core values: the nature of citizenship and national security; equality of sacrifice in times of national crisis; and the legitimate exercise of power within Australia's democracy'.[13]

If any story provides a corrective to populist 'Anzackery', surely this is it. We made a case to Queensland's Anzac centenary funding body that a dramatic script based on authentic sources and critical historical research would have substantial educational value during the centenary and beyond. The script, we contended:

> will faithfully represent the historical record, citing public rhetoric, songs, and official statements of various kinds, but with creative licence to personalise the human dilemmas that pulsed through the great conscription question. The result will be a dramatic historical realism on the stage; audiences will find themselves drawn to one point of view and then another, experiencing in this the pull of loyalty, kinship and community through the language, emotion and narrative action mobilised by the play.

With funding through the Queensland Anzac Centenary Lasting Legacies program, research undertaken by historian Susan Kellett was provided to Brisbane writer Michael Futcher, author or co-author of the plays *The Wishing Well*, *The Drowning Bride*, *A Beautiful Life* (Currency Press) and *Citizen Jane* (Playlab).[14] Using the speeches and letters of historical individuals, together with songs and posters, Futcher wrote *The Blood Votes* to capture the pressures, anxieties and divided loyalties of civilian Australia during 1914–18. The play addressed the issues and emotions of the conscription debates through the experiences of a cast of fictional characters interwoven with historical personalities including Prime Minister Hughes and the prominent Quaker and Women's Peace Army (WPA) activist and anti-conscriptionist, Margaret Thorp. Verbatim transcripts of speeches, private letters and newspaper reports were braided with fictionalised dialogue to sustain the dramatic intensity and impact. After workshopping, revisions and rehearsals, *The Blood Votes* premiered in November 2018 as a full dramatic production, with period costumes and props, in a late-colonial church hall in Brisbane's Fortitude Valley. Six performances were staged, including one for schools and a finale matinée on Sunday 11 November. A cast of eight professional actors, each taking on multiple roles and filling places in the chorus, brought the script to life under the direction of Rob Pensalfini and Kat Dekker.

The project brief required a balanced treatment of both sides of the conscription debate, and close fidelity to historical documents, but beyond these terms Futcher had the creative freedom to ensure an effective stage drama. He experimented accordingly, juxtaposing speeches alongside letters from soldiers abroad; in one scene, Thorp's speech urging pacifism to the National Council of Women overlaps a scarifying letter from Gallipoli. The effect is to drive home the paralysing distance between protagonists in Australia and the distant, horrific, slowly unfolding events of the war.[15] Immersed in the rich, impassioned debates documented in the historical sources, the playwright was struck by the contemporary resonance of his material. Speaking at a Q&A session in September 2017, at a time of heightened tension between the United States and North Korea, Futcher said:

> As a theatre-maker my job is to bring stuff from the past,
> but bring it up to relevance to the modern day. And I have to
> say, it's very easy to get hysterical about all the media, really
> beating up the North Korea thing, but you can't help but
> think that it starts off with rhetoric, everything begins with
> rhetoric. And the rhetoric that is happening from America,
> what it does at the moment is it normalises the use of force,
> which at this time, in 1914, was actually the case as well.

With the period's bellicose and richly textured language at its heart, Futcher's play roves across three quite distinct spheres: the domestic, the activist and the political. It interweaves scenes and plot developments across all three to generate a cumulative historical and dramatic account. In the 'domestic' sphere, we are introduced in the first scene to the Quaker activist Margaret Thorp (our main protagonist, played by Paige Poulier) as she arrives in Brisbane in November 1915 to campaign against the war. We meet Thorp's landlady (another Quaker, of German descent), and two other tenants, Mrs O'Neill and her son Robert (of Irish descent). Robert has just turned 18, and his mother is unmoved by Britain's imperialist war. Robert has not enlisted, but will be compelled to go if conscription is introduced. He has a girlfriend, Ruby, whose brother is at the front and whose mother heads the local branch of the (pro-conscription) patriotic association, the 'All Loyal League'.[16] To begin with, neither Ruby nor Robert gives much thought to conscription, but the audience knows that is set to change. Futcher expertly sets up a tangle of ordinary human situations, the foundation of a dramatic narrative centred on the young lovers, which demonstrates powerfully the human impact of the unfolding conscription debate.

In the activist sphere, we follow Margaret Thorp, who is recruited by the Women's Peace Army (WPA), and in turn is part of an anti-conscription alliance between the WPA and Queensland trade unions. Thorp's story brings historical figures into the action, including Queensland socialist Ernie Lane and his wife Mabel, and two leading WPA figures from Melbourne, Cecilia John and Adela Pankhurst. While much of the drama is revealed through fictionalised exchanges, Thorp's speech about 'The Menace of Militarism' is delivered verbatim to the audience as a town hall set piece. Another historical incident, the riot at the Brisbane School of Arts on 9 July 1917, during which Thorp was shouted down by loyalist hecklers, dragged from the lectern and assaulted, is recreated in dramatic style.[17]

The third sphere of formal politics takes us to the grand political rhetoric of Billy Hughes, played by Matthew Filkins. We follow the Prime Minister as his supporters and opponents react to his bloody-minded determination to implement compulsory military service. The divisive, galvanising presence of Australia's most inscrutable Prime Minister is captured through extracts of his own shrill, insistent words, which are worked into the script. Audiences witness the Labor Party split, Hughes' coalition with conservative rivals, the poisonous sectarianism and the farcical incident at Warwick in Queensland, at which an egg was thrown at the Prime Minister. The drama is carried along by the vivid imagery and impassioned tones of period slogans, speeches and songs.

As the conscription debate unfolds in Australia, a 'choric' element assembles periodically to evoke the pitiless horror and bloodshed of the conflict far away. For Futcher, the actors stand before the audience 'like a series of ghosts from the past'.[18] The chorus recites casualty statistics, newspaper reports about political affairs and letters home from the trenches. Amid the acrimony of the second plebiscite, Futcher's text draws on a 1917 propaganda leaflet called 'The Anti's Creed', which lists a malignant set of 'beliefs', that paraphrase and distort the anti-conscription case. A voice starts: 'What do you believe?' and the chorus follows in rapid fire, slightly overlapping:

> VOICE: I believe in general strikes.
> VOICE: I believe that the men at the Front should be sacrificed.
> VOICE: I believe in taking all the benefit and none of the risks.
> VOICE: I believe that Britain should be crushed and humiliated.
> VOICE: I believe in the murder of women, and baby-killing.
> VOICE: I believe that treachery is a virtue.
> ALL: I BELIEVE I'M WORM ENOUGH TO VOTE NO.
> VOICE: Those who don't believe in this creed –
> ALL: VOTE YES![19]

Through characters such as Robert, Ruby, Margaret Thorp and Billy Hughes and the power of the choric ensemble, *The Blood Votes* captures the passion and hysteria of the conscription debate, and challenges Australians to reboot their understanding of the Great War. We find similar ambition in *A Lost Story of the Great War*. In outlining Stanley's archetypical military career, Daley Donnelly's script explores how a sense of intrinsic purpose was framed by the men and women who endured the war, and how that frame buckled under enormous pressure. Unlike shallower forms of commemoration with their bland, dutiful acknowledgment of 'service' and 'sacrifice', historically grounded theatre supports complex understandings of the Great War. By taking audiences through – and beyond – emotional connection towards critical, evidence-based insights, documentary theatre is potentially the kind of popular memory work that good history needs.

16

REMEMBERING AND FORGETTING THE FIRST WORLD WAR AT THE SIR JOHN MONASH CENTRE

Bruce Scates

Australia's new interpretive centre on the Somme was the single most expensive undertaking of the Anzac centenary. With a price tag of over $100 million, it was ten times the cost of the National Anzac Centre in Albany and considerably more than educational digitisation projects favoured by historians. The Sir John Monash Centre (SJMC) was built around Australia's national memorial at Villers-Bretonneux and involved a formidable engineering challenge. Mindful of the heritage properties of the site, and that they would have to build around a cemetery, the designers placed their complex behind Edwin Lutyen's original memorial tower. Or rather beneath it. To retain sweeping sightlines across the Anzac battlefields, the museum was set several metres below ground level and a 'floating meadow' installed on the roof above it.[1] Inside, the centre 'utilises a range of leading edge communication media ranging from contemplative display to high impact audiovisual presentations'. This 'multi-media experience' was delivered by Convergence Associates, an interpretive design and planning consultancy based in Melbourne. Their objective was 'to create a visitor experience that is credible, emotive and memorable'.[2]

The opening lines of Convergence's tender merit particular attention. Over 400 cubic metres of concrete was not enough. To be 'credible' Australia's national museum on the Western Front must rest, the company announced, on the firm foundations of history:

> The historians for the project have been chosen on the basis of their special expertise on particular aspects of the project brief; their outstanding contributions to the literature, the capacity to communicate effectively with a popular audience, their objectivity and on the basis of peer-reviewed checks. We believe they represent a combination of relevant skills and perspectives that will engender respect for the project from international scholars and the visiting public in Europe. We take the view that aims at anything less than objective excellence is to disrespect those who fought and those who died.[3]

Within a year of this statement being issued, over half of the historians commissioned by Convergence – including this author – had withdrawn from the project. 'International scholars', including those Convergence nominated, disputed the value of a museum that adopted so singular and exclusive a national narrative, and 'the visiting public in Europe' were astonished by Australia's claim to have turned back the German offensive of 1918 virtually single-handed. Far from 'objective excellence' safeguarded by processes of peer review, the historians who valiantly remained on the project faced persistent intervention, their text was rewritten and their analysis blunted. Scholars might question whether a 'highly emotional theatrical experience' delivers a 'broad and deep understanding' of war.[4] Taxpayers may baulk at a $100 million bill for an installation most will never see. But there is an even more urgent question this chapter will address, and one flagged by Convergence's principled preamble. When the integrity of academic inquiry is sacrificed for 'emotive effect', when a global catastrophe is presented as a national triumph, when 'a multi-media experience' strives to 'relive' a horror beyond our imagination, when battle is packaged as a kind of entertainment, do we not 'disrespect those who fought and who died'?

Australian exceptionalism: Nationalism and the soldier-centric narrative

The leading international adviser to the SJMC was the distinguished Great War historian Jay Winter. He had been involved in the design of war museums before, and (with Stéphane Audoin-Rouzeau, Annette Becker and others) helped to fashion the Historial de la Grande Guerre, France's principal museum of the First World War. The Historial is situated on the Somme, as is the SJMC. Located at Péronne and Villers-Bretonneux respectively, they stand at the epicentre of battle, a place where the Great Powers' armies collided and (in Ernst Jünger's memorable phrase) the 20th century was born.[5] And yet, there the similarity between the two installations ends. Like the In Flanders Fields Museum in Ypres, the Historial adopts a comparative, transnational and multi-vocal perspective.[6] The 'story' of the war is told not as a nation-building narrative, but a catastrophe that engulfed Europe and indeed much of the world. Both institutions widen our gaze beyond the experience of combatants; a 'total war' 1914–18 shattered the lives of civilians as well as men and women in the field. One might contrast this with the galleries of the SJMC. Contrary to the advice of historians, Australia's role on the Western Front is the museum's singular focus. Although the AIF fielded only five divisions in France and despite the fact that, in the words of Joan Beaumont, 'Australia's role in World War 1 must be seen as a small part of a much larger British Imperial effort', the purpose of the museum was to 'demonstrate' the way Australia helped 'win the war'.[7]

Nor does the museum look far beyond the battlefield. Its narrative is driven by a grinding succession of battles, 'Fromelles –

A Terrible Charge'; 'Pozières – Unthinkable Losses'; 'Messines – the Earth Trembled' and so on. There is token representation of life 'Behind the Front' – how could there not be when soldiers spent less than a third of their time in the front lines?[8] But the most promising themes identified by historians – 'the grand tour' that attracted men and women to active service, encounters with new people and cultures, social interaction with the civilian population, the entertainments and illusions that sustained a fighting force far from home, the plight of refugees – receive far less attention.[9] How the war came home and how it came to be commemorated, areas of new and burgeoning scholarship, are considered only in the final galleries, and then again the discussion is disproportionately brief. Much is said about 'Anzac values' and the 'legacy' of the First AIF. Far less about the way 'facts turn into myths and legends' and the way 'meanings' of war memory are mobilised for current political purposes.[10]

One of the most significant aspects of Australia's commitment to this conflict is the political and gendered tensions war brought in its train. Industrial unrest, hunger at home, women's unprecedented and often disruptive mobilisation in wartime and two immensely divisive conscription referenda are barely mentioned by the museum. This was the clearly stated preference of the museum's sponsors. The SJMC was funded and managed by a partnership of two state-based commemorative agencies, the Office of Australian War Graves and the Department of Veterans' Affairs (DVA). Neither body had much tolerance of historical inquiry. 'The SJMC', the Chair of the Planning Committee announced, 'is not the place for radical interpretations of the experience of war'.[11] Despite claims to be an educational facility, the SJMC offers no extended analysis of the impact war had on our society. Rather, it is a largely uncritical tribute to the men and women sent to fight it. The marginalisation of these 'radical' topics (commonplace, one would add, in any high school syllabus) can be measured simply enough by the number and placement of artifacts on display. A compelling manifesto opposing the war is hidden away near the entrance to the immersive galleries – recruitment posters far more likely to catch the visitor's eye. A similar bias is evident in biographical panels lining the installation. Mobile phone apps deliver the Great War's testimony from these speaking exhibits. But again, some voices are privileged over others and very few speak of civilians' experience of war. At the SJMC you will hear the words of John Monash, never Tom Barker, the socialist activist who was imprisoned for his opposition to the war. As such, Villers-Bretonneux runs counter to museological practice. 'War museums began to change in the fourth quarter of the twentieth century,' Winter observed. 'They began to privilege non-combatant victims of war alongside civilian and military mobilisation in the war efforts of combatant countries.'[12] The SJMC looks backwards – to a singular, nationalist and soldier-centred vision of war.

These omissions, elisions and exclusions are serious enough. But, as the placement of the anti-conscription material suggests, remembering as a form of forgetting is braided through the centre's very design. Again, Winter's reflections on the making of museums are instructive. How, in the geography of exhibition spaces, does the SJMC compare with its 'sister' installation on the Somme, the Historial de la Grande Guerre at Péronne?

A right way to remember? Representing war in museums

Winter has identified three distinctive ways in which the Historial 'breaks new ground'. 'The first major innovation', he explains, 'is the development of the horizontal axis (the axis of mourning, as the vertical is the axis of hope) as the key visual organising principle'. This is achieved in part by the shallow pits, or fosses, that sit in the very centre of the Historial's galleries. They contain the empty uniforms of men sent to fight. Placed around them are traces of their belongings, affirming their individuality amid the appalling and often anonymous losses of 1914–18. As one walks through these evocative spaces one's gaze is directed downward. 'This avoids the upward inflection of the design of many war museums and hence', Winter explains, 'their implicit optimism'.[13]

If horizontality is the signature of the war museum at Péronne, verticality defines Villers-Bretonneux. Lutyens' original memorial tower is a triumphant statement. It rises above the flat rolling landscape of the Somme; here the missing have symbolically reclaimed the landscape that consumed them.[14] By the same token, visitors entering the SJMC will find the experience uplifting. High vaulted ceilings feature displays of upright poppies. The exposed columns that support that floating meadow reinforce a sense of light and space. As one moves through the galleries themselves, past each of the tall biographical panels, one's gaze is again directed upward – the men and women of the first AIF literally speak from above. Such installations are aptly styled 'plinths' in Convergence's Master Interpretive Schedule. Clearly, they serve a commemorative as much as an 'educational' purpose.[15]

The Historial's second innovation was to 'avoid verisimilitude in favour of authenticity'.[16] There is no attempt at what Winter calls 'pseudo-realism' – no recreation of dugouts, no battle simulations. This is because no museum 'can bring the visitor into something [even] approximating the experience of combat'. Rather, 'it is the business of war museums to resist [a] stylised fascination with combat and … offer a series of alternative ways of approaching the terror of the battlefield'.[17] Instead of a visual representation of combat, the Historial's designers included a blank wall that confronts the visitor with the 'radical impossibility' of representing the Somme: 'This absence, or silence, or void if you will, is an anti-monument, a challenge to our comprehension of the anticipation, the terror, the exhaustion, and pain, and ugliness, which constitute ... [battle]'.[18]

Villers-Bretonneux takes the opposite position. The SJMC purports to 'relive' the Great War, an illusion delivered through an 'immersive multimedia experience'. The 'journey' (as it is styled) begins with the spoken text of biographical panels. Professional actors dressed in AIF uniforms recite passages from diaries and letters, inviting us to imagine the unimaginable and 'share' in their 'experience'. This 'slippage' between the present and the past involves a form of reenactment.[19] Real-life characters speak and act with the authority of the witness. They 'connect' us to events of a century ago and no attempt is made to contextualise let alone critique their testimony. Much store is placed on the 'authenticity' of their stories: 'Above all [they] must play a role in consolidating a real view [my emphasis] of the war – at the place of actual events'.[20]

Between the biographical panels, Convergence has created a kind of digital battlefield. And here we see that 'slippage' once again, the 'collapse of temporality' and 'controlled entry of the present into the past' in the words of historian Jerome de Groot.[21] At one moment a screen several metres across reproduces black and white photographs of men marching to the front. The next, we see the 'same' men in the frenzy of fighting, flashes of artillery bursting around them. The front is a male experience, but (mindful of their brief) the designers have also found a space for women. Nurses feature alongside soldiers – these honorary Anzacs tend to an army of wounded.

There is an element of voyeurism in the recreation of a Casualty Clearing Station.[22] An Australian nurse, her white uniform splashed with blood, places the rosary in the shaking hand of a dying soldier. It is difficult to say how visitors will respond to this dramatisation – and the complex realm of individual, subjective response is beyond the scope of this chapter. What one can state with confidence is that scenes of death and carnage mark a dramatic departure from what Winter called an 'unstated rule of decorum'. It was not so long ago that museum representations ruled out such 'ugly or shocking images'; the SJMC abounds with them. Again the reasons for this are many and complex. One is the ascendant discourse of trauma in civil society; another (paradoxically) an attempt to counter the claim that the centenary sanitised and romanticised military conflict.[23] Whatever the designers' motivation, their efforts ride the tide of what historian Vanessa Agnew dubbed history's 'affective turn'.[24]

Nowhere is that more evident than in 'the heart of the SJMC', an 'immersive gallery' which 'presents an impressionistic and emotive overview of the battles of Villers-Bretonneux and Le Hamel'. 'Emotive' and 'impressionistic' are hardly the hallmarks of critical and analytical history, nor is the bid 'to interact with the battles', as if one was actually present on the field.[25] Moving into the gallery, visitors face a continuous wall of screens, one announcing the 'Show' is about to begin. The installation warns of 'graphic war scenes', 'loud audio' and 'a number of special effects'. Then one is plunged into the thick of battle, gas rises up from the floor, planes strafe the trenches and tanks rumble by. There is something more sinister here than a laboured attempt to 'connect' with the events of 1918. Battlefield simulations evoke simple moral dichotomies of 'us' and 'them'. German soldiers are dehumanised. Their faces concealed by gas masks, they are the enemy. And vicariously we are invited to take part in the killing. Fighting on the Somme has become a kind of computer game – you stalk your quarry through fields and villages – and you shoot him. This is what Winter calls 'a pornography of violence'.[26] Among 'the millions of visitors to war museums', he observes, 'there are many looking for the blood and guts of the victims, and the weapons that tear them apart'.[27] They would not be disappointed by Villers-Bretonneux.

The third innovation at the Historial was an 'attempt to maintain silence in the Museum'. One moves through the galleries in quiet contemplation. There is no dramatic music, no kitsch renditions of soldiers' songs, no rolling thunder of artillery. These, Winter tells us, 'are artificial triggers of emotion or thought'. They have no place in a museum grappling with the sheer enormity of human conflict.[28]

By contrast, the war is in your head at Villers-Bretonneux. Quite literally. Entering the museum, visitors download an app to their mobile phones. An ear plug streams the sound of battle, screams, shell fire and, of course, the plaintive 'voices' of a lost generation. The only escape is by removing the device altogether. And then the hapless visitor is completely detached from busy displays erupting around her – driven by technology, the museum lacks much conventional text-based narrative. This elective silence at the SJMC is a queer sensation. Ironically, it is the closest the centre comes to recapturing anything like 'the experience' of 1914–18 – war's total irreality.

The final distinguishing element of the Historial, Winter concludes, is 'the suggestion of the sacred'. It is true that museums are the cathedrals of our age. But not all are sacred places. The Historial is. The 'funeral shape of the fosses', 'the strict rule of silence', the assembly of relics, the injunction to remember, all create (as Winter puts it) 'a respectful and reflective comportment'.[29] But there is little of the sombre or the sacred in the SJMC. A gigantic screen frames the museum's exit. Words from epitaphs featured in the cemetery outside are superimposed over an Australian flag stretched stiff in the wind. We are told, again, to be proud of their sacrifice – not to ponder the immense futility of a war that claimed the lives of millions. And again, the guidelines issued to the museum's historians are telling. 'There are certain feelings we want to instil in visitors', a senior DVA official commented, and that affective use of history – the cultivation of emotion and empathy at the expense of understanding – is worrying enough. Even more troubling are the feelings he hoped to create. 'Quiet pride' was one of them, moderated, he quickly added, 'by a touch of sadness'.[30]

The DVA claims the SJMC is faithful to Edwin Lutyens' vision for a memorial. I wonder if many of Lutyens' generation would agree. Writing to a woman who lost her son in the Great War, Herbert Baker, Lutyen's fellow adviser to the Imperial War Graves Commission, struggled to justify 'huge expenditure' on work 'so few' would see. 'We are making sanctuaries', he wrote of Villers-Bretonneux, 'not mere monuments', places of peace, 'where the sentiment of the sacred' might 'grow in the future', a refuge for the bereaved, as quiet and contemplative as a village churchyard.[31] But at Australia's national museum on the Somme, in caverns carved from the earth, the war rumbles on – as if we had learned nothing.

Discordant stories, disruptive narratives

What might we have learned at Villers-Bretonneux? How might we have fostered a more complex and nuanced understanding of war? Here we return to the fraught deliberations between government, consultative firm and historians. In the closing months of December 2014, the historical advisory board nominated several individuals, drawn from history, for what the designers called 'biographical content'. Each historical figure was central to the 'story' of Villers-Bretonneux and yet all came to pose a challenge to the project itself as they were not in keeping with the overall aims and objectives of the Convergence-led project. Three cases in particular signal a more inclusive narrative and all suggest ways that history and commemoration, education and 'emotional immersion', diverge.

Arthur Rae showed a different kind of courage to that of a soldier. A founder of the Shearers' Union and one of the first Labor members of parliament, Rae was a fervent internationalist, called for a negotiated peace and opposed the introduction of conscription. He also had three sons who served. Two of them, William and Donald, died.

It was almost certainly Arthur Rae who composed young Billy's epitaph, an inscription set in stone at the entrance of Villers-Bretonneux:

ANOTHER LIFE LOST
HEARTS BROKEN
FOR WHAT

Arthur Rae's story reminds us how the Great War tore a family and a nation apart. It affirms a dissenting voice many Australians seem to have forgotten in our mis-memory of that conflict. The war divided the Commonwealth, it laid to waste a generation and it laid the basis of an even more terrible war to follow. And arguably the greatest victory for democracy to emerge from that war was not over Prussian militarism but the defeat of two bitterly contested conscription referenda. Thanks to the principled voice of Arthur Rae and many like him, Australians affirmed a great principle: no man should be forced to bear arms against another.[32]

The gendered politics of war were equally contentious, as the case of Ettie Rout suggests. Rout was raised in Wellington, New Zealand, and like thousands of women on both sides of the Tasman, threw herself into war work. No doubt knitting socks and distributing comforts provided relief for many soldiers. It also bridged the distance between home and the battlefield, an emotional as well as physical labour that built a connection to the trenches.[33] But Rout's activities abroad proved far more transgressive.

The Anzac forces had the highest rate of sexually transmitted diseases of any army serving abroad, and the authorities' response, at first, was one of ineffective discipline and pious moral outrage. Rout (and a small band of sex reformers) took a different approach to what contemporaries liked to call 'the social evil'. She put together a prophylactic kit, distributed condoms and directed diggers on leave in Paris to a number of safe brothels she helped to supervise. She also wrote to generals, political figures and clergy, exploring (in what must have seemed confronting detail) the 'physical relief of sexual [pleasure]'.[34]

The sexual health of soldiers and sex workers was one of Rout's concerns, the safety of the women and children back home another. The long-term consequences of venereal diseases included sterility, insanity and death – before the discovery of penicillin there was no safe or lasting cure and disease was often transmitted to unborn children. Gonorrhoea and syphilis, like tuberculosis and shell shock, came home with the men and wrought havoc on their families. Australia lost 60 000 men during the Great War; around that same number contracted venereal disease.

Rout stayed in Europe after the fighting ended. She was one of the first Australian women to visit the red zone, a jagged corridor of land cut through the heart of Europe, devastated by four years of conflict. Hers is a woman's story we seldom hear in a narrative that valorises the story of combatants over civilians. It is also a story centred on Villers-Bretonneux. Rout visited the ruined town after the Armistice, distributing aid to both soldiers and civilians. Even so, Rout's story, like Arthur Rae's, sat outside the authorised framework of remembrance. To discuss venereal disease was deemed 'inappropriate' by the Office of Australian War Graves, and, we were told, risked offending 'the sensibilities of the French'.[35]

Allen Charles Kingston was perhaps the most controversial case nominated for the exhibition spaces of Villers-Bretonneux. Again, his connection to the site itself was incontestable. In the immediate post-war period, Captain Kingston was posted to the Australian War Graves Detachment at Villers-Bretonneux. He and his men laid the basis of the cemetery that stands there today.

Charlie Kingston, like Rae and Rout, presents us with an alternative narrative, one that problematises the past. 'The war is over', he told his men, 'don't call me sir'. Men under Kingston's command dressed the German prisoners they had been allocated in Australian uniforms, sparing them the abuse of the locals, took them on 'joy rides' into Amiens, shouted them a drink. Several drinks actually. Under Kingston, the war graves depot at Villers-Bretonneux went by the name of Captain Charlie's Boozer and was frequented by what the locals called 'loose women' as well. Captain Kingston turned a blind eye while soldiers 'entertained' women in the compound and borrowed War Graves Commission vehicles for excursions into town. And when he was not burying the dead, Charlie Kingston was mixing what he called the Villers-Bretonneux cocktail, a potent blend of rum, whisky and sauce of an alcoholic intensity imaginable only in France.[36]

In 1920 the government initiated an official inquiry into the management of Villers-Bretonneux. Kingston was accused of behaviour unbecoming of an officer and sent home. He was sent home by the same military authorities who had decorated him for bravery just a few years before.[37]

We can read Charlie Kingston's story in a number of different ways: perhaps he was a man struggling with demons; perhaps the drink was an escape from the grim work of exhumation; perhaps he had simply had enough. But arguably, there was great humanity in befriending those German prisoners and discarding the brutal authority that ordered men to their deaths. And whatever the 'truth' of Charlie Kingston, it is surely a story that we should tell today at Villers-Bretonneux.

These three cases signalled a parting of ways. Not long after the names of Arthur Rae, Ettie Rout and Charlie Kingston fell off the list of approved biographies, four historians (independent of government and acting in an advisory role) withdrew from the

Villers-Bretonneux project. I was one of them. I still believe historians have a social responsibility to engage with community and government. If we fail to do so (as the advocates of public history often remind us), there are others who will take our place. How many journalists peddling their Anzac blockbusters today also claim to speak with the authority of 'history'? But that engagement, imperative as it is, cannot be at the expense of our discipline. Genuine historical inquiry is just that – searching and expansive, interrogating our own and others' subjective understandings, stretching the very boundaries of knowledge. History is not a consultancy 'service', culling content deemed problematic, delivering a message dictated by others. On that note, I acknowledge the work on the project of Michael McKernan, Ross McMullin and Robin Prior, three accomplished historians of immense professional integrity. In retrospect, the decision by Rae Frances, Al Thomson, Jay Winter and myself to quit the project was an easy option. Remaining, and demanding something better, proved a far harder task.

There is more at stake here than the professional discomfort of a few disputatious academics. At issue is the character of historical remembrance. Do we want a memory of war that's confined to a singular and unitary national narrative, or a past that's open to complexity, multiplicity, even disagreement? Should an interpretive centre tell us what to feel, or should it present us with questions, challenges, uncomfortable, unsettling narratives? The SJMC, the DVA assures us, will be a major educational resource on the Western Front. If so, can it wilfully turn away from the terrible question Arthur Rae had carved in stone; a challenge to his and future generations?[38]

Conclusion

Those who design war museums face 'a stark choice', in the words of Jay Winter: 'either they aim at an interrogation as to how war can be represented or they continue to deepen lies and illusions about it'. The Historial fulfils what Winter calls the 'moral responsibility' of all who examine military conflict. It also serves an educative purpose. 'By the time the visitor finishes the slow journey through the war and its aftermath, assisted by objects and documentary alike, the impossibility of describing the Allies as, in any straight forward sense, victorious becomes apparent.'

By contrast, Australian visitors to the SJMC will be told their country secured 'victory' in 1918. Some will cling to the illusion that the AIF won the war single-handed. They may develop a better understanding of the forces that plunged the world into chaos, and the nature of Australian society in 1914. An introductory, interactive quiz examines the imperial alliances that drove European politics and outlines the early achievements of Australia's social laboratory. But there is an irony here. The prosperous and progressive society deemed worth defending was shaped by a strong and assertive labour movement, not by a military machine placed at the service of the British Empire. Some visitors will believe they have 'relived' the war themselves. By presenting the 'unpresentable', the SJMC trivialises the trauma that afflicted a generation.[39] Some may even enjoy the wilful fetishism of violence.

The Historial is a museum that serves the purpose of a new Europe. A hundred years since the carnage that tore the world apart, it is time to speak across borders and focus on the common tragedy shared by combatants and civilians on all sides of the conflict. In 2018 Australia had the opportunity to do just that. We failed to do so. Rather, we clung to the 'old lies': that war is a measure of the greatness of a nation, that the slaughter of 1914–18 was something other than a sordid waste.

COMMEMORATING THE GREAT WAR

17

REMEMBRANCE DAY: THE POOR COUSIN OF AUSTRALIAN WAR COMMEMORATION

Romain Fathi

When Australia's then largest memorial to the Great War – the Shrine of Remembrance – was unveiled in Melbourne in 1934, it included a specific commemorative feature that attracted widespread praise from the public. The Shrine had a small aperture in its dome through which a ray of sunlight shone at the 11th hour of the 11th day of the 11th month: Remembrance Day. The tunnelled beam of light illuminated the word 'love' onto the tombstone located at the heart of the Shrine. The tombstone, which symbolised the absent dead, was inscribed with the words 'Greater love hath no man' from John's Gospel.[1] In an overwhelmingly Christian society, the inscription provided comfort to grieving families, for it drew a parallel between the sacrifice of Christ and the death of their loved ones.

Significantly, it was Armistice Day (later known as Remembrance Day) rather than Anzac Day that was chosen to showcase the Shrine's most distinct and solemn commemorative feature, the Ray of Light.[2] From the perspective of 2019, wherein Anzac Day dominates Australian war commemoration, it is curious to imagine that Armistice Day once held such a significant place in Australians' commemorative calendar. This chapter considers the evolution of Remembrance Day in Australia from 1918 to 2018. From its first iteration to its hundredth one, the chapter explores why

Remembrance Day – a major commemorative day in inter-war Australia – has mostly held a secondary position in orchestrating Australians' commemorations of World War I. The chapter highlights the reasons behind a progressively fading popularity, in particular pointing to the role of Anzac Day and the absence of a public holiday for Remembrance Day.

The 'end' of the First World War

In the early hours of 11 November 1918, aboard the Supreme Allied Commander Marshal Ferdinand Foch's train carriage, a few plenipotentiaries of Germany and the principal Allied nations signed a short document that ordered, among other demands, a ceasefire effective from 11 am that day. Their signatures put an end to the conflict that had killed more than ten million combatants and six million civilians. Germany, the last belligerent standing among the Central Powers, had collapsed militarily, economically and politically. Although the Armistice prompted a ceasefire, it did not formally end the war. Indeed, Germany had sought an armistice in order to negotiate a formal peace treaty. This peace was secured eight months later, on 28 June 1919, at the Paris Peace Conference. The Armistice also did not resolve localised conflicts resulting from the war, which continued in parts of Eastern Europe and the Middle East until the early 1920s. But for most combatant nations, including Australia, the armistice of 11 November came to represent the end of the war. Armistice Day has since been commemorated annually in Australia and many former Allied nations.

Australia's first Armistice Day

The terms of the Armistice were signed shortly after 5.15 am on 11 November 1918. News spread quickly in Europe that the agreement would be effective from 11 am. In the meantime, the United States broke the news to Australia which, given the time difference, learned about the Armistice at around 7 pm, Melbourne time, on the day it was signed. The news spread immediately across the nation, and tens of thousands of people crowded the streets of towns and cities to celebrate. In Melbourne, *The Age* reported:

> The news spread with extraordinary rapidity to the suburbs. Everyone was awaiting the signal, everyone expectant. And when the first cheer was given all realised that the moment for rejoicing had come. Bells began to peal, and tins were rattled, and the people assembled in the streets and sang songs. Fireworks were seen on all sides. People from every direction sought a way to the city, and trains and trams, motors and other vehicles, were crowded with those who were eager to join in the big demonstration.[3]

Later in the night, cables from London confirmed the news. The mood was festive, and national, state and local newspapers attest to the thousands of celebrations and services that were held across Australia, and indeed the world, in the following days. Finally, that dreadful conflict had ended. Anecdotally, Australia's Armistice Day celebrations had started several days earlier, on 8 November, when misleading press reports announced that an armistice had been signed on the Western Front on 7 November. In fact, an authorisation to cross no-man's-land had been granted to German representatives with a short ceasefire in order to negotiate the Armistice, which was only signed in the early hours of the 11th. These details had been misinterpreted by a number of press officials, and Australians were not alone in celebrating what then became known as the false armistice.

The news of the Armistice produced relief as much as joy. Despite being among the victors, the war had been profoundly shocking for the newly federated nation. Sixty thousand Australians lay dead in France, Belgium, Gallipoli and the Middle East – a significant blow for a country of less than five million people, but a drop in the ocean of death that was the First World War. The unprecedented number of dead young men lying on faraway battlefields called for new commemorative practices. From 1919, Armistice Day became a vital element of the rituals and commemorative practices that Australians put in place to live with their loss.

Armistice Day in the inter-war period

After the celebrations of 1918, Armistice Day subsequently became a more formal and sombre occasion on which people were encouraged to remember the dead with respect and solemnity. A dedicated time for silence became part of the ceremony and has been central to Armistice Day commemorations ever since. In Britain, King George V requested a two-minute silence, which was observed from 1919 onward across the empire. This feature was not unique to the British Empire. France, among other examples, instituted a *minute de silence* in 1922. Silence meant time for contemplation, reflection, introspection and, above all, respect. In multi-faith empires and countries in which atheism was becoming more common, the gesture could conveniently replace a prayer.

Veterans would often take a leading role in Armistice Day commemoration, which was deemed a civic duty for many. It was an occasion not just to remember the dead, but to call attention to the plight of those who came home and were suffering the effects of their war service. In France, veterans' organisations began selling *bleuets* (cornflowers) to raise money for returned soldiers and their families. A similar practice was begun throughout the British Empire using poppies, which became an iconic representation of the war in the British world, following Canadian John McCrae's 'In Flanders

Fields' poem, first published in 1915. The notion of sacrifice also became central to Armistice Day, as those who survived tried to cope with and give meaning to the deaths of their loved ones. The language of memory honoured the deceased, acknowledging that they had not sacrificed themselves in vain but for institutions and values such as God, King and Country, and freedom. However, as time passed, this language came to be increasingly contested.

In the inter-war years, Armistice Day became a focus for protesting against war and campaigning for peace. Some mourners and veterans refused to attend official commemorations. In doing so, they showcased their anger at the state-sanctioned carnage that the First World War had been, and voiced their disgust of war and the loss that it caused. During the 1920s and 1930s in France and Belgium, large pacifist movements used Armistice Day to stress the futility of war and the dangers of nationalism. French historian Antoine Prost has analysed the virulent 'patriotic pacifism' displayed by French veterans who resented the lack of civilian understanding of what they had endured during the war. Those veterans declared 'war to the war' and nourished little hatred against the German soldiers they fought.[4] Their revulsion was towards militarism, imperialism and the propaganda that had sent them to war. To counter those doctrines, they championed peace and the common interests of everyday people who should no longer be fooled by those in power. As historian Marilyn Lake has shown, Australia was not exempt from such movements.[5] On 11 November 1929, protesters marched in Adelaide and adopted 'a resolution [...] against war expressing the hope that the peace would be a lasting one'.[6]

What's in a name?

During the inter-war years in Britain, Australia and other parts of the British Empire, Armistice Day became increasingly referred to as Remembrance Day. This shift reflected a change in the nature of the commemoration. The act of marking the Armistice itself – the cessation of combat, the 'end' of the war – became less of a priority, as increased emphasis was placed on remembering and grieving the dead. By the mid-1920s, both 'Armistice Day' and 'Remembrance Day' were commonly used in Australia, and by the 1930s, the latter term was dominant.

It was the end of the Second World War that compelled an official change in nomenclature within the (soon to be defunct) British Empire. As a result of the war, there were hundreds of thousands more dead and a host of new anniversaries to commemorate. The scope of the war meant that these occasions varied substantially across the empire. To avoid a proliferation of commemorative days, preserve the unity of imperial commemorations, and ensure that the day would remain relevant to newer generations, London suggested that a common commemoration be inaugurated on the closest Sunday to 11 November, or on 11 November if that day happened to be a Sunday. This commemoration would henceforth be known as 'Remembrance Sunday'. By compressing commemorations into one non-work day, the new policy cleverly limited a rush of claims for new public holidays. The Chifley government approved London's suggestion in March 1946.[7] For many years, the British monarch determined the day on which Remembrance Sunday should fall, though nowadays in the United Kingdom it is always held on the second Sunday of November.[8]

The restoration of Remembrance Day

From 1946 until the 1970s, Australians joined with Britons in observing Remembrance Sunday. The occasion conveniently encapsulated the commemoration of different conflicts and enabled the memory of the Great War's Armistice to endure, despite the passing of its

Remembrance Day: The poor cousin of Australian war commemoration

veterans and their families. But things started to change and, progressively, some returned to honouring 11 November in a special Remembrance Day service. In the 1980s and the 1990s in particular, with the resurgence of Anzac and the 'memory boom', Australia witnessed the multiplication of official commemorative days, some of which had been recognised by particular groups before being made national commemorative days, such as VP Day, Korean War Day, Long Tan Day, Battle for Australia Day and Reserve Forces Day. Each group wished to mark the importance and specificity of its service, something Remembrance Sunday sought to standardise. Perhaps this idea was doomed from its inception: different wars had different significations – how could they be remembered under one banner? Commemorating the idea of service was not a commemoration of the values or circumstances under which each different generation had fought. Therefore, as each group of veterans pushed for their own special day, Remembrance Sunday lost traction. The new commemorative days gained both official and community support, contributing to the rejuvenation of Remembrance Day as the one day to mark the end of the First World War in Australia and remember those who died in the conflict. In addition, from the late 1980s the government did not want fewer commemorative days (the principle underpinning Remembrance Sunday), but more and more commemorative events to celebrate Australia's military past and fuel the Anzac revival.

With newer generations of veterans replacing those of the First World War, one could have thought that the 11 November commemoration in Australia, regardless of its name, would become extinguished. Once First World War veterans had all gone, who would come to mark their special day? However, since the 1990s the prime place that the First World War has occupied in Australia's redesigned national narrative – the Anzac legend – has given a new boost to Remembrance Day. While Remembrance Sunday faded from the Australian commemorative calendar, Remembrance Day continued its revival, riding on the coat-tails of a resurgent Anzac Day and the nation's rapacious appetite for war commemoration. For instance, one of Australia's most significant Remembrance Days (its 75th anniversary) happened in 1993 when Australia's Unknown Soldier was exhumed from Adelaide Cemetery in Villers-Bretonneux and reinterred with a national ceremony at the Australian War Memorial (AWM) in Canberra. Two years earlier, staff at the AWM had been encouraged to devise projects to celebrate the 50th anniversary of the opening of the memorial. The reburial of an unknown Australian soldier in Canberra was proposed to fill the void of the AWM's Hall of Memory, a commemorative space imagined by the founders of the AWM, which had remained until then rather empty of rituals. The national ceremony, held on Remembrance Day 1993, was well attended and well publicised, and contributed to its return to favour. The resurgence of Remembrance Day was formalised on 30 October 1997, when the Governor-General, under the Howard government, proclaimed that '(a) 11 November in each year shall be known and observed as Remembrance Day; and (b) all Australians are urged to observe, unless impracticable, one minute's silence at 11:00 on Remembrance Day each year'.

Remembrance Day now

The 11th of November is observed in many countries (mostly on the 'winning' side of the war) under various names: Armistice Day, Remembrance Day, Poppy Day, 11 Novembre, National Independence Day and Veterans Day, for instance. For some, the day is a public holiday. Notably, every state celebrating Remembrance Day grants different meanings to its commemoration. During official ceremonies in France, speeches deplore the loss of lives and insist on the value of peace. In Poland, however, the day marks the rebirth of the nation and a time to celebrate as Remembrance Day is also Poland's National Independence Day. In the United States, the commemoration recognises the veterans of all wars.

Australians have a clear preference for Anzac Day over Remembrance Day – the former offers a more patriotic service and a public holiday. Since the 2000s, crowds at official Remembrance Day state services in Australia have rarely exceeded a few hundred, whereas those at Anzac Day services are counted by the thousands and, more recently, the tens of thousands. Historian Ken Inglis has noted that 'quieter uses of war memorials large and small are made in commemoration of 11 November'.[9] While attendance is far greater at Anzac Day services, both days see only a marginal fraction of the Australian population turn out. Anzac centenary services in 2015 drew record crowds to war memorials, helped by unprecedented government funding. Attendance at Remembrance Day services increased in comparison to the 1990s and 2000s, but remained low when measured against 25 April.

In Australia, there was much more excitement surrounding the beginning of the Anzac centenary than its conclusion. Large and costly commemorative events were organised in 2014 and 2015, in particular.[10] The centrepiece was 25 April 2015. Ten thousand members of the public, most of whom had been selected by ballot, gathered at Gallipoli with Prime Minister Tony Abbott and dozens of other dignitaries for the dawn service. There were significant commemorative occasions in the remaining years, including the opening of the $100 million Sir John Monash Centre on Anzac Day in 2018, but public enthusiasm climaxed in April 2015.

Despite the fact that Remembrance Day in 2018 marked the end of the centenary period, it attracted little public attention. In Adelaide, Veterans SA oversaw Remembrance Day commemorations in South Australia and wished to mark its hundredth anniversary with a little more fanfare than usual. Four Tiger Moth aircraft flew over the state's war memorial in formation. After the observation of a minute's silence, a Cessna dropped thousands of poppies over the ceremony. These poppies had been coloured by local school children to honour those South Australians who died in the war. Officials and security made for a third of the attendees, who numbered a few hundred in total. The story was similar in Canberra, where Remembrance Day in 2018 attracted 12 000 attendees, a tenth of the record crowd of 120 000 people who attended the Australian War Memorial's dawn service on 25 April 2015.[11]

Remembrance Day versus Anzac Day

It was commonly believed in the late 19th century that nations were only truly made during war. According to this martial nationalist ideology, the peaceful federation of six British colonies to create the Commonwealth of Australia on 1 January 1901 was not entirely legitimate. Thus, Australia's first significant involvement in a global conflict, the landing at Anzac Cove on 25 April 1915, was ripe to be heralded as a rite of great significance; the 'birth of the nation', the 'martial baptism'.[12] Anzac Day was celebrated from 1916 with troop parades, patriotic rallies, sporting events, recruitment campaigns and extravagant displays of national pride. In contrast to other Allied nations, Australia (and New Zealand) had created a commemorative tradition well before the end of the war. By 1927, Anzac Day was legislated as a public holiday in every state, and by the 1930s it had acquired its now-familiar features of the dawn service, march and memorial service. Remembrance Day never became a public holiday in Australia.

From the outset, Anzac Day and Remembrance Day had quite distinctive associations. Remembrance Day was primarily about acknowledging grief and facilitating mourning. These functions explain why it had most salience in the decades immediately following the war, when the despair of parents, siblings, spouses and children was most acute. Anzac Day, on the other hand, was a brighter occasion. While there was much solemnity at the dawn vigil and formal morning service, Anzac Day was also an occasion to celebrate the martial achievement of the First AIF and the awakening of a distinctively Australian national consciousness. Unlike most combatant nations, such as Belgium, Germany, France, Austria, the United States, Britain and Serbia, the First World War had given white Australia the story of national genesis which, according to the martial nationalism it hung on to, the country so conspicuously lacked. The shame of Australia's convict heritage and its violent dispossession of Indigenous peoples were swept aside by the able showing of its fighting men. In Australia, the war was not without meaning because it had made – allegedly – the Australian nation. The rituals of Anzac Day were a powerful expression of this purpose and a consolidation of the 'birth of the nation' narrative. By contrast, among the nations of Europe and other parts of the world, the most important day of the war was the day on which it ended (for most): Armistice Day. It is no coincidence that Australia produced few of the bleak modernist representations of the war that appeared in Europe during the 1920s and 1930s and were described by historian Paul Fussell in *The Great War and Modern Memory* (1975). If the European war was tragic and futile, the Australian war was marketed as an epic.

The difference between 25 April and 11 November was described by historian Ken Inglis, who recalled his childhood experience in Melbourne during the 1930s: 'on Armistice Day classes were suspended between morning playtime and lunch while we stood in line, heard addresses like those of Anzac Eve but dwelling more on death than birth and on the world rather than the nation'.[13] Inglis further explained:

> briefer and simpler rituals were performed on 11 November
> ... Where people in most countries had chosen for their
> principal wartime anniversary the day the killing stopped and
> the soldiers began to pack their kitbags for home, Australians
> and New Zealanders looked back at the beginning, the
> separation of soldier from civilian, the national baptism
> of fire.[14]

Thus, the meanings associated with Anzac Day in Australia also explain why Remembrance Day was of secondary importance in the nation's commemorative agenda.

Conclusion

The history of Armistice/Remembrance Day in Australia is fundamentally linked to that of Anzac Day. The British historian Adrian Gregory concluded his history of Armistice Day in Britain by observing that: 'At the centre of Armistice Day was a silence'.[15] In contrast, there is clamour at the centre of Anzac Day. Both Armistice Day and Remembrance Day sought to find meaning in the First World War. Most European countries initially conceived Remembrance Day as an occasion to honour the redemptory sacrifice of those who had died in the 'war to end all wars'. In the decades following the Second World War, Remembrance Sunday became a day to remember those who had perished in all conflicts. In Australia, Anzac Day has addressed the question of the meaning of the war far better than Remembrance Day or Remembrance Sunday. It can acknowledge loss and suffering with a nod to the sacred, while simultaneously representing imagined distinct national values such as mateship, laconic humour and stoicism. This capacity to connect the national community to the numinous explains Anzac Day's primacy over Remembrance Day.

Though the 'shelf life' of Remembrance Day was extended in Australia in the 1990s as the government sought to valorise the First World War generation for political purposes, Remembrance Day services across the nation still attracted relatively small crowds when compared to concerts, shows or sporting events.[16] Remembrance Day drew larger crowds over the Anzac centenary period, but its salience appears highly dependent upon state sponsorship. It has little of the grass-roots, emotional appeal of Anzac Day. In 2004, an article in the *Victorian Historical Journal* lamented that 'Remembrance Day remains virtually a *tabula rasa* for Australian historians'.[17] Fifteen years later, little has changed. Remembrance Day remains the poor cousin of Australian war commemoration and historiography.

18

WHAT IS WRONG WITH ANZAC?

Henry Reynolds

I had just finished speaking to a small but engaged audience about what I had called the militarisation of Australian history. An earnest young man came up to speak to me. I thought he was in his early twenties. He asked if there were any other ways of interpreting Australian history and, if not, why not? It was a good question and one that caused me to reflect that he represented a generation that had experienced the full force of the heavily funded government propaganda that insisted the war was Australia's defining experience. The ubiquitous shorthand was that the nation was founded in April 1915 on the shores of the Ottoman Empire. This is a view that is now deeply embedded in the national psyche.

In the short time I had with the inquisitive young man I explained that, while Anzac Day had been commemorated throughout my childhood, when I was his age the prevailing interpretation of Australian history was quite different. To refresh my memory I later went back to look at the historiography of the 1950s and 1960s when there was both a great expansion of the teaching of Australian history and many new general histories written by the leaders of the profession.[1] In retrospect the striking feature of these general histories was that most of them were reprinted many times ... Gordon Greenwood's *Australia: A Social and Political History* 13 times between 1955 and 1974, AGL Shaw's *The Story of Australia* nine times between 1955 and 1983, RM Crawford's *Australia* eight times between 1952 and 1963, Manning Clark's *A Short History of Australia* four times between 1963 and 1967.

While most, but not all, of these histories mentioned the Gallipoli campaign and the significance of Anzac Day, the authors' main focus was on social and political developments in Australia itself. This is particularly apparent when they deal with the years of the First World War. It was domestic developments that captured their attention whether it was economic innovation, industrial relations, political tumult or the great campaigns about conscription. It seems unlikely that among the students who studied these widely prescribed text books that many would have concluded the nation was born in April 1915 on the other side of the world.

So, what changed? And why? The short answer is that history was swept up into the culture wars that have characterised the generation since the final years of the 20th century. The change of government in 1996 was a watershed moment principally because the incoming Prime Minister, John Howard, took a personal interest in history and was engaged in a crusade against what he called the black armband version of our past. He had come to believe that the historiographical revolution that had thrust Indigenous history to the front of the public stage had distorted the national story. In doing so it had undermined the positive sagas about national development and failed to inspire the nation's children with pride in their country. In a direct way it had seriously compromised the most enduring themes of the popular history that had focused on exploration, pioneering and the heroic struggle with the land itself in regard to distance, drought, flood and fire. The rediscovery of frontier violence had changed all that. This was true whether it was the conservative version of the pioneering saga with its intrepid families who tamed the wilderness, or the radical story about the nomad tribe of bush workers bound together by mateship and outback unionism. Both squatters and workers had blood on their hands or were complicit with those who did, while the exploitation of Aboriginal women was almost universal.

The conservative counter-attack came from two directions. The most obvious manoeuvre was to cast doubt on the credibility of leading scholars in the contentious field of Indigenous history with a full-scale onslaught by Keith Windschuttle in his 2002 polemic *The Fabrication of Australian History*.[2] Much controversy followed, but in the long-run a new generation of scholarship pursued in many parts of the country confirmed the extent and brutality of frontier conflict. But the more enduring response to the troubling reality of life and death on the ragged fringes of settlement was to shift the focus to foreign wars. As Marilyn Lake observed in 2005, John Howard used his power to outflank his enemies in the history wars by choosing to fight his battles on his own terms. 'Foreign battlefields', she declared, 'have displaced frontier wars as sites of memory'. Who cares, she continued, whether Aboriginal people were dispossessed by British settlement or that colonial history was marred by massacres? Real Australian history begins with Gallipoli.[3]

The militarisation of our history has been remarkably enduring. It has been by far the most successful campaign in the culture wars in part because it has not been seen for what it actually was: a counter-revolution in Australian historiography. Many things have produced this result. The drive from government and the lavish expenditure channelled through the Australian War Memorial and the Department of Veterans' Affairs have been decisive. We have never before seen so much money expended over such a long period to promote an official version of history. The sanctimony surrounding the war dead deters critical assessment. So too does quotidian patriotism. Then there is the drama and even the dark glamour associated with war across the ages. The slow and quiet achievements of civil society are easily overshadowed. But that still leaves us with a political conundrum. Why has a project initiated by a conservative Prime Minister received overwhelming bipartisan support? Has any political figure come out in opposition to the blatant militarisation of our history? Has anyone objected to the expenditure of millions of dollars that have fuelled the project? How has the truly improbable claim that the nation was created on the shores of Gallipoli been sustained against a galaxy of cogent counter-arguments? How has it been shielded from widely ramified scepticism relating to the Gallipoli campaign itself, to the nature of Australian society before 1914 and to the consequences of the war for the nation during the 1920s and 1930s?

Australians are so familiar with the story of Anzac Day that they miss what is glaringly obvious to outsiders. While it is quite appropriate as a general day of mourning for lives lost in war, it is an extraordinary occasion to commemorate our national sovereignty, even the birth of the nation itself. It is doubtful if any other nation state has a commemorative day anything like it. The Australian troops were fighting far from home in places they knew very little about, as part of an imperial venture, where the true purpose was unknown to them. Australian children are taught the young men who died during the campaign were fighting for our freedom, when the greatest beneficiary of the assault on the Ottoman Empire would have been Czarist Russia, which would have achieved a centuries-old aspiration to gain control of Constantinople and access to the Mediterranean Sea. And while Australian rhetoric is all about sacrifice, little is mentioned about killing and the shattered families the Anzac's fighting spirit left behind. And the enemy dead were men who could never have been a threat to the distant homeland. In the circumstances, the Australian emphasis has been about how the men fought, not why they fought and whether their efforts were of any demonstrable benefit to the nation itself. And many of the characteristics lauded in nationalistic rhetoric – mateship, courage, resourcefulness – were on display in many contemporary armies and were clearly not distinctively Australian.

The rhetoric replayed again and again on Anzac Day points to further claims about the benefits that flowed from Australia's deep involvement in the First World War. Few of them could withstand scrutiny. It is argued that the exploits of the First AIF in the Middle East and the Western Front stimulated Australian national pride. But if the war did anything it tied the country even more firmly to the empire. So much blood had been shed in the cause that loyalty to king and empire were stronger after the war than it had been prior to 1914. When in the 1920s Canada, Ireland and South Africa agitated to achieve a form of independence within the Commonwealth, Australia fell far behind. Doubt about the empire was denounced as disloyalty.

A second spurious claim about the consequences of the war is that it united the country. Nothing could be further from the truth. In 1919 Australia was far more deeply divided than it had been in 1914. Class divisions were exacerbated by rising costs of living and sharp industrial conflict. The campaigns about conscription had split families, friendships and communities. The alienation of many Catholics of Irish descent triggered by the Easter Rising in Dublin in 1916 grew worse during the conscription campaigns, to be personified in the personal antagonism between Prime Minister Hughes and Archbishop Mannix. Regional assertiveness also troubled the post-war nation. This was intense in Western Australia, which voted in a referendum in 1933 to secede from the Commonwealth. Two-thirds of the voters and every electorate but one voted in favour of secession and a return to the status of a crown colony. The war-induced trauma was probably more pervasive than this. In a powerful essay written in 2014, Marilyn Lake argued that during the war Australia suffered severe social and political damage. By the end of the war 'the Labor Party had split, conservative forces had triumphed, and the British Empire had gained a new lease of life in Australia. In World War 1 Australia lost its way. Its enmeshment in the imperial European war fractured the nation's soul'.[4]

Post-war Australia, then, provides little support to the centrepiece of militaristic rhetoric – the insistence that the Anzac campaign founded the nation. Pre-war Australia delivers much the same message. What did the Australian nation lack in 1913 or 1914 that was supplied by the young men who stormed ashore at Anzac Cove in April 1915? How could a few weeks of fighting be commensurable with the achievements of thousands of men and women across generations and over the vast distances of the continental homeland? How could brief moments of intense fighting be measured favourably against the slow accretion of nation-building in civil society?

The reality was that pre-war Australia was a remarkably successful society. Along with New Zealand it stands out in any international comparison. They were two of the wealthiest countries with a more equal distribution of wealth than in any comparable nation. They had pioneered significant advances in the welfare state. They were arguably the most democratic societies in the world. They had high literacy rates and were reaping the benefits of earlier introduction of free, compulsory education. They had high levels of union membership and had seen the rapid rise to power at state and federal levels of union-based labour parties. Their parliaments and bureaucracies worked well and the level of corruption was low by world standards. The same question forces its way forward once more. Whatever did Australia lack in the early months of 1914 that was supplied by warriors fighting half a world away? How was Australia a better or more complete nation at the end of April 1915 than it had been in the same month a year before?

The yawning gap between legend and reality can be narrowed by a consideration of beliefs that were current in the early years of the war. There was a widespread belief in Australia, as in other

Western countries, that nations were either born in, or reached full maturity in, war. Congenial metaphors cluttered contemporary speeches. There were references to baptisms of fire, to mettle being tested, to nations experiencing the ultimate test of manhood, to their bloody rite of passage. It was all part of the romanticism of war passed on to the early 20th century from the era of braid, epaulettes and flashing sabres. It scarcely survived the terrible reality of trench warfare typified by high explosives and gas attacks. It was maintained in Fascist Italy and Nazi Germany until they experienced crushing defeat.

It is then easy to explain why many Australians believed in April 1915 that the nation was either born or achieved full maturity on the battlefield. But how can we continue to assimilate, along with the rhetoric of the time, ideas both anachronistic and profoundly irresponsible? War is no longer accepted as an untrammelled right of the nation state. And while such views prevailed among the small number of European powers and their vast empires in the second decade of the 20th century, the world has now changed beyond recognition. When it parades its Anzac Day rhetoric about the battlefield birth, does Australia intimate to the almost 200 nation states that they need a good war to achieve national maturity? Are we suggesting that nations that have avoided major wars are somehow unformed or immature?

The renewal of the Anzac legend and the much more general militarisation of our history has distorted the story relayed to children of this generation. It valorises war ahead of peace, the military over the civic and action over reflection. It also cheapens Australia's distinctive political and social developments. The need to rebalance our public history is now clear. We could profitably return to that generation of historians who were writing and teaching in the 1950s and 1960s and recognised the importance of overseas wars, but did not let them eclipse what had been achieved in civil society in Australia itself. They paid as much attention to the great political battles over conscription as they did to the Anzac landing and the Western Front. In retrospect that seems entirely appropriate.

Australian society openly and publicly debated, as no other country did, profound questions about war and peace and the proper boundaries of state power. And the ultimate decision was put to one of the most democratic electorates in the world. It was inimitably Australian and a far more distinctive development than all of the countries' exploits on the battlefields of the old world.

19

HONEST HISTORY: LESSONS IN THE POLITICS OF HISTORY

David Stephens

There is a politics of history as well as a history of politics. The discipline of history involves collecting and arranging evidence to support an interpretation. The next step is publicly arguing for the interpretation, and that takes the historian into the realm of politics. A historian need not take this step, of course. That leaves the field to bolder historians. And to mythologists, who are concerned less with evidence than with fairy tales.

I was the secretary of the Honest History association between 2013 and 2019. I continue to edit and contribute to the Honest History website (honesthistory.net.au), and co-edited with Alison Broinowski *The Honest History Book* (2017). We in the Honest History enterprise have argued – as a coalition and a website – for the interpretation that Australia is more than Anzac, and always has been. In other words, there is a lot more to Australian history than tales of men in khaki travelling overseas to fight – and sometimes die – bravely, serving allegedly noble causes. Secondly, while war is important in Australian history, this is not so much because of what Australians have done in war but because of what war has done to Australia and Australians.

We targeted 'Anzackery', defined in the *Australian National* and *Australian Concise Oxford* dictionaries as 'the promotion of the Anzac legend in ways that are perceived to be excessive or misguided'. Anzackery is loud, nationalistic and jingoistic, and is frequently taken up by people wanting to make a political point or a commercial killing. We argued instead for a version of Anzac which is quieter, more private, free of euphemisms (not 'made the supreme sacrifice' and 'the fallen' but 'killed' and 'the dead'), which considers what happens after our wars as well as during them and how those wars affected people other than white Australians. Our Anzac has been considerate rather than celebratory, universal rather than parochial; it has tried to steer away from khaki-tinged maudlin nostalgia and towards a peaceful future.

Starting Honest History

Honest History had its origins in a campaign that supported the traditional role of the Australian War Memorial. Around 2004, some Canberra citizens (the Memorials Development Committee or MDC) began calling for the erection in the national capital of memorials to commemorate the dead of the First World War and the Second World War. The MDC argued that the Australian War Memorial was for the dead of *all* our wars, and that Canberra lacked memorials explicitly for the two major wars.[1] To oppose the MDC, the Lake War Memorials Forum (the Forum) was established in 2010. We argued that the existing War Memorial performed the commemorative task more than adequately, and that the proposed new structures would detract from the Memorial and spoil the vision of Canberra imagined by Walter Burley and Marion Mahony Griffin. The Forum included everyone from peace activists, landscape architects and historians to veterans' advocates and retired senior military officers. It attracted hundreds of supporters in Canberra and beyond.

By 2012, it was clear that the rival war memorials would not be built. This was due to both the MDC's inability to raise funds (from donors that included arms manufacturers) and the effectiveness of the Forum's lobbying campaign, which gained support from the National Capital Authority (responsible for planning) and, eventually, the Council of the War Memorial. Some Forum activists then turned their attention to the centenary of the First World War. By mid-2013, there existed a loose coalition of historians and others determined to contest the official approach to the centenary, an approach that saw the occasion as a commemorative extravaganza not requiring intellectual analysis. An Honest History incorporated association was established for administrative purposes, and the Honest History website was launched in November 2013. Some weeks later, we had our first brush with official Anzackery – the extreme, jingoistic version of the Anzac legend – when retired Brigadier Andrew Nikolic, a federal politician at that time, accused the ABC of lacking 'situational awareness' for showing on the eve of the Anzac centenary a news item about our website launch, including remarks by Professor Peter Stanley on the need to exercise critical judgment about Anzac.[2] Many more such skirmishes were to follow.

A concept, a coalition, and getting the message across

The historian EH Carr said 'history means interpretation'.[3] Honest history as a concept is interpretation robustly supported by evidence. We in Honest History sought *balanced* history, making evidence-based interpretations available to students, teachers, universities, journalists and the public, and trying to ensure that history was not distorted to serve political or other agendas. We respected differences of interpretation but tried to call out any history that was tendentious, unjustified, exaggerated, distorted, partial or unbalanced. And we tried to bust myths.

Since 2013, there have been more than 3000 posts to the Honest

History website, almost 22000 Tweets, and nearly 60 newsletters going to around a thousand addresses. *The Honest History Book* (NewSouth, 2017) has sold well over 2000 copies. We have gathered more than 2300 Twitter followers and over 1200 Facebook likes. Visits to our website have steadily increased. Some of our key themes (Anzackery, Australia's prodigious spending on the Anzac centenary, and the Australian War Memorial's links with arms manufacturers) have been picked up by the mainstream media. We have made many presentations to school and community groups and our *Alternative Guide to the Australian War Memorial* has been downloaded more than 2500 times by students and teachers. In this chapter, I distill some of the lessons we have learned from the Honest History project.

Marshalling forces

Author Don Watson has noted a characteristic of people who work in corporate or government communications, people sometimes called 'spinners' or 'spinmasters'. Spinners 'begin to believe [their] own bullshit', said Watson. 'Spin is the stuff that myths are made of.'[4] Anzackery is an example of what Watson skewered: it deals in myth and spin, and the spinners believe it – or give the impression that they do. One of our tasks has been to oppose the Anzackery-spinners, to push back against the wave of bullshit. This has not always been pleasant, but it has been necessary. Bullshit unresisted expands to fill the space available; unless spin is unravelled it just goes on spinning. There has been a lot of spin during the Anzac centenary and not enough of it has been resisted.

Pushing back needs to be coordinated, however; messages from one source need to be reinforced by similar messages from other sources and in other media. As secretary of the Honest History coalition and editor of its website, I lost count of the number of times

I found out by accident (sometimes too late) about a published article or public event that reinforced the message that we had been pushing and that we could have promoted. Far too often among the critics of Anzackery the left hand did not know what the right hand was doing. The majority of historians (with honourable exceptions, like some of the contributors to this book) are not only poor publicists of their own work but often shrink from public debate in fields where their views would carry weight. Meanwhile, the well-funded – by government and book publishers – Anzackery-spinners just go on spinning, and local history societies, press clubs, RSL branches and shock jocks are all too ready to provide platforms.

The reticence of critics of the Anzac-heavy image of Australia helps that image to endure. Of course, as the historian Peter Cochrane has said, history is 'a cautious and ever-questioning discipline' but some historians are cautious to a fault.[5] It should be possible to produce different sorts of history – on the one hand, peer-reviewed and studious work primarily for publication behind pay-walls or presentation to academic conferences and, on the other, crisp, hard-hitting and timely (but still evidence-based) contributions on matters of public interest. Historians need to talk to the world, not just to each other, to take to Twitter and Facebook, as well as to Taylor & Francis journals. This necessarily means engaging in politics, not the frothy, myth-based, shouty politics of the Anzackery-spinners, but politics based on evidence and research.

So, anti-Anzackery advocates need to be prepared to sign on for the long haul, to employ a range of weapons, and keep them honed and primed. We have been well aware of the strength of ridicule as a weapon – and some Anzackery is ridiculous – but we have been careful to gather evidence as well – and to present it forcefully. Criticism needs to be sustained, soundly based and public; catty asides on television talk shows or coded remarks to the converted may prick balloons and bring laughs, but more is needed.

(Commentator Catherine McGregor on ABC TV's *The Drum* described the War Memorial's Director, Brendan Nelson, as 'bouncing around like a sort of an electrocuted imp asking for money for commemoration of wars he never found the time to go to'.[6])

Nor should historians suspend their critical faculties in the presence of sentimental words. We are all entitled to shed a tear over 'Auld Lang Syne' or 'Away in a Manger', as memories of past New Years and Christmases flood in. But for historians to give a 'leave pass' to the 'Those heroes that shed their blood ...' – words allegedly coined by Turkish statesman Mustafa Kemal Atatürk – because they are beautiful words encapsulating worthy sentiments, even though their provenance is doubtful in the extreme – is a denial of the historian's calling. We have piled up evidence of the highly political origin of those words.[7] To mix metaphors, historians should be active in spearing such sacred cows.

Keeping up to date

To be effective, contestants in the politics of history need to be very aware of what is being said and done by other players. In the case of Honest History, this meant keeping up to date with the tactics of the Anzackery-spinners. During the years 2013 to 2018, most critics of Anzackery became reasonably well versed in the total Australian cost of the centenary of Anzac (around $600 million, counting Commonwealth, state and territory, and corporate money).[8] We in Honest History assiduously kept track of and publicised the tally. Indeed, the costs became so well known that Australian government spokespeople tried to diminish them by making spurious comparisons with total veterans' affairs expenditure (most of which is committed by legislation) or total defence expenditure.[9]

To take another example, however, critics of the failure of the Australian War Memorial to properly acknowledge the frontier wars and massacres (the conflicts between Indigenous and non-Indigenous Australians between 1788 and at least 1928) have too often not taken account of the ways in which the Memorial, albeit in a clumsy and ambivalent fashion, has acknowledged the role of Aboriginal warriors, provided they wore the queen's or king's uniform. The Memorial, particularly in its *For Country, for Nation* exhibition and purchases of Indigenous art depicting massacres, has developed a theme of Indigenous warriors magnanimously fighting for Australia since 1901 – 'they denied their Aboriginality', according to Memorial Director Brendan Nelson – despite the wrongs done to their ancestors.[10] Essentially, the Memorial has tried to divert attention from the frontier wars by reframing the issue in terms of what great and goodhearted fighters Indigenous people have been – in uniform. While many Indigenous people have appreciated the acknowledgment that their soldier forebears have belatedly received, this tactic of conceding an inch to save a mile is unlikely to quell the need to address frontier conflict in the nation's premier war museum.

The lesson is that there are always new ways of analysing the stance of other players in the politics of history. Dean Ashenden, an academic and author, has suggested that the War Memorial's blind spot about the frontier wars and massacres is a symptom of a national silence about these events.[11] Noting the willingness of Director Nelson to acknowledge the events (while saying they should be commemorated somewhere other than the Memorial), I had attributed to bureaucratic politics the failure to go further than that, specifically the unwillingness of successive senior military officers on the Memorial's Council to recognise and commemorate 'the queen's enemies', which is what Indigenous warriors were in colonial times. Ashenden's explanation is also very plausible: the Memorial is a microcosm of national denial. The prospect of the Memorial recognising the frontier wars certainly upset a Tweeter from the Military History Society of New South Wales, who wrote in early 2019 that recognition 'would be a terrible mistake, would transform the @AWMemorial from a site of remembrance and gratitude to one of shame and recrimination'.[12] Perhaps that prospect is what has upset the senior officers on the Council, too.

Understanding context

The best way of attacking Anzackery is by emphasising other parts of Australian history, the 'non-khaki' parts. As Eualeyai-Kamillaroi historian Larissa Behrendt said in her chapter of *The Honest History Book*, we need to 'acknowledge that there is no one dominant national narrative but many concurrent, competing and conflicting stories that reflect the diverse backgrounds and perspectives within Australian society'.[13] Our Honest History project has encouraged Australians to deal with the 'non-khaki' parts of our history, from bushfires to the Great Depression, great and powerful friends to multiculturalism. In particular, that means confronting what Behrendt calls 'the invasion moment', for 'until we do that we will never have found a way to truly share this colonised country'. The invasion of 1788 and its consequences deserve far more of our attention today than does the failed invasion of the Ottoman Empire in 1915 and our military ventures since. As we give 1788 its due significance, we can begin to rectify the anomaly that leads Australians to remember Anzac sacrifice from a century ago, while eschewing remembrance of frontier wars and massacres.

Context has another aspect, too. Anzackery is bipartisan and the struggle against it goes on, regardless of which government is in power. Ever since Andrew Fisher, as leader of the opposition during the 1914 election campaign, rushed to gazump Prime Minister Joseph Cook in promising 'the last man and the last shilling', Labor has waxed and waned in its attitude to Anzac.[14] In a waxing phase, we had Bill Shorten, opposition leader at the time, complaining about reduced commemoration activity, undertaking to make John Monash a field marshal, and pledging Labor's support for a proposed $500 million extension of the War Memorial.[15] State Labor governments are just as assiduous as non-Labor ones in offering Anzac-themed programs to schoolchildren.[16] Standing against the khaki tide can be a courageous decision for members of the political class. Patient and continuous persuasion of parties by advocates and voters – to provide evidence that the public is not as rusted on to Anzackery as politicians believe – will be needed if political attitudes are to change. Even then, there may be the unedifying spectacle of politicians making fine calculations between courage and their fear of being wedged by their opponents.

That perceived need to make such calculations arises partly from awareness of the political milieu. Revolutions, it has often been said, occur as expectations rise, yet expectations met may breed conservatism. Recent Australian history, particularly an uninterrupted 27 years of economic growth, may have bred complacency, even smugness, in areas of life that are not explicitly material. Having our economic expectations continuously met may have made us – or at least those of us who have benefited from prosperity – not just inclined to protect our material wealth but also less prepared to ask questions about non-material matters. Prosperity may make it easier for received myths, like those attached to Anzac, to maintain their grip. While there are, of course, other reasons why Anzac has taken on a 'sacred' status for many Australians, the link to prosperity is still worth exploring further. One test would be whether reduced economic prosperity in future makes Australians more inclined to question received cultural myths like Anzac.

On the other hand, as social researcher and commentator Hugh Mackay has recognised, recently we Australians seem to have become more anxious and depressed, as we confront terrorism, climate change and economic disruption.[17] Perhaps Anzac offers comfort as other certainties crumble. As Carolyn Holbrook notes in the following chapter, historian Ken Inglis famously referred to Anzac as a 'secular religion' or a 'civic religion'. Some of us love the Anzac rituals (Last Post ceremonies, the Dawn Service) and yearn for liturgy (well-known hymns, comforting words about poppies or deathless soldiers, and always 'Lest We Forget'). Others are agnostic or atheist about Anzac. It is not compulsory to worship at Anzac altars, although it is democratic and polite to respect people who do.

Anzackery – the extreme version of Anzac – is about myth masquerading as history. Some myths are harmless; most of us grow out of them (Santa Claus, the Easter Bunny). Communities like to have origin myths and they find them comforting, which provides fertile ground for official and other 'top-down' spinners. Other myths, however, can be harmful, particularly when they are reinforced by repetition and false attributions of significance. The people most conned by the 'Atatürk words' referred to earlier are the children who are trotted out on every Anzac Day to recite them. A former Minister for the Centenary of Anzac, Senator Michael Ronaldson, regularly reminded us that children had to understand that their freedom had been won in blood – with a clear implication that future children should prepare to shed blood also.[18] War Memorial Director Nelson has been at his most unctuous when he insists in his speeches that soldiers a century ago died 'for us'.[19] This glosses over the important question of whether soldiers ever die *for* something, rather than *because of* something – an enemy shell, an exploding hand grenade, an aeroplane shot down, disease; these causes did for four relatives of mine in two wars. Claims about dying *for* something are often after-the-event constructions by governments and officials wanting to make grieving relatives feel better. And claims that people today derive a benefit from deaths a century ago – they died 'for us' – are a stretch at best and nonsense at worst.

The reckoning – and what next?

Despite the ubiquity and 'shoutiness' of Anzackery-spinning, it is still possible to detect latent uneasiness beneath the public response to the spin. Sometimes people who abhor Anzac excesses are wary of saying so, for fear of being thought disloyal or unpatriotic. Frank Bongiorno has noted that 'those who refuse to participate [in the Anzac legend] can readily be represented as beyond the pale. To question, to criticise – to doubt – can become un-Australian'.[20] Despite that pressure to conform, every time a controversy arises in the mainstream media about Anzac Day or commemoration there are plenty of voices critical of the received approach to Anzac and its slippages into Anzackery. There is scope to build on such feelings. 'Here's a prediction [said *Guardian Australia* columnist Paul Daley in 2016]: with the end of the centenary celebrations of the first world war in 2018 ... Anzac could assume a more low-key, contextual place in popular Australian consciousness'.[21] Let's hope so.

The German sociologist and politician Max Weber said that 'politics is the strong and slow boring of hard boards'.[22] The Honest History experience confirms this aphorism and adds that the bored holes are usually small. It is hellishly difficult to make an impression on a juggernaut like officially sanctioned Anzackery. It is easy for Anzackers to dismiss criticism as 'the usual stuff' from a few recalcitrants.[23] The quiet stirrings of unrest, the growing recognition of the non-khaki strands of our history, the distaste at Anzackery, all carry promise of improvement, but there will be hard going for a while yet. In the meantime, what difference, if any, has Honest History made in five years? Through our website, our book, social media, the *Alternative Guide* to the War Memorial, and presentations to school classes, we have given teachers, students and citizens a different perspective on their country's history. We take some credit for increased community awareness of the obscene expenditure on commemoration, of the links between the commemoration industry and arms manufacturers, of the complicity in Anzackery of media outlets and commercial interests, and the unwillingness of politicians to step out of the Anzac line. We know we have irritated some of the Anzackery-spinners and we are pleased about that. They deserve to be irritated; bullshit is still bullshit even when dressed up as something sacred.

Busting myths, pushing back against the tide of bullshit, and restoring balance in the study of Australian history is what Honest History has tried to do. On 8 November 2018, more than one hundred people attended the *Honest History 5 Years Symposium* at the Australian National University in Canberra. They heard Michael Brissenden of the ABC launch Paul Daley's book, *On Patriotism*, which carried the dedication 'For Honest History'. The symposium recognised that the planned lifespan of the Honest History association had been reached. The association has been wound up, but the website continues and people who browse it will see that Australians 'do' memory well; we just need to remember more of our past. Australia is more than Anzac, and always has been.

20

MAKING SENSE OF THE GREAT WAR CENTENARY

Carolyn Holbrook

Channel Nine's chief executive, David Gyngell, felt confident that the network's *Gallipoli* TV series, set to debut on 9 February, would be the 'television event' of 2015. Research panels had heaped praise on Christopher Lee's seven-part series, critics were admiring, and the lavish production, directed by Glendyn Ivin, had been heavily promoted over the summer months.

Yet, less than three weeks after its debut, Gyngell pronounced *Gallipoli* 'my biggest disappointment of the year … Research panels across the country said *Gallipoli* was going to be the biggest show on television and it hasn't been'.[1] Though the first episode had attracted a healthy 1.1 million viewers, the audience halved to 580 000 by the second week and was being soundly beaten by the reality cooking show, *My Kitchen Rules*. The show shed a further 58 000 viewers the following week and fell outside of the nation's top 20 programs.[2] The downward trajectory prompted Channel Nine to 'burn off' the remainder of the series, showing it in two-hour blocks.

Television commentators began to see a pattern in the fortunes of Anzac-themed television. The ABC's *Anzac Girls* series, which screened in September 2014, slumped in the ratings after a promising start. Stellar documentaries like *The War that Changed Us*, *Lest We Forget What?* and *Why Anzac* with Sam Neill were met with an indifference that seemed to belie popular interest in Anzac. Channel

Seven's Anzac contribution, *The Power of Ten*, was an expensive, two-part series hosted by Victoria Cross winner, Ben Roberts-Smith, which included a re-enactment of Gallipoli's Lone Pine battle – like those that had gone before, it failed to fulfil ratings expectations. Foxtel's series *Deadline Gallipoli*, which starred Sam Worthington as war correspondent Philip Schuler, presented an original and thoughtful perspective on the Gallipoli story. Again, Australian audiences were uninterested.

While there were murmurings about the curious failure of Anzac TV, it was Woolworths' public relations disaster that ignited public debate about the centenary commemoration. Commercial interests of the kind that put hot cross buns on supermarket shelves in late December, and cash in on the increasing commodification of Australia Day, must have rubbed their hands as the April 2015 bonanza approached. Woolworths was by no means alone in seeking to profit from the Anzac centenary, but it was uniquely inept. The grocery duopolist engaged a public relations firm called Carr-space, expert in 'experiential' marketing, to devise its Anzac strategy. The result was 'Fresh in Our Memories', a campaign that encouraged members of the public to upload pictures of 'those affected by war' to a picture generator. The generator inserted the Woolworths logo and the words 'Fresh in Our Memories' – a nod to the company's 'Fresh Food People' slogan.

The campaign was launched in the early afternoon of Tuesday 14 April. The public backlash was swift and vicious. Outrage spread like bushfire; 'IT'S ALL ABOUT PROFIT, PROFIT, PROFIT!' read one response; 'it is disgusting … There is nothing that this company won't do in the name of the almighty $$$ …Worst company ever and this is so disrespectful I will never shop at one of the Woolworth's business ever again', read another.[3] The picture generator was hijacked by memes that quickly went viral; everything from pictures of Tony Abbott and Kevin Rudd, to cute cats, piles of rotting corpses, Batman and Hitler appeared.[4] By early evening 'Fresh in Our Memories' had been canned.

Woolworths' excoriating experience must have sent shivers down the spines of executives who had long-eyed the Anzac centenary as a cash cow. Fearing that Australians were suffering from 'Anzac fatigue' and in an effort to avoid the backlash against Anzac opportunism, Channel Seven and Channel Nine cancelled plans to send breakfast television celebrities to Turkey for Anzac Day.[5] 'Brandzac Day' abuses continued to be called out on social media and in the mainstream media. Retailer Target was forced to withdraw merchandise that bore the word 'Anzac' because the company had not sought approval from the Department of Veterans' Affairs to use the highly regulated word.[6] Camp Gallipoli, an organisation run by a South Australian businessman called Chris Fox, which coordinated sleep-outs on Anzac eve around Australia, came under scrutiny for its many commercial linkages. When Fox was later found to have failed to donate Camp Gallipoli profits to Legacy and the RSL, the organisation's charity status was withdrawn.[7] An American website called Zazzle was required by the Department of Veterans' Affairs to remove its Anzac Pin Up Girl T-shirt from sale, and men's magazine *Zoo* withdrew its Anzac-themed edition, which featured on its cover the bikini-clad model Erin Pash holding a poppy between her teeth. Country singer Lee Kernaghan cancelled his plans for an Anzac Arena Spectacular, featuring Jack Thompson and Lisa McCune, citing poor ticket sales.

How was this retreat on the Anzac front by commercial interests to be interpreted? Media academic Jason Sternberg argued that the failure of Channel Nine's *Gallipoli* series showed that 'some people are fatigued by the story and that is compounded when they are presented with another TV show about roughly the same thing, Australia's national identity'.[8] ABC presenter James Valentine claimed that he was suffering from 'Gallipoli fatigue':

> Every media outlet, every gallery, every concert, every surf lifesaving club, every park, every council, every artist, every institution is marking this centenary. Individually, they probably all should. Collectively, it's smothering me and any actual emotion I might feel.[9]

Historian Clare Wright agreed that Australians were tired of the ubiquity of Anzac and wary of its commercialisation:

> we're seeing a sense of ennui, almost a kind of nausea in a way where everybody is just over it. I don't think it's that there is a sense that they want to show disrespect towards the soldiers or the memory of the Anzacs but the way that that is being exploited presently.[10]

In reviewing the highlights and lowlights of television programming in 2015, a Fairfax journalist considered the failure of Anzac-themed TV:

> Sociologists and historians will long debate why Australians did not embrace the 100th anniversary programming with which the networks honoured the Anzacs … Perhaps we were already in pacifist mode in April, perhaps we feared that accurate reconstructions would shatter our illusion that the Aussies died occupying the high moral ground, or perhaps we felt the networks were exploiting an event that should be marked more modestly.[11]

I don't believe that diagnoses such as 'Gallipoli fatigue' match the symptoms of the Anzac centenary. While Clare Wright's claim that people were eager for a 'more complex, a more nuanced version of the Anzac story' certainly applied to a section of the population in

2015, the bulk of Australians demonstrated by their actions that they were uninterested in extending or challenging their understanding of Australian involvement in the First World War.[12] But that lack of desire to engage intellectually with Anzac commemoration or seek new perspectives on historical events did not indicate a lack of attachment to the mythology itself. Far from it.

Those who thought that popular fatigue and disillusion would be reflected in reduced numbers at Anzac Day ceremonies in 2015 must have been surprised by the massive turn-outs. The Australian War Memorial dawn service attracted a crowd estimated at 120 000, an increase of 80 000 from the previous year. A further 31 000 attended the service and march later in the morning.[13] Wet weather did not deter a record 85 000 people from attending the dawn service at Melbourne's Shrine of Remembrance, while an extraordinary 80 000 people turned up to the dawn service at the Western Australian War Memorial in King's Park, nearly double the usual crowd.[14] There was similar enthusiasm around the country and in other parts of the world with Australian connections.

If commentators needed proof of the sacrosanct status of Anzac to many Australians, they needed to look no further than social media. On 25 April 2015, an SBS sports journalist called Scott McIntyre posted a series of tweets to his 30 000 followers, in which he referred to those who mark Anzac Day as 'poorly-read, largely white, nationalist drinkers and gamblers'. Among a number of other provocative statements was McIntyre's claim that he was 'Remembering the summary execution, widespread rape and theft committed by these "brave" Anzacs in Egypt, Palestine and Japan'. McIntyre was heavily criticised, including by then Communications Minister Malcolm Turnbull, who tweeted that McIntyre's 'despicable comments … deserved to be condemned'.[15] Such was the perceived gravity of McIntyre's offence, that his employment at SBS was terminated the following day (he later reached a settlement with SBS).

Even more controversial than the McIntyre tweets was the Facebook post by prominent young engineer and television presenter Yassmin Abdel-Magied on 25 April 2017. When Abdel-Magied wrote 'Lest we forget (Manus, Nauru, Syria, Palestine)' in reference to asylum seekers and victims of conflict, the fury of the social media mob descended upon her. In addition to the accusations of being 'disrespectful', 'disloyal', 'treasonous' and committing a 'vile slur' against the Anzacs, she was subjected to an extraordinary level of religious, racial and gender-based vitriol and abuse.[16] Abdel-Magied received death threats and calls for her deportation from media presenters and politicians. Prime Minister Turnbull and other senior federal ministers condemned her comments and Sydney tabloid newspaper the *Daily Telegraph* called the tweet: 'a sickening insult to the nation's war dead'.[17] Abdel-Magied was compelled to move house, change her phone number and close her social media accounts. She has since left Australia.

So how are we to weigh the evidence from the centenary commemoration? There was an unanticipated lack of interest in new perspectives on the Gallipoli story, no matter their artistic and historical merit, and a morally driven intolerance, however inconsistently applied, of the commercialisation of Anzac. We also witnessed immense enthusiasm for the rituals of Anzac Day and a level of indignation, fuelled by social media, towards those who besmirched Anzac. The rage of the social media mob – elevated when the critic was Muslim, Sudanese-Australian and female – recalled that of the religious zealot against the blasphemer. I believe that our curious behaviour during the centenary commemoration is best explained if we understand that Anzac functions as a kind of faith. The religious analogy was first mooted by historian Ken Inglis in the 1960s.[18] It remains the most apt formulation in the 21st century, because it accounts for our lack of intellectual curiosity about Anzac, our enthusiastic participation in its rituals, and our sensitivity to its exploitation and disparagement.

History shows that Anzac commemoration has always filled an emotional rather than an intellectual function in the Australian psyche. In its original manifestation up until the 1960s, Anzac commemoration was primarily an outlet for mourning and remembrance. While it contained an element of celebratory nationalism – Australians' pride in the martial achievements of their soldiers was all the greater because of the shame about their convict origins – it was anchored in the fact that 60 000 men died in the war and 150 000 were wounded from a population of less than five million.

Anzac commemoration endured a period of apathy and hostility that is discernible from the mid-1950s, because it ceased to fulfil this emotional role. The war generation was dying out and younger people found little to offer in the rituals of Anzac. Even as the nation was commemorating the 50th anniversary of the Gallipoli landing in 1965 with a grand ceremony at the Australian War Memorial attended by the Duke and Duchess of Gloucester, controversy was swirling around the Anzac legend. The churches were engaged in a nasty dispute with the RSL because Anzac Day fell on a Sunday, and the RSL insisted that the annual march would proceed, despite Christian sensitivities. Newspapers became a forum for debate about the contemporary relevance of the Anzac legend. Mr GJ Walsh, a member of the ACT Advisory Council, intervened with a perspective that sounds decidedly modern. He claimed that 'an attempt was being made to brainwash Australians into believing that Anzac Day had been the day in Australia's history that the nation was welded. It was a day to remember those who died', Walsh claimed, 'not the mightiest day in the calendar'.[19] Much of the criticism was directed towards the RSL, which many people feared was injecting Anzac Day with militarist values. Betty Archdale, principal of a Sydney girls' school, participated in a panel discussion for the *Sydney Morning Herald* about the future of Anzac Day. She worried whether we were 'really commemorating the people who paid the highest price or are we bolstering up a rather out-of-date false conception of war – glorifying war'? Another panellist, a university student called David Graupner, felt that Anzac represented values from another time:

> As Australia becomes a more sophisticated nation, and a more mature nation, a myth of the type of Anzac Day simply doesn't fit. It's a bad suit. Another one has to be found. If Anzac Day is to be used, then it is certainly going to be changed from its present state.[20]

The decline of Anzac during this period can be explained by generational change; the meaning of the Anzac legend had been transformed during its transmission from the First World War generation to the young men and women who were growing to adulthood in the decades after the Second World War. Where the veterans and their children's generation saw in the Anzac legend noble sacrifice for nation and empire, their grandchildren saw a bunch of bigoted old blokes stumbling around on Anzac Day, gambling and drinking too much beer. This sacrilegious interpretation of Anzac Day was controversially presented in an editorial in the Sydney University student newspaper *Honi Soit* in 1958, and more famously by Alan Seymour in his play, *The One Day of the Year* (1960). Like any mythology, once a new audience failed to find its personal experience and aspirations reflected in the Anzac legend, it lost its potency.

The seeds of the revival of Anzac can be found during the period of its decline, in the growing interest of family historians during the 1970s and 1980s in the experiences of their soldier fathers and grandfathers. A new perspective on the war, far removed from the anachronistic values of the RSL, could also be found in works of history, such as Bill Gammage's *The Broken Years* (1974) and Patsy Adam-Smith's *The Anzacs* (1978). University student David Graupner's observation that the Anzac legend would need to change if it were to survive proved prescient. Anzac 2.0 discarded the imperial connotations and emphasis on Australian soldiers' martial prowess that lay at the heart of the original Anzac legend, for a focus on the personal experiences of ordinary troops. This intimate focus was facilitated by the diaries and letters that were increasingly used by descendants, academic historians and others to understand the experience of the war. Anzac 2.0 valorised inoffensive values such as mateship, suffering and sacrifice. It provided Australians with a mythology around which to craft a distinctive sense of nationhood, following the demise of the British-Australian identity. With its sympathetically crafted main characters, played by Mark Lee and Mel Gibson, and its anti-British sensibility, Peter Weir's 1981 film *Gallipoli* remains the most influential representation of the reforged Anzac legend.

The Hawke government discerned this renewed interest among the Australian public in Anzac commemoration when it agreed to fund the 75th anniversary 'pilgrimage' to Gallipoli of a group of elderly veterans in 1990.[21] The success of the trip marked the dawn of the age of political patronage of Anzac, and the tradition of Australian prime ministers travelling to Gallipoli for the Anzac Day dawn service. That tradition was greatly enabled during the prime ministership of John Howard (1996–2007) and has continued under both conservative and Labor governments. Australia spent more than any other nation on commemoration of the centenary of the Great War; Germany outlaid approximately A$2 for each soldier and civilian killed during the war; France $52, and the United Kingdom $109, while Australia spent $8889 per soldier and civilian killed.[22] Despite these extraordinary figures and the desire of political leaders to use Anzac to stoke nationalist sentiment, Anzac remains a grass-roots phenomenon; a mythology that survives and flourishes because the seeds of political patronage fall on fertile ground.

Like all mythologies, whether they are nationally, ethnically, religiously or otherwise based, Anzac commemoration invites emotional rather than intellectual engagement from its adherents. There is no need for the reflections prompted by Christopher Lee's *Gallipoli* or Sam Neill's *Why Anzac*, because the Anzac religion already has its sacred 'text' in Peter Weir's film *Gallipoli*. This perennially popular film moulds the basic form of modern Anzac commemoration by masterfully presenting the classic conceit of tragic sacrifice; in this case, the sacrifice of innocent young soldiers to give birth to the Australian nation. In addition to its celluloid scripture, Anzac commemoration has developed an annual ritual of great emotional and aesthetic power; the dawn service. In cities and towns around Australia, at Anzac Cove in Gallipoli, at Villers-Bretonneux in Picardy, and in dozens of other places overseas, thousands of Australians commune in the evocative conflation of human sacrifice and national birth.

Those who are dismayed by the ubiquity of Anzac must understand that its power cannot be countered by rational argument, that Anzac commemoration is an experience not an intellectual exercise. In the absence of an alternative national mythology, and in the face of continuing sponsorship by the state on a massive scale – witness the $498 million expansion of the Australian War Memorial – it is hard to imagine that Anzac commemoration will be supplanted any time soon. Already we have seen it stretch to embrace women, Indigenous Australians, gay and lesbian service men and women, and others of non-Anglo backgrounds.[23] Perhaps the efforts of sceptics are best devoted to resisting those who strive to impose Anzac on the national imagination to the exclusion of other aspects of Australian history – and, even worse, those who seek to revive its old militarist and racist connotations. After all, an Anzac legend that is steeped in the language of trauma and suffering, and conjures values such as mateship, sacrifice and courage is a relatively benign foundation on which to rest a national identity.

NOTES

1. The Great War: Aftermath and commemoration

1 Carolyn Holbrook interview with Kim Beazley, 15 May 2012.
2 Carolyn Holbrook interview with Bob Hawke, 21 May 2012.
3 *Sydney Morning Herald*, 26 April 1990.
4 Foreword to D Day, *Reluctant Nation: Australia and the Allied Defeat of Japan, 1942–45*, Oxford University Press, Melbourne, 1992, p. iii.
5 M Ryan (ed.), *Advancing Australia: The Speeches of Paul Keating, Prime Minister*, Big Picture, Sydney, 1995, p. 280.
6 J Curran, *The Power of Speech: Australian Prime Ministers Defining the National Image*, Melbourne University Press, Melbourne, 2006, p. 326.
7 J Hawkins, *Consuming Anzac: The History of Australia's Most Powerful Brand*, UWA Publishing, Perth, 2018, p. 78.
8 Hawkins, 2018, p. 78. See also B Ziino, 'Who owns Gallipoli? Australia's Gallipoli anxieties 1915–2005', *Journal of Australian Studies*, vol. 30, no. 88, pp. 1–12.
9 B Scates, *Return to Gallipoli: Walking the Battlefields of the Great War*, Cambridge University Press, Cambridge, 2006, p. 215.
10 M McKenna and S Ward, '"It was Really Moving, Mate": The Gallipoli Pilgrimage and Sentimental Nationalism in Australia', *Australian Historical Studies*, vol. 38, no. 129, 2007, p. 141.
11 C Holbrook, *Anzac: The Unauthorised Biography*, NewSouth, Sydney, 2014, pp. 194–204.
12 McKenna and Ward, '"It was Really Moving, Mate"', p. 144. For a response to McKenna and Ward, see Scates, B, 'The First Casualty in War: A Reply to McKenna and Ward's "Gallipoli Pilgrimage and Sentimental Nationalism"', *Australian Historical Studies*, vol. 38, no. 130, pp. 362–71.
13 M Lake, H Reynolds, J Damousi, M McKenna and C Donaldson, *What's Wrong with Anzac? The Militarisation of Australian History*, NewSouth, Sydney, 2010, p. vii.
14 Lake *et. al.*, *What's Wrong with Anzac?*, p. 165.
15 G Davison, 'The Habits of Commemoration and the Revival of Anzac Day', *Australian Cultural History*, no. 22, 2003, pp. 73–82; I Clendinnen, 'The History Question: Who Owns the Past', *Quarterly Essay*, no. 23, 2006, pp. 8–15. Alistair Thomson's landmark book *Anzac Memories: Living with the Legend* looked at the intersection between personal and official memory, Oxford University Press, Melbourne, 1994.
16 J McKay, 'A Critique of the Militarisation of Australian History and Culture Thesis: The Case of Anzac Battlefield Tourism', *Journal of Multidisciplinary International Studies*, no. 1, vol. 10, 2013, <epress-dev.lib.uts.edu.au/journals/index.php/portal/article/view/2371/0>, viewed online 2 April 2019.
17 C Twomey, 'Trauma and the Reinvigoration of Anzac: An Argument', *History Australia*, vol. 10, no. 3, 2013, pp. 90, 106.

2. Conscription and the strange case of Captain Father Thomas O'Donnell

1. J Kildea, *Anzacs and Ireland*, UNSW Press, Sydney, 2007.
2. P O'Farrell, *The Irish in Australia,* Sydney, University of NSW Press, Sydney, 1984, p. 260ff.
3. M Hogan, *The Sectarian Strand; Religion in Australian History,* Ringwood, Penguin, 1987.
4. LL Robson, 'O'Donnell, Thomas Joseph (1876–1949)', *Australian Dictionary of Biography*, National Centre of Biography, Australian National University, <adb.anu.edu.au/biography/odonnell-thomas-joseph-7880>, first published in hardcopy 1988, viewed online 27 January 2019.
5. E Malcolm and D Hall, *A New History of the Irish in Australia*, Sydney, NewSouth, Sydney, 2018, p. 308.
6. *Daily Standard*, Brisbane, 30 December 1919, interview with O'Donnell.
7. M Lake, *A Divided Society: Tasmania During World War 1,* Melbourne University Press, Melbourne, 1975, p, 30.
8. Lake 1975, p. 70
9. *Daily Herald*, Adelaide, 20 December 1917.
10. *Tribune,* Melbourne, 20 December 1917.
11. C McConville, *Croppies, Celts and Catholics: The Irish in Australia,* Edward Arnold, Melbourne, 1987, p. 109ff; Val Noone, 'Class Factors in the Radicalisation of Archbishop Daniel Mannix, 1913–17', *Labour and the Great War, Labour History,* no. 106, May 2014, p. 192.
12. *Ballarat Courier,* 25 March 1918, p. 1; *Age,* 25 March 1918.
13. P Bastian, 'Vice-Regal Intervention in Australian Domestic Politics; Ronald Munro Ferguson and the ALP Split of 1916', *Labour History,* no. 114, May 2018, pp. 1–16.
14. *Evening Echo*, 28 March 1918.
15. *WA Record,* 9 February 1918.
16. *Advocate*, 9 March 1918, 'The Sinn Fein Movement'.
17. R Kee, *Ireland: A History*, Abacus, London, 2003, p. 179ff.
18. L Robson, '"Mad Ireland Made Me": The Arrest and General Court Martial of Captain (4th Class) the Reverend Father Thomas Joseph O'Donnell, AIF 1919', in Tasmanian Historical Association, *Papers,* December 1987, pp. 100–17.
19. *Ballarat Star,* 3 November 1919.
20. Robson 1987, p. 107.
21. *Advocate,* 6 December 1919.
22. F Murphy, *Daniel Mannix; Archbishop of Melbourne*, Advocate Press, Melbourne, 1948, pp. 86–102.
23. *Ballarat Star,* 16 August 1920, p. 1.
24. *Burnie Advocate,* 6 November 1920.
25. *Southern Cross,* Adelaide, 21 January 1921 (a Catholic paper).
26. *The World* (Hobart), 28 March 1921.
27. *The World,* 28 March 1921.
28. Kee 2003, chapter 11; Malcolm and Hall 2018, p. 330.
29. Malcolm and Hall 2018, p. 307.

Notes to pages 34–42

3. The 1918 Armistice and the civilian experience of war

1. Isabella Parkes to Murray Parkes, 29 September 1918, Australian War Memorial (AWM) PR03015, box 2, folder 9.
2. *The Age*, 13 November 1918, p. 7.
3. A James, *New South Wales Parliamentary Debates*, 8 November 1918, p. 2676.
4. J Wright, *New South Wales Parliamentary Debates*, 8 November 1918, pp. 2677–8.
5. Jessie Street to Kenneth Street, 10 November 1918, National Library of Australia (NLA) MS2683/1/147. Box 1, Folder 3.
6. Street to Street, 10 November 1918, NLA MS 2683/1/147, Box 1, Folder 3.
7. E Millen, *Commonwealth Parliamentary Debates*, 12 November 1918, p. 7645.
8. W Watt, *Commonwealth Parliamentary Debates*, 12 November 1918, p. 7779.
9. G Black, *New South Wales Parliamentary Debates*, 13 November 1918, p. 2718.
10. HSW Lawson, *Victorian Parliamentary Debates*, 12 November 1918, pp. 2099–2100.
11. AH Peake, Chief Secretary, *South Australia. Official Reports of the Parliamentary Debates*, 12 November 1918, p. 1280.
12. DJ Gordon, *South Australia. Official Reports of the Parliamentary Debates*, 12 November 1918, p. 1278.
13. P Collier, *Western Australia. Parliamentary Debates*, 7 November 1918, p. 1058.
14. A Robinson, *Victorian Parliamentary Debates*, 12 November 1918, p. 2096.
15. JP Jones, *Victorian Parliamentary Debates*, 12 November 1918, p. 2098.
16. J Garland, President, *New South Wales Parliamentary Debates*, 13 November 1918, p. 2708.
17. G Ritchie, *South Australia. Official Reports of the Parliamentary Debates*, 12 November 1918, p. 1281.
18. WS Manifold, *Victorian Parliamentary Debates*, 12 November 1918, p. 2097.
19. Sir J Carruthers, *New South Wales Parliamentary Debates*, 13 November 1918, p. 2711.
20. Jacoba Palstra to Will Palstra, 27 December 1918, University of Melbourne Archives (UMA), A.1984.0057, Box 1.
21. William Jones to Ray Jones, 10 November 1918, UMA, A.1981.0081
22. J Le Gay Brereton to Duncan Hall, 4 November 1918, NLA MS 7229.
23. Rose Keast to Jim Keast, 11 November 1918, AWM PR0064, Folder 10.
24. Reuben Hallenstein to Lt Archie Michaelis, 14 November 1918. UMA, A.2002.0060, Box 20, Series 15/3.
25. WJ George, *Western Australia. Parliamentary Debates*, 12 November 1918, p. 1065.
26. G Black, *New South Wales Parliamentary Debates*, 13 November 1918, p. 2718.
27. Arthur Fry to Katie, 14 November 1918. Mitchell Library, State Library of New South Wales, ML MSS 1159, ADD-ON 2076/BOX 1, Item 1.
28. HSW Lawson, *Victorian Parliamentary Debates*, 12 November 1918, p. 2101.
29. *Commonwealth Parliamentary Debates*, 12 November 1918, p. 7647.
30. Ada Jones to Ray Jones, 17 November 1918, UMA, A.1981.0081.
31. Margaret Thorp to Dr and Mrs Thorp, 14 November 1918. National Archives of Australia (NAA), MP95/1, 167/46/56, QF2358; Mary Boote to George Calderwood, 11 November 1918, QF2443, MP95/1, 167/57/68.
32. J Damousi, *The Labour of Loss: Mourning, Memory and Wartime Bereavement in Australia*, Cambridge University Press, Melbourne, 1999, p. 30; T Luckins, *The Gates of Memory: Australian People's Experiences and Memories of Loss in the Great War*, Curtin University Books, Fremantle, 2004, pp. 159–70.

33 Luckins 2004, p. 168.
34 *Australian Women's Weekly*, September 1939, p. 37, quoted in H Muirhead, 'The Shadow Battalion: The Red Cross on the Victorian Homefront, 1939–1945', BA (Hons) Thesis, Deakin University, 2016, p.17.
35 John B (Steel) to FJ Dunleavy, 21 November 1918, NAA, MP 95/1, 168/30/39, RE1498.

4. Bringing the AIF home: The organisation of repatriation 1918–19

1   E Scott, *Official History of Australia in the War of 1914–1918*, vol. XI, *Australia During the War*, Angus & Robertson, Sydney, 1936, p. 825.
2   AWM 4/30/1/1 Pt. 1, 'Minutes of a Conference re Demobilisation AIF between Prime Minister of Australia and Brig. Genl. Dodds, Commandant, Administrative HQ', undated.
3   AWM 4/30/1/1 Pt. 1, Note by Sherington on minutes of Prime Minister and Dodds conference.
4   AWM 4/30/1/1 Pt. 1. Sherington's emphasis.
5   Scott 1936, p. 825.
6   AWM 4/30/1/1 Pt. 1, Unofficial press release, 'British Australasian', 21 November 1918, in 'AIF Repatriation Precis of Correspondence from 27.12.16 to 18.11.18'.
7   AWM 4/30/1/1 Pt. 1, 'Repatriation, Demobilisation and Rehabilitation of the AIF', 26/10/1917.
8   AWM 4/30/1/1 Pt. 1, 'Policy Matters for the Consideration of the Prime Minister of Australia', 26/8/1918.
9   AWM 4/30/1/1 Pt. 1, 'Proceedings of Conference on Repatriation and Demobilisation', 9/8/1918.
10 Lieutenant GH Goddard, *Soldiers and Sportsmen*, Roseberry Press, London, 1919, p. 9.
11 AWM 30/4/1/2 Pt. 1, 'Repatriation and Demobilisation: An Address to Divisional and Brigade Commanders on November 26th, 1918, by Lieut.-General Sir J. Monash, KCB, VD.'
12 Monash address, 26/11/1918.
13 Scott 1936, p. 826.
14 Monash address, 26/11/1918.
15 AWM 4/30/1/17 Pt. 1, 'Return R.47: Repatriation and Demobilisation Statistical Summary', 27 February 1920.

5. The veteran challenge: Repatriation benefits for Australian soldiers

1   AWM 4/30/1/17 Pt. 1, 'Return R.47: Repatriation and Demobilisation Statistical Summary', 27 February 1920.
2   AG Butler, *Official History of the Australian Army Medical Services in the War of 1914–1918,* vol. III, *Problems and Services,* Australian War Memorial, Canberra, 1943, p. 965.
3   The best single study of the fortunes of Australian returned soldiers after World War I is in S Garton's *The Cost of War: Australians Return*, Oxford University Press, Melbourne, 1996.
4   C Twomey, 'Trauma and the Reinvigoration of Anzac: An Argument', *History Australia*, vol. 10, no. 3, pp. 85–108.

5   See M Larsson, *Shattered Anzacs: Living with the Scars of War*, UNSW Press, Sydney, 2009, and E Nelson, *Homefront Hostilities: The First World War and Domestic Violence*, Australian Scholarly Publishing, Melbourne, 2014.
6   For a full history of the Repatriation administrative structures in Australia, see C Lloyd and J Rees, *The Last Shilling: A History of Repatriation in Australia*, Melbourne University Press, Melbourne, 1994.
7   For the leading work on how Australian veterans were honoured and memorialised, see KS Inglis, *Sacred Places: War Memorials in the Australian Landscape*, Miegunyah Press, Melbourne, 1998.
8   Garton 1996, pp. 74–17; M Crotty and M Edele, 'Total War and Entitlement: Towards a Global History of Veteran Privilege', *Australian Journal of Politics and History*, vol. 59, no. 1, 2013, pp. 15–32.
9   Such comparisons are, however, difficult because of differences in pension rates, eligibility criteria and non-pension compensation. For information informing this assessment, see, among others, P Reese, *Homecoming Heroes: An Account of the Reassimilation of British Military Personnel into Civilian Life*, L Copper, London, 1992; D Cohen, *The War Come Home: Disabled Veterans in Britain and Germany, 1914–1939*, University of California Press, Berkeley, 2001; and S Ortiz, *Beyond the Bonus March and GI Bill: How Veteran Politics Shaped the New Deal Era*, New York University Press, New York, 2009.
10 Crotty and Edele 2013, pp. 15–32.
11 Cornell University Press, forthcoming.
12 The GI Bill's formal title was the *Servicemen's Readjustment Act*. For an excellent overview, see GC Altschuler and SM Blumin, *The GI Bill: A New Deal for Veterans*, Oxford University Press, Oxford, 2009.
13 As well as the sources cited above, see M Edele, *Soviet Veterans of the Second World War. A Popular Movement in an Authoritarian Society, 1941–1991*, Oxford University Press, Oxford, 2008; JM Diehl, 'Germany: Veterans' Politics under Three Flags', in SR Ward (ed.), *The War Generation: Veterans of the First World War*, Kennikat Press, Port Washington, 1975, pp. 135–86; JM Diehl, *The Thanks of the Fatherland: German Veterans after the Second World War*, University of North Carolina Press, Chapel Hill, 1993.
14 On the weakness of the British Legion, see N Barr, *The Lion and the Poppy: British Veterans, Politics, and Society, 1921–1939*, Praeger, Westport, 2005.
15 M Crotty, 'The Returned Sailors' and Soldiers' Imperial League of Australia, 1916–46', in M Crotty and M Larsson (eds), *Anzac Legacies: Australians and the Aftermath of War*, Australian Scholarly Publishing, Melbourne, 2010, pp. 166–86.
16 See P Stanley, *Bad Characters: Sex, Crime, Mutiny, Murder and the Australian Imperial Force*, Pier 9, Sydney, 2010.

6. Australian naval activities in the Pacific at the end of the Great War

1   In some cases spelled 'Malakula'.
2   Resident Commissioner, New Hebrides, to High Commissioner, 7 October 1918, *Despatch of warships to Mallicolo Is, New Hebrides to punish natives who murdered a French planter names Meglia – despatch of HMAS Una and Fantome*, 'Decipher of telegram from the British Consul, Noumea, 26th September 1918', NAA: MP1049/1, 1819/0623.

3   RC Thompson, *Australian Imperialism in the Pacific: The Expansionist Era 1820–1920*, Melbourne University Press, Melbourne, 1980, pp. 178–202.
4   Captain JF Robins, 'Despatch regarding punitive expedition landed from H.M.A.S. "Fantome" against natives of north Mallicollo', NAA: MP1049/1, 1819/0623.
5   AM Jose, *The Royal Australian Navy, 1914–1918*, vol. IX, *Official History of Australia in the War of 1914–1918*, Angus & Robertson, Sydney, 1935, pp. 370–71.
6   Robins, 'Despatch regarding punitive expedition landed from H.M.A.S. "Fantome" against natives of north Mallicollo', NAA: MP1049/1, 1819/0623.
7   M King, 'Re No. I. in Western Pacific despatch, Confidential, of the 14th October, 1918, NAA: MP1049/1, 1819/0623.
8   RM Neilly to Navy Office Melbourne, 6 October 1918 (letter translated by JF Robins), NAA: MP1049/1, 1819/0623.
9   'Trouble in the New Hebrides', *The Mercury*, 18 January 1919, p. 7.
10 Department of Veterans' Affairs, 'Patrolling the Oceans', <anzacportal.dva.gov.au/multimedia/publications/royal-australian-navy/patrolling-oceans>, viewed online 9 February 2019.
11 M Lake and H Reynolds, *Drawing the Global Colour Line: White Men's Countries and the Question of Racial Equality*, Cambridge University Press, UK and USA, 2008, p. 4.
12 S Bedford, '"A Good Moral Effect?": Local Opposition and Colonial Persistence in Malakula, New Hebrides, 1875–1918', *Journal of Colonialism and Colonial History*, January 2017, <https://muse.jhu.edu/article/655211>.
13 S Bullard, *In Their Time of Need: Australia's Overseas Emergency Relief Operations, 1918–2006*, Official History of Australian Peacekeeping, Humanitarian and Post-Cold War Operations, vol. VI, Cambridge University Press, Melbourne, 2017, p. 61.
14 Driver ER Linklater, 2nd Field Artillery Brigade, Australian War Memorial (AWM) 3DRL/5098.
15 'Report of Samoan Epidemic Commission', *Samoanische Zeitung*, vol. 19, no. 37, September 1919.
16 Influenza Epidemic Samoa, NAA: A2, 1919/701.
17 'Helpers for Samoa', *Sydney Morning Herald*, 26 November 1918, p. 6.
18 D Stevens, 'The RAN and the 1918–19 Influenza Epidemic', <www.navy.gov.au/history/feature-histories/ran-and-1918-19-influenza-pandemic>, viewed online 13 February 2019.
19 'Report of Samoan Epidemic Commission', Bullard 2017, p. 75.
20 'Fighting the 'Flu in Samoa', *Richmond River Herald and Northern Districts Advertiser*, 14 February 1919, p. 6.
21 See, for example, 'At Samoa', *Darling Downs Gazette*, 16 December 1918, p. 5; 'Flu Epidemic', *Daily Standard*, 16 December 1918, p. 5; 'From Samoa', *Sydney Morning Herald*, 27 December 1918, p. 7.
22 Bullard 2017, p. 77.
23 RC Thompson 1980, pp. 1–7.
24 H McQueen, *A New Britannia*, University of Queensland Press, Queensland, 2004, p. 50.
25 M Peel and C Twomey, *A History of Australia*, Palgrave Macmillan, Basingstoke, UK, 2011, p. 108.
26 M McKenna, 'Anzac Day: How Did it Become Australia's National Day?', in

M Lake, H Reynolds, J Damousi, M McKenna and C Donaldson, *What's Wrong with Anzac? The Militarisation of Australian History*, NewSouth, Sydney, 2010, p. 110.
27   W Watt, Commonwealth of Australia, *Hansard*, House of Representatives, 14 November 1918, pp. 7833–7838; F Tudor, *Hansard*, 14 November 1918, p. 7842.
28   Watt, *Hansard*, 14 November 1918, p. 7836.

7.   Plans for peace, fears of war: Defending Australia in 1919

1   WJ Hudson, *Billy Hughes in Paris: The Birth of Australian Diplomacy*, Thomas Nelson with the Australian Institute of International Affairs, West Melbourne, 1978; P Spartalis, *The Diplomatic Battles of Billy Hughes*, Hale & Iremonger, Sydney, 1983, pp. 132–44, 150; J Cotton's 'William Morris Hughes, Empire and Nationalism: The Legacy of the First World War', *Australian Historical Studies*, vol. 46, no. 1, 2015, pp. 100–18, provides a useful assessment of the nationalist legacy associated with Hughes and the First World War.
2   TD Saxon, 'Anglo-Japanese Naval Cooperation, 1914–1918', *Naval War College Review*, vol. 53, no. 1, 2000, pp. 63, 66–69; J Latham, 'Australia's Claim to the German Islands', 19 December 1918, Papers of Sir John Latham, National Library of Australia (NLA), MS 1009/19/1342. By no means the origin of Australia's invasion fears, Japan's 1905 victory in the Russo-Japanese War – the first significant non-European victory against a great European power – heightened suspicion of Japan and Australia's sense of vulnerability in the Pacific. German New Guinea consisted of the northeastern part of the island of New Guinea, Bismarck Archipelago, North Solomon Islands, Marshall Islands, Mariana Islands (excluding Guam) and Caroline Islands.
3   N Meaney, *A History of Australian Defence and Foreign Policy*, vol. 2, *Australia and World Crisis, 1914–1923*, Sydney University Press, Sydney, 2009, pp. 407–09; [Official History, 1914–18 War: Naval records of Arthur W Jose: Navies Japanese – Miscellaneous telegrams AWM36 1914–1915], National Archives of Australia (NAA): AWM36, Bundle 32/1; 'The Importance to Australia of German New Guinea and the Islands (lately German) North of the Equator', 11 July 1918, A981 Mars 5.
4   J Latham, 'German Islands', 24 February 1919, NLA: MS 1009/ 19/1390–95 (original emphasis).
5   'Australia to Have a Monroe Doctrine', *New York Times*, 1 June 1918, p. 9. The Monroe Doctrine (1823) stipulated that the western hemisphere was the US sphere of interest and attempts by European powers to colonise or extend influence in this area would not be tolerated.
6   Spartalis 1983, pp. 6–15, 55–58.
7   C Bridge, *William Hughes: Australia*, London, Haus, 2011, pp. 60, 65–67; Spartalis 1983, pp. 96–98. The League of Nations was an international organisation tasked with resolving disputes. The League was first proposed in 1918 by Wilson in his Fourteen Points speech and was operational from 1920. Among the points concerning Australia was the removal of economic barriers and absolute freedom of maritime navigation.
8   Bridge 2011, pp. 77–81; JV Fuller (ed.), *Foreign Relations of the United States: Papers Relating to the Paris Peace Conference, 1919*, vol. 3, US Government Printer, Washington, 1943, pp. 720–22; Spartalis 1983, p. 123. The League of Nations was

an international organisation tasked with resolving disputes. The League was first proposed in 1918 by Woodrow Wilson and was operational from 1920. The Council of Ten was the primary decision-making body at the Paris Conference, composed of the leaders of Britain, France, Italy, Japan and the US and their foreign ministers.

9   JR Poynter, 'The Yo-yo Variations: Initiative and Dependence in Australia's External Relations, 1918–1923', *Historical Studies,* vol. 14, no. 54, 1970, p. 234.

10 D Lee, 'Sir John Latham and the League of Nations', in J Damousi and P O'Brien (eds), *League of Nations: Histories, Legacies and Impact,* Melbourne University Press, Melbourne, 2018, pp. 86–91; Meaney 2009, pp. 411–13; 'Australia's Claim to the German Islands', 19 December 1918, NLA: MS1009/19/1342; J Latham, 'Control of the Pacific', 9 July 1918, NAA: MP1049/1, 1919/0118; 'The Peace Treaty of Versailles, 28 June, 1919: Articles 1–30 and Annex – The Covenant of the League of Nations', *The World War I Document Archive,* <net.lib.byu.edu/~rdh7/wwi/versa/versa1.html>, viewed online 13 February 2019.

11 W Hughes, 'Australia and the Pacific Island Memorandum', 6 February 1919, NLA: MS 1009/19/1300–04.

12 J Latham, 'Mandatory System and the German Pacific Islands', 21 February 1919, NLA: MS 1009/19/1378–89.

13 Latham 1919, NLA: MS 1009/19/1378–89.

14 Bridge 2011, pp. 83–86; Lee, 'Sir John Latham', 2018, pp. 90–91; LF Fitzhardinge, *The Little Digger, 1914–1952: William Morris Hughes: A Political Biography,* vol. 2, Angus & Robertson, Sydney, 1979, p. 398; 'The Peace Treaty of Versailles, 28 June, 1919'. The Japanese delegation's insistence on freedom of entry and residence in the C-class mandates – a position that was not abandoned until late 1920 – coupled with their failed attempt to include a racial equality clause in the League Covenant, galvanised for Australia the value of immigration restriction afforded by the mandate system.

15 J Latham, 'Australia's Claim to the German Islands', 19 December 1918, NLA: MS 1009/19/1342.

16 Enclosure to Admiralty letter, 23 December 1918, NAA: A981, Def 350 Part 1; Naval Bases, n.d. on or after 3 January 1919, NAA: A981, Def 350 Part 1. In 1910 Admiral Reginald Henderson visited Australia to advise on naval infrastructure. On the basis of his recommendations, base construction commenced in Victoria, New South Wales and Western Australia. With the outbreak of the First World War, however, the British ordered construction to be slowed or halted until the end of the war.

17 Watt to Jellicoe, 2 May 1919, NAA: A981, Def 350 Part 1.

18 Jellico Report – 1919, n.d., NAA: A5954, 1080/1 (original emphasis); Admiral of the Fleet Viscount Jellicoe's Naval Mission to Colonies, 3 February 1920, National Archives (NAA): ADM 116/1831.

19 M Murfett, 'The Singapore Strategy', in *Between Empire and Nation: Australia's External Relations from Federation until the Second World War,* C Bridge and B Attard (eds), Australian Scholarly Publishing, Melbourne, 2000, pp. 188–204; HH Cuffe, 'The Limits of Empire: Australia, Eastern Appeasement and the Drift to War in the Pacific, 1937–41', *History Australia* vol. 15, no. 4, 2018, pp. 766–84.

20 See J Cotton, *The Australian School of International Relations,* Palgrave Macmillan, New York, 2013, particularly pp. 7–20, 49–72.

8. Anzacs and Australasians

1. E Wallace, 'Anzacs', *The Anzac Book Written and Illustrated in Gallipoli by the Men of Anzac* (Sydney, 1916), 3rd edn, UNSW Press, Sydney, 2010, p.113.
2. S Gower, 'Preface to the Third Edition', *The Anzac Book*, p. v.
3. *Sydney Morning Herald*, 26 April 1922 quoted in M Lake, 'Mission Impossible: How Men Gave Birth to the Australian Nation. Nationalism, Gender and Other Seminal Acts', *Gender and History*, vol. 4, no. 3, 1992, p. 307.
4. See, for example, B Gammage, *The Broken Years: Australian Soldiers in the Great War*, ANU Press, Canberra, 1974 (and the associated film *Gallipoli*). Arguably the most influential and one of the finest historical accounts of the Anzacs, *The Broken Years* has no index entry for 'Australasians' and just three for New Zealand Anzacs. Gammage's book effectively turned Anzac into an Australian story. Anzac was subsumed in the same kind of nationalising story in New Zealand.
5. Lake, *Progressive New World: How Settler Colonialism and Transpacific Exchange Shaped American Reform,* Harvard University Press, Cambridge, MA, 2019; D Denoon and P Mein Smith with M Wyndham, *A History of Australia, New Zealand and the Pacific*, Blackwell, Oxford, 2000; M Lake, 'Colonial Australia and the Asia-Pacific Region', in A Bashford and S Macintyre (eds), *Cambridge History of Australia,* vol. 1, *Indigenous and Colonial Australia*, Cambridge University Press, Melbourne, 2013, pp. 547–50.
6. Lake 2019.
7. W Pember Reeves, *State Experiments in Australia and New Zealand*, vols 1 and 2, Grant Richards, London, 1902.
8. Denoon and Mein Smith 2000, p. 302.
9. J Royce to Alfred Deakin 21 June 1888, 28 February 1889, MS 1540/1/48, 1540/1/73–74, National Library of Australia.
10. J Royce, 'Reflections after a Wandering Life in Australasia', *Atlantic Monthly*, vol. LXIII, 1889.
11. Lake 2019, p. 8.
12. Lake 2019, p. 194.
13. Lake 2019, p. 4.
14. Lake 2019, pp. 136–37.
15. Lake 1992.
16. A Curthoys and M Lake (eds), *Connected Worlds: History in Trans-National Perspective*, ANU Press, Canberra, 2005, pp. 5–20, 23–43.
17. M Lake and H Reynolds, *Drawing the Global Colour Line: White Men's Countries and the International Challenge of Racial Equality*, Cambridge University Press, Cambridge, 2008; on the Anzacs' sense of racial superiority over Arabs and Bedouins see P Daley, 'The Moment that Forever Changed my Perspective on Anzac Mythology', *Guardian*, 10 December 2018, and *Beersheba: A Journey Through Australia's Forgotten War*, Melbourne University Press, Melbourne, 2009.
18. *The Anzac Book*, 2010, pp. 171, 180.
19. Wallace, 'Anzacs', 2010 *The Anzac Book*, p. 113.
20. Royce 'Reflections', 1889, p. 681.
21. Lake 2019, pp. 57–9.
22. VS Clark 'Present State of Labor Legislation in Australia and New Zealand', *Annals of the American Academy of Political and Social Sciences*, vol. 33, no. 2, 1909, p. 223.

23 E Tregear, 'How New Zealand is Governed', *Arena* (USA), 32, no. 181, 1904.
24 Quoted by K Fewster, 'Ellis Ashmead Bartlett and the Making of the Anzac Legend', *Journal of Australian Studies*, 10, June 1982, p. 19.
25 Gammage 1974, p. 268.
26 S Garton, 'Demobilization and Empire: Empire Nationalism and Soldier Citizenship in Australia after the First World War – in Dominion Context', *Journal of Contemporary History*, vol. 50, no. 1, 2015.
27 M Lake, 'The Power of Anzac', in M McKernan and M Browne (eds), *Australia: Two Centuries of War and Peace*, Australian War Memorial in association with Allen & Unwin, Canberra, 1988, p. 221.
28 M Lake, *The Limits of Hope: Soldier Settlement in Victoria 1915–38*, Oxford University Press, Melbourne, 1987, p. 31.
29 For a detailed account of the political struggle between returned soldiers over the meaning and legacy of Anzac, see Lake 1988, pp. 200–12.
30 M Lake, H Reynolds, M McKenna, J Damousi and C Donaldson, *What's Wrong with Anzac?: The Militarisation of Australian History*, NewSouth, Sydney, 2010.

9. Australian politics in the wake of the First World War

1 B Gammage, *The Broken Years: Australian Soldiers in the Great War*, Penguin, Ringwood, 1987 [1974], pp. 1–3, 276–79.
2 N McLachlan, *Waiting for the Revolution: A History of Australian Nationalism*, Penguin, Ringwood, 1989, pp. 209–38.
3 M Cathcart, *Defending the National Tuckshop: Australia's Secret Army Intrigue of 1931*, McPhee Gribble/Penguin Books, Melbourne, 1988, p. 91.
4 R Bollard, *In the Shadow of Gallipoli: The Hidden History of Australia in World War I*, NewSouth, Sydney, 2013, pp. 165–67.
5 R Evans, *The Red Flag Riots: A Study of Intolerance*, University of Queensland Press, Brisbane, 1988.
6 Bollard 2013, pp. 157–86.
7 N Wise, *Anzac Labour: Workplace Cultures in the Australian Imperial Force During the First World War*, Palgrave Macmillan, Basingstoke, UK, 2014.
8 *Age*, 29 May 1919, p. 8.
9 M Crotty, 'The Returned Sailors' and Soldiers' Imperial League of Australia, 1916–46', in M Crotty and M Larsson (eds), *Anzac Legacies: Australians and the Aftermath of War*, Australian Scholarly Publishing, North Melbourne, 2010, pp. 166–86.
10 C Coulthard-Clark, *Soldiers in Politics: The Impact of the Military on Australian Political Life and Institutions*, Allen & Unwin, Sydney, 1996, pp. 122–25.
11 D Lee, *Stanley Melbourne Bruce: Australian Internationalist*, Continuum, London and New York, 2010, p. 17.
12 R Darroch, *DH Lawrence in Australia*, Macmillan, Melbourne, 1981, pp. 58–66.
13 B Nairn, 'Carmichael, Ambrose Campbell (1866–1953)', *Australian Dictionary of Biography*, National Centre of Biography, Australian National University, <adb.anu.edu.au/biography/carmichael-ambrose-campbell-5506/text9369>, published first in hardcopy 1979, viewed online 2 March 2019.
14 *Sydney Morning Herald*, 26 March 1919, p. 14.
15 *Examiner* (Grafton), 25 October 1919, p. 4.
16 *Daily Telegraph*, 28 November 1919, p. 5.

17 *Sydney Morning Herald*, 9 February 1920, p. 7.
18 J Hagan and K Turner, *A History of the Labor Party in New South Wales: 1891–1991*, Longman Cheshire, Melbourne, 1991, pp. 114, 118; Hogan, *The Sectarian Strand: Religion in Australian History*, Penguin, Melbourne, pp. 186–91.
19 BD Graham, *The Formation of the Australian Country Parties*, Australian National University Press, Canberra, 1966, p. 132.
20 S Garton, *The Cost of War: Australians Return*, Oxford University Press, Melbourne, 1996, chapters 3–4.
21 M Roe, 'The Establishment of the Australian Department of Health: Its Background and Significance', *Historical Studies*, vol. 17, no. 67, 1976, pp. 176–92.
22 J Brett, *From Secret Ballot to Democracy Sausage: How Australia Got Compulsory Voting*, Text Publishing, Melbourne, 2019, pp. 134–38.
23 B Attwood and A Markus, *Thinking Black: William Cooper and the Australian Aborigines' League*, Aboriginal Studies Press, Canberra, 2004.
24 J Maynard, *Fight For Liberty and Freedom: The Origins of Australian Aboriginal Activism*, Aboriginal Studies Press, Canberra, 2007.
25 B Attwood, *Rights for Aborigines*, Allen & Unwin, Sydney, 2003, p. 59.
26 WH Richmond, 'SM Bruce and Australian Economic Policy, 1923–9', *Australian Economic History Review*, vol. 23, no. 2, 1983, pp. 238–57.
27 NG Butlin, A Barnard and JJ Pincus, *Government and Capitalism: Public and Private Choice in Twentieth Century Australia*, Allen & Unwin, Sydney, 1982, pp. 74–107.
28 SL Wilks, '"Now is the Psychological Moment": Earle Page and the Imagining of Australia', PhD Thesis, Australian National University, 2018, p. 108.
29 N Kirk, '"Australians for Australia": The Right, the Labor Party and Contested Loyalties to Nation and Empire in Australia, 1917 to the Early 1930s', *Labour History*, no. 91, 2006, pp. 95–111.
30 S Macintyre, *The Reds: The Communist Party of Australia from Origins to Illegality*, Allen & Unwin, Sydney, 1998, p. 55.
31 I Turner, *Industrial Labour and Politics: The Dynamics of the Labour Movement in Eastern Australia 1900–1921*, Hale & Iremonger, Sydney, 1979 [1965], pp. 223–35.

10. 'They should at least be given a voice': Aboriginal veterans and the RSSILA

1 Based on an estimate by the Australian War Memorial in 2016. The true figure may be greater. See N Riseman, *In Defence of Country: Life Stories of Aboriginal and Torres Strait Islander Servicemen & Women*, Australian National University Press, Canberra, 2016, p. 3.
2 Throughout this chapter I largely focus on Aboriginal soldiers, excluding, for reasons of space, those from the Torres Strait Islands.
3 N Riseman and R Trembath, *Defending Country: Aboriginal and Torres Strait Islander Military Service Since 1945*, University of Queensland Press, Brisbane, 2016, pp. 6–9.
4 J McCalman and R Kippen, 'Diggers to Veterans: Risk, Resilience and Recovery in the First AIF', <figshare.com/articles/Diggers to Veterans database/5936899>, viewed online 29 January 2019.
5 A Gerrard and K Harman, 'Lives Twisted Out of Shape: Aboriginal Soldiers and the Aftermath of the First World War', *Aboriginal Studies*, vol. 39, 2015, pp. 183–201.
6 S Furphy, 'The Home Front in the First World War', in J Beaumont and A Cadzow,

Notes to pages 115–123

    Serving Our Country: Indigenous Australians, War, Defence and Citizenship, NewSouth, Sydney, 2018, pp. 94–112.
7 *Australian Abo Call*, 1 May 1938, p. 2.
8 *Morning Bulletin* (Rockhampton), 11 March 1939, p. 9. Also see *Central Queensland Herald* (Rockhampton), 16 March 1939, p. 59.
9 *Daily Advertiser* (Wagga Wagga), 27 April 1939, p. 2.
10 J Horton, '"Willing to Fight to a Man": The First World War and Aboriginal Activism in the Western District of Victoria'*, Aboriginal History*, vol. 39, 2015, p. 213.
11 C Clark, 'Grant, Douglas (1885–1951)', *Australian Dictionary of Biography*, National Centre of Biography, Australian National University, <adb.anu.edu.au/biography/grant-douglas-6454>, published first in hardcopy 1983, viewed online 29 January 2019.
12 'The Late Jack Dunn', *Cootamundra Herald*, 9 May 1934, p. 2.
13 'Mr Walter McCready', *Healesville and Yarra Glen Guardian*, 18 May 1935, p. 2.
14 'All Cobbers Again', *Adelaide News*, 25 April 1938, p. 5. Point McLeay is now known as Raukkan.
15 P Scarlett, 'Aboriginal Service in the First World War: Identity, Recognition and the Problem of Mateship', *Aboriginal History*, vol. 39, 2015, pp. 163–81.
16 'Abo Ex-Soldiers Detained Are Prisoners on Palm Island', *Daily Standard* (Brisbane), 14 May 1930, p. 1.
17 'Aborigines. Ex-Soldiers Want Inquiry', *Workers' Weekly*, 13 July 1934, p. 1.
18 C Clark, 'A Question of Numbers – First World War', <www.awm.gov.au/articles/indigenous-service/report-first-world-war>, viewed online 12 February 2019.
19 'Rights of Aboriginal Soldiers', *Darling Downs Gazette*, 29 January 1920, p. 4.
20 See *Queensland Times* (Ipswich), 27 February 1939, p. 3; *Dalby Herald*, 28 February 1939, p. 1; *Townsville Daily Bulletin*, 28 February 1939, p. 12; *Cairns Post*, 1 March 1939, p. 14; *Morning Bulletin* (Rockhampton), 1 March 1939, p. 3; *Daily Mercury* (Mackay), 1 March 1939, p. 8; *Northern Herald* (Cairns), 4 March 1939, p. 2; *Cloncurry Advocate*, 4 March 1939, p. 7; *Proserpine Guardian*, 11 March 1939, p. 2; *Warwick Daily News*, 11 March 1939, p. 7; *Johnstone River Advocate and Innisfail News*, 21 March 1939, p. 5.
21 'Soldiers Notes. Citizen Rights for Aboriginal Diggers Sought', *Brisbane Telegraph*, 22 February 1939, p. 6.
22 RA Hall, *The Black Diggers: Aborigines and Torres Strait Islanders in the Second World War*, Allen & Unwin, Sydney, 1989, p. 20.
23 Riseman and Trembath 2016, pp. 36–37.
24 Riseman and Trembath 2016, pp. 17–20.
25 CW Joyce, Secretary, Victorian Branch, RSL to JC Neagle, Federal Secretary, RSL, 16 April 1946, RSL papers, series 1, MSS 6609, box 158, File 2248c, National Library of Australia (hereafter NLA), Canberra.
26 General Secretary, RSL to JB Chifley, Prime Minister, 20 November 1946 in RSL papers, series 1, MSS 6609, box 158, file 2248c, NLA, Canberra. Also see *Argus*, 2 November 1946.
27 *The Argus,* 25 March 1947.
28 *The Age*, 1 September 1948.

11. Anzac trauma and frontier violence? Re-examining the Coniston Massacre

1. Elements of the section entitled 'The Coniston killings' were first published in *Wartime* 85, January 2019, pp. 36–40, and are reprinted here with permission. That article in turn stemmed from my paper 'The Coniston Massacre in the context of the Australian frontier', delivered at the Australian Historical Association's annual conference in July 2018 at the Australian National University, Canberra. I would like to thank my Australian War Memorial colleagues Christina Zissis, Dr David Sutton, Dr Karl James, Dr Meleah Hampton and Dr Lachlan Grant for reading and commenting on earlier drafts of this chapter.
2. For example, A Thomson, *Anzac Memories: Living with the Legend*, Oxford University Press, Melbourne, 1994; S Garton, *The Cost of War: Australians Return*, Oxford University Press, Melbourne, 1996; M Larsson, *Shattered Anzacs: Living with the Scars of War*, UNSW Press, Sydney, 2009; M Crotty and M Larsson (eds), *Anzac Legacies: Australians and the Aftermath of the War*, Australian Scholarly Publishing, Melbourne, 2010; B Scates, R Wheatley and L James, *World War One: A History in 100 Stories*, Penguin, Melbourne, 2015.
3. B Wilson and J O'Brien, '"To Infuse an Universal Terror": A Reappraisal of the Coniston Killings', *Aboriginal History*, vol. 27, 2003, pp. 66–68.
4. G Briscoe, *Racial Folly: A Twentieth-Century Aboriginal Family*, ANU Epress, Canberra, 2010, p. 13.
5. S Downer, *Patrol Indefinite: The Northern Territory Police Force*, Rigby, Adelaide, 1963, p. 126.
6. 'Attacks on White Men by Natives – Killing of Natives – Central Australia', National Archives of Australia (NAA): A431, 1950/2768, Part 2, p. 66. Page numbers refer to the digitised document.
7. William George Murray, service record: NAA: B2455, MURRAY WILLIAM GEORGE service number 308; Embarkation Roll, 4th Light Horse Regiment (October 1914), p. 9, Australian War Memorial (AWM), AWM8 10/9/1; 4th Australian Light Horse Regiment, unit history, AWM, <www.awm.gov.au/collection/U51038>, viewed online 16 January 2019; CEW Bean, *The Story of ANZAC from May 4 1915 to the Evacuation of the Gallipoli Peninsula*, vol. 2, *Official History of Australia in the War of 1914–1918*, Angus & Robertson, Sydney, 1937, p. 381; II ANZAC Corps Mounted Regiment, unit history, AWM: <www.awm.gov.au/collection/U51051>, viewed online 17 January 2019; D Holloway, *Endure and Fight: A Detailed History of the 4th Light Horse Regiment, AIF, 1914–19, Gallipoli, Sinai and Palestine, France and Belgium*, 4th Light Horse Regiment Memorial Association, Melbourne, 2011, pp. 129–30; N Smith, *Men of Beersheba: A History of the 4th Light Horse Regiment, 1914–1919*, Mostly Unsung Military History Research and Publications, Melbourne, 1993, p. 53; D Carment, 'Murray, William George', *Northern Territory Dictionary of Biography*, Charles Darwin University Press, Darwin, 2008, p. 423.
8. Wilson and O'Brien 2003, pp. 60, 62–63; 'Attacks on White Men by Natives', part 2, pp. 69, 80; Blind Alec Jupurrula in P Read and J Read (eds), *Long Time, Olden Time: Aboriginal Accounts of Northern Territory History*, Institute for Aboriginal Development, Alice Springs, 1991, pp. 35–36.
9. 'Attacks on White Men by Natives – Killing of Natives – Central Australia',

Notes to pages 129–139

NAA: A431, 1950/2768, Part 1, p. 20, p. 64.
10 See, for example: 'Shooting of 17 Natives is Told: "Mowing Them Down Wholesale"', *Weekly Times*, 17 November 1928, p. 9; 'Natives Shot: "Mowed Down Wholesale"', *Chronicle*, 17 November 1928, p. 55; 'Casual Attitude', *Northern Star*, 18 January 1929, p. 7; 'Attacks on White Men by Natives', part 2, pp. 86–88.
11 R Nungarrayi in P Vaarzon-Morel (ed.), with G Napangardi and J Nakamarra Long, *Warlpiri karnta karnta-kurlangu yimi/ Warlpiri Women's Voices: Our Lives, Our History*, Institute for Aboriginal Development Press, Alice Springs, 1995, pp. 53, 46.
12 RG Kimber, *Man from Arltunga: Walter Smith, Australian Bushman*, Hesperian Press, Perth, 1986, p. 109; F Jupurrurla Kelly, 'Coniston', *Cosmopolitan Civil Societies Journal*, vol. 6, no. 3, 2014, p. 3.
13 A Nettlebeck, 'Writing and Remembering Frontier Conflict: The Rule of Law in 1880s Central Australia', *Aboriginal History*, vol. 28, 2004, p. 203.
14 *South Australian Government Gazette*, 2 August 1855, p. 575.
15 'Another Tragedy on the Telegraph Line', *South Australian Advertiser*, 16 July 1875, p. 11.
16 Foelsche to Montagu, 19 July 1875, cited in T Austin, *Simply the Survival of the Fittest: Aboriginal Administration in South Australia's Northern Territory, 1863–1910*, Historical Society of the Northern Territory, Darwin, 1992, p. 15.
17 *Northern Territory Times and Gazette*, 4 July 1890, p. 2.
18 A Searcy, *In Australian Tropics*, 2nd edn, George Robertson & Co, London, 1909, p. 174.
19 'Attacks on White Men by Natives', part 2, pp. 71–73.
20 'Attacks on White Men by Natives', part 2, pp. 69, 66, 113.
21 'Casual Attitude' 1929, p. 7. This is a condensed version of Murray's evidence: see 'Attacks on White Men by Natives', part 2, p. 94. The chairman's comments are not recorded in that file.
22 'Attacks on White Men by Natives', part 2, p. 73.
23 J Sémelin, 'In Consideration of Massacres', *Journal of Genocide Research*, vol. 3, no. 3, 2001, p. 377, 382.
24 Kelly 2014, p. 2.
25 *Coniston*, dir. D Batty and F Jupurrurla Kelly (Yuendumu, NT: PAW Media, 2012).

12. Remembering the resilient

1 The account that follows draws on the definitive biography by R McMullin, *Pompey Elliott*, Scribe, Melbourne, 2002, paperback edition 2008, pp. 653–55.
2 The details of Hawker's life and personality provided in this chapter are drawn largely from the extensive correspondence in the 1960s between friends of Hawker and his sister, Lilas Needham when she was conducting research for the biography, *Charles Hawker, Soldier-Pastoralist Statesman*, Griffin Press, Adelaide, 1969. See Lilas Needham papers, MS 4847 Box 1, National Library of Australia (NLA).
3 The account that follows of Throssell's death and life draws on the memoirs of his wife, KS Prichard, *Child of the Hurricane: An Autobiography*, Angus & Robertson, Sydney, 1963; and those of his son, R Throssell, *My Father's Son*, William Heinemann, Melbourne, 1989.
4 See McMullin 2008, p. 640.
5 Throssell 1989, p. 46.

6	Prichard 1963, p. 251.
7	'Throssell Hugo Vivian Hope', B2455, NAA.
8	Repatriation Commission 'M' file, Throssell, Hugo Vivian, PP645/1 M5273, NAA.
9	Prichard 1963, p. 261.
10	Throssell 1989, p. 4.
11	The details that follow are taken from 'Chief Events in Charles Hawker's Life', Needham Papers, NLA.
12	The discussion that follows draws on: R Reid and L Courtenay Botterill, 'The Multiple Meanings of "Resilience": An Overview of the Literature', *Australian Journal of Public Administration*, vol. 72, no. 1, 2013, pp. 31–40; R Pendall, KA Foster and M Cowell, 'Resilience and Regions: Building Understanding of the Metaphor', *Cambridge Journal of Regions, Economy and Society*, vol. 3, 2010, pp. 71–84; and HB Kaplan, 'Toward an Understanding of Resilience: A Critical Review of Definitions and Models', in MD Glantz and JL Johnson (eds), *Resilience and Development: Positive Life Adaptations*, Kluwer Academic Publications, New York, 2002, pp. 17–83.
13	FH Norris *et al.*, quoted in Reid and Botterill 2013, p. 32.
14	AS Marsten and M Rutter, both quoted in Kaplan 2002, p. 20.
15	For a detailed discussion of risk factors see Kaplan 2002, pp. 36 ff.
16	E Losel, T Bleisener and P Koferl 1989, quoted in Kaplan 2002, p. 39.
17	M Conrad and C Hammen, quoted in Kaplan 2002, p. 46.
18	Later research into PTSD has shown that one of the most important factors in post-deployment adjustment is a veteran's social support system: R Hearder and T Moss, Appendix C, in J Bou, B Breen, D Horner, G Pratten and M de Vogel (eds), *The Limits of Peacekeeping*, vol. 4, *The Official History of Australian Peacekeeping, Humanitarian and Post-Cold War Operations: Australian Missions in Africa and the Americas, 1992–2005*, Cambridge University Press, Melbourne, 2018, p. 591.
19	M Topf, quoted in Kaplan 2002, p. 34.
20	Quotations from A Antonovsky 1984, in Kaplan 2002, p. 49.
21	Throssell 1989, pp. 52–53.
22	McMullin 2008, pp. 332–33.
23	Repatriation M file PP645/1 M5273.
24	Department of Repatriation and Demobilisation, Medical Report, 6 May 1919, Repatriation 'R' file B73, M691813, NAA.
25	McMullin 2008, pp. 503, 504, 509.
26	Quoted in McMullin 2008, p. 641.
27	Memorandum for O.I.C. Medical & General Section by B Phillips (?) Investigating Officer, 31 March 1931, B73, M691813, NAA.
28	An extensive search of the National Archives unearthed one slim file, A2487 1921/12306, which revealed only that in 1921 Hawker was deemed by Repatriation to be eligible for assistance and was in receipt of a pension.
29	This conclusion is based on the correspondence in the Lilas Needham papers. There are occasional deletions in these letters, presumably by Needham, but the picture they provide of Hawker's personality and courage is overwhelmingly positive.
30	Typescript of Corporal W Hughes memories, Needham papers.
31	Letter from [indecipherable] Hunter, 21 June 1962, Needham papers.
32	Letter of Madge Kitchener, who nursed Hawker at Ridley House hospital, London, 18 April 1963, Needham papers.
33	EW Gordon and LD Song, quoted in Kaplan 2002, p. 52.

34 Typescript by Hughes, letter from Vaughan Squires to Needham, nd, and annotations (by Needham?) on 'Chief Events in Charles Hawker's Life', Needham papers.
35 McMullin 2008, pp. 519, 576.
36 John Hamilton, *The Price of Valour,* Pan Macmillan, Sydney, 2016, p. 277; Prichard 1963, p. 253.
37 See Hamilton 2016, p. 306.
38 Typescript by Hughes, Needham papers.
39 'Hawker, Michael Seymour (1857–1933)', Obituaries Australia, <oa.anu.edu.au/obituary/hawker-michael-seymour-16015>; Needham 1969, p. vii.
40 Throssell 1989, p. 117.
41 McMullin 2008, p. 26.
42 Notes and extract from letter of Mrs R Travers, Needham papers. See also Needham 1969, p. 19.
43 Hamilton 2016, p. 287.
44 Notes taken from Jack Chomley, Needham files.
45 Statement of Identification by William Watt, Investor, nd, Repatriation 'R' file, B73 M691813, NAA.
46 Prichard to Deputy Commissioner, Repatriation Commission, Perth, 25 January 1934, PP645/1, M5273.
47 Parliament of Australia, 'Suicide in Australia', <www.aph.gov.au/About_Parliament/Parliamentary_Departments/Parliamentary_Library/pubs/BN/2011–2012/Suicide#_Toc299625618>, viewed online 23 February 2019.
48 Bou *et al.* 2018, p. 591.
49 Australian War Memorial, 'Harold Edward "Pompey" Elliott', <www.awm.gov.au/learn/schools/resources/1916/fromelles/pompey-elliott>, viewed online 23 February 2019.
50 C Twomey, 'Trauma and the reinvigoration of Anzac', *History Australia,* vol. 10, issue 3, 2013, pp. 105–06.
51 A Thomson, *Anzac Memories: Living with the Legend,* Monash University Publishing, Clayton, Victoria, 2013; K Ariotti, *Captive Anzacs: Australian POWs of the Ottomans during the First World War,* Cambridge University Press, Melbourne, 2018; M Larsson, *Shattered Anzacs: Living with the Scars of War,* UNSW Press, Sydney, 2009; B Scates and M Oppenheimer, *The Last Battle: Soldier Settlement in Australia 1916–1939,* Cambridge University Press, Melbourne, 2016.
52 M Larsson, '"The Part We Do Not See": Disabled Soldiers and Family Caregiving after World War I', in M Crotty and M Larrson (eds), *Anzac Legacies: Australians and the Aftermath of War,* Australian Scholarly Publishing, Melbourne, 2010, p. 40.
53 S Garton, *The Cost of War: Australians Return,* Oxford University Press, Melbourne, 1996, pp. 83–84.
54 See Scates and Oppenheimer 2016, especially pp. 143–99.
55 Garton 1996, p. 86.

13. William Roy Hodgson and the aftermath of the First World War

1 Lieut.-Colonel WR Hodgson, February 24 1945, 'Address to the South African Veterans' Association', National Archives, M1516 M1516/1.
2 A Watt, 'Hodgson, William Roy (1892–1958)', *Australian Dictionary of Biography,* National Centre of Biography, Australian National University, <adb.anu.edu.au/biography/hodgson-william-roy-6695/text11551>, published first in hardcopy 1983,

viewed online 29 March 2019; Education Department Melbourne, 23 November 1923, Letter to National Archives M1516 M1516/1.
3   Hodgson, 'Address to the South African Veterans' Association'.
4   Watt 1983.
5   'Australia's Brisk Delegate at United Nations', 16 August 1947, *Age*, p. 2.
6   NAA: B73, R35433.
7   Memorandum, Department of Repatriation, 24 April 1922, NAA: A2487, 1922/5548.
8   DS Bird, *JA Lyons: The 'Tame Tasmanian' Appeasement and Rearmament in Australia, 1932–39*, Melbourne, Australian Scholarly Publishing, 2008, p. 134.
9   Bird 2008, p.134, See also A Watt, 'The Australian Diplomatic Service 1935–1965', in G Greenwood and G Harper (eds), *Australia in World Affairs 1961–1965*, Cheshire, Melbourne, 1968, pp. 134–76.
10 P Hasluck, *Diplomatic Witness: Australian Foreign Affairs, 1941–1947*, Melbourne University Press, Melbourne, 1980, pp. 7–10; P Edwards, *Prime Ministers and Diplomats: The Making of Australian Foreign Policy, 1901–1949*, Oxford University Press with Australian Institute of International Affairs, Melbourne, 1983, pp. 104–09.
11 Edwards 1983, p. 107.
12 AJ Hill, 'Chauvel, Sir Henry George (Harry) (1865–1945)', Australian Dictionary of Biography, National Centre of Biography, Australian National University, <adb.anu.edu.au/biography/chauvel-sir-henry-george-harry-5569/text9497>, published first in hardcopy 1979, viewed online 29 March 2019; J Grey, 'White, Sir Cyril Brudenell (1876–1940)', Australian Dictionary of Biography, National Centre of Biography, Australian National University, <adb.anu.edu.au/biography/white-sir-cyril-brudenell-1032/text15983>, published first in hardcopy 1990, viewed online 29 March 2019.
13 Edwards 1983, p. 107.
14 Hasluck 1980, p. 4.
15 G Greenwood and N Harper 1968, p. 137.
16 Security Council official records, 3rd year: 390th meeting, 23 December 1948, Palais de Chaillot, Paris, <digitallibrary.un.org/record/637540?ln=en>, viewed online 29 March 2019, and cited in Greenwood and Harper 1968, p. 179. Australia had already recognised the *de facto* authority of the Indonesian Republic in Sumatra, Java and Madura in 1947 and were now voicing strong disapproval of renewed Dutch military action against the Republic. See HC McMichael, 'Australia-Indonesia Relations', *Australian Outlook*, vol. 40, no. 3, 1986, p. 139.
17 See, for example, No. 33, Memorandum prepared by Delegation to Imperial Conference, 28 May 1937, *DAFP* 1 1937–38, p. 90.
18 No. 27, Minutes of Third Meeting of Principal Delegates to Imperial Conference, 21 May 1937, *DAFP* 1 1937–38, p. 74.
19 NK Meaney, *Towards a New Vision: Australia and Japan through 100 Years*, Kangaroo Press, Sydney, 1999, p. 77.
20 Australia's representation at the 1937 Imperial Conference is examined in Waters, *Australia and Appeasement: Imperial Foreign Policy and the Origins of World War II*, IB Tauris, London, 2012, pp. 20–26.
21 Hodgson, 'Address to the South African Veterans' Association'.
22 Hodgson, 'Address to the South African Veterans' Association'.
23 'Australia's Brisk Delegate', 1947, p. 2.
24 'Australia's Brisk Delegate', 1947, p. 2.

25 'William Roy Hodgson', in *United States Handbook No. 2, Human Rights Commission, Third Session*, Eleanor Roosevelt Papers, Box 4595, Roosevelt Library, Hyde Park, New York.
26 *UN Weekly Bulletin*, June 17, 1947, p. 639.
27 'Australia's Brisk Delegate' 1947, p 2.
28 United Nations Library, 'Drafting of the Universal Declaration of Human Rights', <research.un.org/en/undhr/draftingcommittee#s-lg-box-wrapper-3512507>, viewed online 1 February 2019.
29 MA Glendon, *A World Made New: Eleanor Roosevelt and the Universal Declaration of Human Rights*, Random House, New York, 2002, p. 49.
30 Glendon 2002, p. 49.
31 Resolution 22 (1947); NAA, Cable UN 379, 9 April 1947, cited in LW Maher, 'Half Light Between War and Peace: Herbert Vere Evatt, the Rule of International Law, and the Corfu Channel Case', *Australian Journal of Legal History*, vol. 9, no. 1, 2005, p. 61. See also 'Australia's Brisk Delegate', 1947, p. 2.
32 Human Rights Commission, First Session, Summary Records (E/CN. 4/SR.2, p.4; SR.9, p. 3; SR.15, pp. 2–3; SR.16, p.2). Cited in Glendon 2002, p. 38.
33 Report of Australian Representative on Drafting Committee, International Bill of Human Rights, First Session of the Commission on Human Rights, in NAA A 1838/1, 856/13/2/1. Cited in A Devereux, 'Australia and the International Scrutiny of Civil and Political Rights: An Analysis of Australia's Negotiating Policies, 1946–1966', *Australian Year Book of International Law*, vol. 22, 2002, pp. 47, 54.
34 Report on First Session of Commission on Human Rights; in NAA A 1838/1, Item 856/13 Pt I. Cited in Devereux 2002, p. 54.
35 Cablegram from R Hodgson to DEA, 16/12/47. In NAA A 1838/1, Item 856/13/2. Cited in Devereux 2002, p. 59.
36 Devereux 2002, pp. 59–61.
37 'Australia's Brisk Delegate' 1947, p. 2.
38 Edward C Fuller, President Bard College, October 27 1947, Correspondence with William R Hodgson, National Archives, M1516 M1516/1. He received warm congratulations for his Honorary Doctorate from his colleague at the Human Rights Commission, Eleanor Roosevelt, with an invitation to 'stop for tea on your way back from Bard College Saturday, I should be very glad to see you then'. Eleanor Roosevelt, June 19, 1947, Correspondence with William R Hodgson, National Archives, M1516 M1516/1.
39 A Watt 1983.
40 J Suares, *JB Chifley: An Ardent Internationalist*, Melbourne University Press, Melbourne, 2019.
41 Hodgson, 'Address to the South African Veterans' Association'.
42 Hodgson, 'Address to the South African Veterans' Association'.

14. 'A suitable memorial'? Painting, memory and the Great War

1 P Daley, 'How Do We Settle the "Statue Wars"?', *Guardian*, 29 June 2018.
2 M Hutchison, *Painting War: A History of Australia's First World War Art Scheme*, Cambridge University Press, Melbourne, 2019.
3 Will Dyson to Andrew Fisher, 23 August 1916, AWM93 18/7/5 Part 1.
4 Dyson to Fisher, 23 August 1916.
5 A Galbally and A Grey (eds), *Letters from Smike: The Letters of Arthur Streeton, 1890–1943*, Oxford University Press, Melbourne, 1989, p. 34.

6 Fisher to WM Hughes, 31 January 1917, AWM93 12/12/1 Part 2.
7 Henry Smart to Charles Bean, 16 May 1917, AWM38 3DRL6673/286; Arthur Streeton to Tom Roberts, 21 December 1917, Letters from A. Streeton, 1889–1931, MFMG 27511, NLA; Streeton to Walter Baldwin Spencer, 28 November 1917, Walter Baldwin Spencer Papers, MLMSS 875, SLNSW.
8 'Australian Artists at the Fighting Fronts: Progress of War Records', *Argus*, 18 May 1918, p. 7.
9 C Speck, *Painting Ghosts: Australian Women Artists in Wartime*, Craftsman House, Melbourne, 2004, p. 20.
10 Smart to Bean, 16 May 1917, AWM38 3DRL 6673/286.
11 Speck 2004.
12 Speck 2004, p. 32.
13 Excerpt of letter from Norman Lindsay to Premier of New South Wales in letter from Premier's Department to Prime Minister's Department and Department of Defence, 7 August 1918, AWM93 8/2/23.
14 Watt to Pearce, 23 October 1918, AWM93 8/2/23; George Pearce to Bertram Stevens, 3 September 1918, AWM93 8/2/23.
15 See S Butlin, *The Practice of Her Profession: Florence Carlyle, Canadian Painter in the Age of Impressionism*, McGill-Queen's University Press, Kingston and Montreal, 2009, p. 274.
16 William Trahair, 10 June 1918, AWM93 8/2/23.
17 Sydney Ure Smith to the Honourable W Elliot Johnson, 13 July 1918, AWM93 8/2/23.
18 Art and the War, in Minutes of the Meeting of the Historic Memorials Committee, 17 October 1918, A457 B508/7, NAA.
19 Lord Beaverbrook to Edmund Walker, 14 December 1917, 5.41-C, File 1, NGC.
20 M Tippett, *Art at the Service of War: Canada, Art, and the Great War*, University of Toronto Press, Buffalo, p. 49.
21 M Harries and S Harries, *The War Artists: British Official War Art of the Twentieth Century*, M Joseph, London, 1983, p. 87.
22 Speck 2004, p. 57; J Damousi, 'Socialist Women and Gendered Space: Anti-conscription and Anti-war Campaigns 1914–18', in J Damousi and M Lake (eds), *Gender and War: Australians at War in the Twentieth Century*, Cambridge University Press, Cambridge, 1995, pp. 254–73.
23 Bean to Edwin and Lucy Bean, 19 January 1919, AWM38 3DRL 7447/7.
24 Hutchison 2019.

15. Staging history in Brisbane's Anzac centenary

1 See Romain Fathi's chapter in this volume, and M Cryle, 'Making "The One Day of the Year": A Genealogy of Anzac Day to 1918', PhD dissertation, University of Queensland, 2016. For recent perspectives on Charles Bean, see P Stanley (ed.), *Charles Bean: Man, Myth, Legacy*, UNSW Press, Sydney, 2017; for museums and official memory, see J Wellington, *Exhibiting War: The Great War, Museums, and Memory in Britain, Canada, and Australia*, Cambridge University Press, Cambridge, 2017.
2 G Seal, *Inventing Anzac: The Digger and National Mythology*, University of Queensland Press, Brisbane, 2004, p. vii.
3 Wellington 2017, p. 316. See also M Lake, H Reynolds, M McKenna, J Damousi and C Donaldson (eds), *What's Wrong With Anzac? The Militarisation of Australian History*,

NewSouth, Sydney, 2010, and C Holbrook, *Anzac: The Unauthorised Biography*, NewSouth, Sydney, 2014.

4   B Brooker, '100 Years of Anzac: Ludicrous Spending for Nationalist Validation', *Overland* online, 24 April 2018, <overland.org.au/2018/04/100-years-of-anzac-ludicrous-spending-for-nationalist-validation>, viewed online 20 February 2019.

5   J Beaumont, *Broken Nation: Australians in the Great War*, Allen & Unwin, Sydney, 2013.

6   See J Brown, *Anzac's Long Shadow: The Cost of Our National Obsession*, Black Inc., Melbourne, 2014; the various articles and blog posts on the 'Honest History' website <www.honesthistory.net.au/hp/category/centenary-watch>, viewed online 20 February 2019; and Brooker 2018.

7   A Laugesen, 'Word watch: Anzackery' *ANU Reporter* online, <www.anu.edu.au/news/all-news/word-watch-anzackery>, viewed online 20 February 2019; G Serle, 'Godzone 6: Austerica Unlimited?', *Meanjin Quarterly*, vol. 26, no. 3, 1967, pp. 237–50.

8   See the website <www.linkinteractive.com.au> where 'Fort Lytton at Night: A Lost Story of the Great War' features as a key example of the firm's work.

9   This and the following is drawn from an interview with Donnelly and de Plevitz, Brisbane, 15 February 2019, and with Queensland National Parks and Wildlife Service ranger Roland Dowling, 23 February 2019.

10 Queensland National Parks and Wildlife Service, 'Fort Lytton at Night – 01–16' unpublished typescript, p. 16.

11 Interview with D Donnelly and Z de Plevitz, Brisbane, 15 February 2019.

12 Disclosure: the author took a lead role in this project in the UQ School of Historical and Philosophical Inquiry, writing the original grant application and subsequently producing the November 2018 theatre production and its associated educational materials. The initial project team was Martin Crotty as Head of School, Rebecca Hurst as School Manager, and Geoff Ginn as Director of Engagement. As the incoming president of Brisbane theatre group the Queensland Shakespeare Ensemble, Hurst played a key role in developing the relationship with QSE and its creative director Rob Pensalfini.

13 Beaumont 2013, p. 223.

14 The prominent Brisbane playwright Errol O'Neill was originally engaged in late 2015 to undertake the commission, but sadly passed away in April 2016, after which time Futcher took up the project. *The Blood Votes* is dedicated to Errol O'Neill's memory.

15 For this and the following, see Michael Futcher's comments on his drafting process, captured on *The Australian Conscription Debates, 1916–17*, UQ School of Historical and Philosophical Inquiry website <www.hpi.uq.edu.au/australian-conscription-debate>.

16 A semi-fictional entity, created by the playwright based on a number of patriotic and pro-conscription associations.

17 Superbly documented in R Evans, '"All the Passion of Our Womanhood": M Thorp and the Battle of the Brisbane School of Arts', in J Damousi and M Lake (eds), *Gender and War: Australians at War in the Twentieth Century*, Cambridge University Press, Cambridge, 1995, pp. 239–53.

18 See Futcher's comment, <www.hpi.uq.edu.au/australian-conscription-debate>, viewed online 11 February 2019.

19 M Futcher, *The Blood Votes: A Historical Drama*, unpublished typescript 2018, p. 100, <www.hpi.uq.edu.au/australian-conscription-debate>, viewed online 10 February 2019.

16. **Remembering and forgetting the First World War at the Sir John Monash Centre**

1. B Scates, 'Colonising the Commemorative Landscape: The Villers-Bretonneux Project and Australian Interventions on the Western Front', in A Becker and S Tison (dir), *Un siècle de sites funéraires de la Grande Guerre. Enjeux d'une reconnaissance mondiale*, Presses de Paris Nanterre, Paris, 2018, pp. 107–45; see also R Fathi, *Our Corner of the Somme: Australia at Villers-Bretonneux*, Cambridge University Press, Cambridge, 2019. I am especially indebted to Rae Frances, Alistair Thomson and Jay Winter (who helped draft preliminary submissions on historical content for the museum) and Michael McKernan, Ross McMullin and Robin Prior who continued to advise government throughout the construction process. I make no claim to speak for any of these individuals. Thanks are also due to Piet Chielens, Annick Vanderbilke and Annette Becker, and to Rebecca Wheatley and Laura James, co-authors of *World War One: A History in 100 Stories*, Penguin, Melbourne, 2015.
2. Convergence Associates, Expression of Interest: Interpretative Design Consultancy Services, Western Front Interpretative Centre, 14 June 2014, p. 36.
3. Convergence Associates, Revised Tender Submission: Western Front Interpretive Centre Australian National Memorial, 2014, Villers-Bretonneux, France, p. 10.
4. Convergence, Revised Tender, p. 41.
5. J Winter, *Remembering War: The Great War Between Memory and History in the Twentieth Century*, Yale University Press, New Haven and London, 2006, pp. 223–36.
6. K Shelby, *Belgian Museums of the Great War: Politics, Memory and Commerce*, Routledge, New York, 2018.
7. J Beaumont, *Broken Nation: Australians in the Great War*, Allen & Unwin, Sydney, p. 518. A larger *Allied* effort might be a more appropriate way to put this. Interestingly the role of French forces, including their contribution to key actions at Villers-Bretonneux, is displaced by this nationalist narrative.
8. Convergence Associates, 'The Visitor Journey-SJMC', outline kindly provided by Jenni Klempfner.
9. R Frances, B Scates and A Thomson, 'Australian Western Front Memorial Centre: Theme Ideas', notes submitted to Convergence, 19 August 2014.
10. Convergence 2014, p. 39.
11. Correspondence cited in Scates 2018, p. 142; again, this runs counter to the Interpretive Centre's original guidelines. The 'divisions that arose from the conscription referenda' and the 'treatment of German born Australians' were identified as 'key focus questions' in the government's specifications for tender, Department of Veterans' Affairs, 'Western Front Interpretive Centre', guidelines circulated to tenderers, 2014.
12. J Winter, 'Museums and the Representation of War', in W Muchitsch (ed.), *Does War Belong in Museums: The Representations of Violence in Exhibitions*, Transcript Verlag, Bielefeld, 2013, p. 29.
13. J Winter, 'Designing a War Museum: Some Reflections on Representations of War and Combat', in E Anderson, A Maddrell, K McLoughlin and A Vincent (eds), *Memory Mourning Landscape*, Rodopi, Amsterdam, 2010.
14. B Scates, *Return to Gallipoli: Walking the Battlefields of the Great War*, Cambridge University Press, Cambridge, 2006, pp. 55–56. See also J Winter, *War Beyond Words: Languages of Remembrance from the Great War to the Present*, Cambridge, Cambridge University Press, 2017, chapter 6.

15 Convergence Associates, 'Western Front Interpretive Centre, Villers-Bretonneux, Master Interpretive Schedule, Revision A', 15 December 2014, pp. 13–14.
16 Winter 2010, p. 1.
17 Winter 2013, p. 37.
18 Winter 2006, p. 232.
19 I McCalman and P Pickering (eds), *Historical Reenactment: From Realism to the Affective Turn,* Palgrave Macmillan, Basingstoke, 2010, pp. 1–17.
20 Convergence 2014, p. 35.
21 J de Groot, 'Affect and Empathy: Re-enactment and Performance as/in History', *Rethinking History,* vol. 15, no. 4, p. 599.
22 Winter 2013, p. 34.
23 J Beaumont, 'Remembering the Heroes of Australia's Wars: From Heroic to Post Heroic Memory', in S Scheipers (ed.), *Heroism and the Changing Character of War: Towards Post Heroic Warfare,* Palgrave Macmillan, Basingstoke, 2014, pp. 344–46; also C Twoomey, 'Trauma and the Reinvigoration of Anzac: An Argument', *History Australia,* vol. 10, no. 3, 2013, pp. 85–105; B Scates, R Wheatley and L James, *World War One: A History in 100 Stories,* Penguin, Melbourne, 2015, pp. vii–viii.
24 V Agnew, 'History's Affective Turn: Historical Reenactment and its Work in the Present', *Rethinking History,* vol. 11, no. 3, 2007, pp. 299–312.
25 Convergence, 'The Visitor Journey'; 'Revised Tender Submission', Master Interpretive Schedule, p. 19.
26 Conversation with Jay Winter, Canberra, November 2018.
27 Winter 2013, pp. 33–34.
28 Winter 2013, p. 1.
29 Winter 2013, pp. 1, 5.
30 Minutes of initial meeting between Convergence Associates, DVA and historical advisers, 16 December 2014, Monash University. The official DVA website maintains this commitment to 'quiet pride'. A 'touch of sorrow' has been reconfigured as 'deep sorrow for a [single] nation's grief', <www.dva.gov.au/commemorations-memorials-and-war-graves/office-australian-war-graves/current-projects/sir-john-2>, viewed online 6 June 2017.
31 Herbert Baker to Violet Milner, 14 November 19(38?), Violet Milner Papers, Box 58, Bodleian Library, University of Oxford.
32 'Hearts Broken for What', in Scates, Wheatley and James 2015, pp. 149–50.
33 B Scates, 'The Forgotten Sock Knitter: Voluntary Work, Emotional Labour, Bereavement and the Great War', *Labour History,* vol. 81, pp. 113–18.
34 'A Guardian Angel of the Anzacs: Ettie Rout', in Scates, Wheatley and James 2015, pp. 71–73; Ettie Rout Papers, Archives New Zealand/Te Rua Mahara o te Kāwanatanga Wellington, WA107 ZMR1/1/43.
35 Cited in Scates 2018, p. 141.
36 Statement by Driver Bollan, 26 March 1920; Findings of Fact, Court of Inquiry into the Graves Detachment at Villers-Bretonneux, NAA: MP376/1, 446/10/1840.
37 'Captain Charlie's Boozer: Charlie Kingston', in Scates, Wheatley and James 2015, pp. 115–18.
38 The epitaph appears on a screen in the final commemorative gallery. It is visible for a few seconds and its concerns are not addressed.
39 Winter 2010, pp. 17–36; H Brondender, *Presenting the Unpresentable: Renewed Presentations in Museums of Military History,* Legermuseum, Delft, 2003. See also

Becker, 'Museums, Architects and Artists on the Western Front: New Commemoration for a New History?', in *Remembering the First World War*, B Ziino (ed.), Routledge, Abingdon, 2015, pp. 86–103; and R Fathi, 'Look at Me! Look at me! The Sir John Monash Centre at Villers-Bretonneux: A Frenchman's Reflection on his visit', Honest History, <http://honesthistory.net.au/wp/fathi-romain-look-at-me-look-at-me-the-sir-john-monash-centre-at-villers-bretonneux-a-frenchmans-reflection-on-his-visit>, viewed online 15 July 2019.

17. Remembrance Day: The poor cousin of Australian war commemoration

1. B Scates, *A Place to Remember: A History of the Shrine of Remembrance*, Cambridge University Press, Melbourne, 2009, p. 135.
2. The chapter refers to 11 November 1918 as 'Armistice Day' from 1918 & 1946, and as 'Remembrance Day' thereafter. The name had already started to switch from Armistice Day to Remembrance Day in the mid-1920s, and by the 1930s and 1940s most people referred to the day as Remembrance Day. The focus was no longer on the Armistice itself and the end of the war; it became a day to grieve and honour those who had died, to remember them.
3. 'Rejoicings in Australia', *Age*, 12 November 1918, p. 5.
4. A Prost, 'Le patriotique pacifisme des anciens combattants' in A Prost (ed.), *Les anciens combattants et la société française 1914–1939*, Presses de Sciences Po, Paris, 1977, pp. 77–119.
5. C Donaldson and M Lake, 'Whatever Happened to the Anti-war Movement?', in M Lake, H Reynolds, M McKenna and J Damousi, *What's Wrong with Anzac? The Militarisation of Australian History*, NewSouth, Sydney, 2010, p. 77.
6. 'Desire for Lasting Peace', *The Age*, 12 November 1928, p. 10.
7. Minutes of meeting of Full Cabinet held at 2.30 pm, Monday, 25th March 1946, at Parliament House, Canberra in NAA A2703, 124, p. 3.
8. 'Remembrance Sunday', *Brisbane Telegraph*, 6 October 1953.
9. K Inglis, *Sacred Places: War Memorials in the Australian Landscape*, Melbourne University Press, Melbourne, 2008, p. 407.
10. J Beaumont, 'Commemoration in Australia: A Memory Orgy?', *Australian Journal of Political Science*, vol. 50, no. 3, 2015, pp. 536–44.
11. 'Anzac Day 2015: Dawn Services around Australia', *Sydney Morning Herald*, 25 April 2015 and 'Remembrance Day 2018: Canberra Pauses to Honour the Sacrifice', *Canberra Times*, 11 November 2018.
12. M Crotty, '25 April 1915: Australian Troops Land at Gallipoli: Trial, Trauma and the "Birth of the Nation"', in M Crotty and DA Roberts (eds), *Turning Points in Australian History*, UNSW Press, Sydney, 2009, pp. 100–14.
13. Inglis 2008, p. 4.
14. Inglis 2008, p. 230.
15. A Gregory, *The Silence of Memory: Armistice Day 1919–1946*, Berg, Oxford, 1994, p. 225.
16. J Winter and E Sivan, *War and Remembrance in the Twentieth Century*, Cambridge University Press, New York, 1999, p. 16.
17. DX Powell, 'Remembrance Day. Memories and Values in Australia since 1918', *Victorian Historical Journal*, vol. 75, no. 2, 2004, p. 167.

18. What is wrong with Anzac?

1. See, for instance, R Ward, *Australia*, Horwitz, Sydney 1965; RM Crawford, *Australia*, Hutchinson, London, 1952; CMH Clark, *A Short History of Australia*, Mentor, New York, 1963; AGL Shaw, *The Story of Australia*, Faber, London, 1955; D Pike, *Australia: The Quiet Continent*, Cambridge University Press, Cambridge, 1962; G Greenwood (ed.), *Australia: A Social and Political History*, Angus & Robertson, Sydney, 1955.
2. K Windschuttle, *The Fabrication of Australian History*, Macleay Press, Sydney, 2002. See the scholarly riposte, R Manne (ed.), *Whitewash: On Keith Windschuttle's Fabrication of Aboriginal History*, Black Inc Agenda, Melbourne, 2003.
3. M Lake, 'The Howard History of Australia', *The Age*, 20 August 2005.
4. *Pearls and Irritations*, 23 April 2014, <johnmenadue.com/marilyn-lake-fracturing-the-nations-soul-2>, viewed online 21 February 2019.

19. Honest History: Lessons in the politics of history

1. D Stephens, 'When a Motley Crew of Canberra Stirrers Protected the War Memorial from Competition', Honest History, 11 November 2016, <honesthistory.net.au/wp/when-a-motley-crew-of-canberra-stirrers-protected-the-war-memorial-from-competition/>, viewed online 12 February 2019.
2. D Stephens, 'Should We Softpedal on Gallipoli?' Honest History, 4 February 2014, <honesthistory.net.au/wp/should-we-softpedal-on-gallipoli/>, viewed online 12 February 2019.
3. EH Carr, *What is History?* Penguin, Harmondsworth, new edn, 1978, p. 23.
4. D Watson, 'Enemy Within: American Politics in the Time of Trump', *Quarterly Essay* no. 63, September 2016, p. 61.
5. P Cochrane, 'The Past Is Not Sacred: The "History Wars" Over Anzac', The Conversation, 25 April 2015, <theconversation.com/the-past-is-not-sacred-the-history-wars-over-anzac-38596>, viewed online 12 February 2019.
6. G Henderson, Gerard Henderson's Media Watch Dog, issue no. 435, 7 December 2018, <thesydneyinstitute.com.au/blog/issue-435/>, viewed online 12 February 2019.
7. 'Talking Turkey', Honest History, <honesthistory.net.au/wp/talking-turkey/>, viewed online 12 February 2019.
8. D Stephens, 'Total Australian Spending on World War I Centenary: An Aide Memoire for the Curious', Honest History, 19 February 2019, <honesthistory.net.au/wp/stephens-david-total-australian-spending-on-world-war-i-centenary-an-aide-memoire-for-the-curious/>, viewed online 27 May 2019.
9. D Stephens, 'Faulty Abacus? DVA and the Cost of Commemoration', Honest History, 30 November 2017, <honesthistory.net.au/wp/stephens-david-faulty-abacus-dva-and-the-cost-of-commemoration/>, viewed online 12 February 2019.
10. D Stephens, 'Paradoxical Purchase: War Memorial Acquires APY "Defence Of Country" Painting Kulatangku Angakanyini Manta Munu Tjukurpa', Honest History, 17 November 2017, <honesthistory.net.au/wp/paradoxical-purchase-war-memorial-acquires-apy-defence-of-country-painting-kulatangku-angakanyini-manta-munu-tjukurpa/>, viewed online 23 February 2019.
11. D Ashenden, 'Saving the War Memorial from Itself', Inside Story, 15 January 2019, <insidestory.org.au/saving-the-war-memorial-from-itself/>, viewed online 12 February 2019.
12. Military History Society of New South Wales, Twitter, 16 January 2019, <twitter.com/MHS_NSW>, viewed online 12 February 2019.

13 L Behrendt, 'Settlement or Invasion? The Coloniser's Quandary', in D Stephens and A Broinowski (eds), *The Honest History Book*, NewSouth, Sydney, 2017, pp. 238–39.

14 N Dyrenfurth, 'Labor and the Anzac Legend, 1915–45', *Labour History*, no. 106, May 2014, pp. 163–88, <search.informit.com.au/documentSummary;dn=380550988612084;res=IELHSS;subject=Music>, viewed online 24 March 2019.

15 Power, 'Outrage as Lone Pine Ceremony at Gallipoli Axed', *Sydney Morning Herald*, 16 February 2016, <www.smh.com.au/national/outrage-as-lone-pine-ceremony-at-gallipoli-axed-20160213-gmt8ba.html>; Shorten, 'Bill Shorten: Giving John Monash the Ultimate Honour Is Long Overdue', *Sydney Morning Herald*, 18 April 2018, <www.smh.com.au/politics/federal/bill-shorten-giving-john-monash-the-ultimate-honour-is-long-overdue-20180418-p4zacs.html>;
A Rishworth, 'Address to Australian War Memorial Development Launch, Thursday, 1 November 2018', Amanda Rishworth MP, <www.rishworth.com.au/news/portfolio-media-releases/1203-speech-address-to-australian-war-memorial-development-launch-thursday-1-november-2018.html>. All websites viewed online 14 February 2019.

16 Department of Education, Queensland, 'Anzac and Education', <education.qld.gov.au/about-us/events-awards/events/anzac-and-education>, viewed online 27 May 2019; Department of Education, Victoria, 'ANZAC Centenary Commemoration', <www.education.vic.gov.au/school/teachers/teachingresources/discipline/humanities/history/Pages/anzac.aspx>, viewed online 27 May 2019.

17 H Mackay, email to author, 4 February 2019.

18 D Stephens, 'Ministers Tell Future Generations: There Will Be Blood, Your Blood', *Sydney Morning Herald*, 9 September 2015, <www.smh.com.au/opinion/ministers-tell-future-generations-there-will-be-blood-your-blood-20150908-gjhwhd.html>, viewed online 12 February 2019.

19 '[I]n the Australian War Memorial conceived in blood they shed for one another, for us and the ideals of mankind': B Nelson, 'Address to the National Press Club: We're All Australians Now: 1918 and the War that Changed Us', 19 September 2018, <www.awm.gov.au/commemoration/speeches/AllAustraliansNow>, viewed online 19 February 2019.

20 F Bongiorno, quoted in Cochrane 2015.

21 P Daley, 'Why Australia Day and Anzac Day Helped Create a National "Cult of Forgetfulness"', *Guardian*, 16 October 2016, <www.theguardian.com/australia-news/postcolonial-blog/2016/oct/16/why-australia-day-and-anzac-day-helped-create-a-national-cult-of-forgetfulness>, viewed online 12 February 2019.

22 M Weber, 'Politics as a Vocation [1919]', <anthropos-lab.net/wp/wp-content/uploads/2011/12/Weber-Politics-as-a-Vocation.pdf>, p. 27, viewed online 12 February 2019.

23 C Kininmonth, 'Dr Brendan Nelson: To Lead People You Have to Know Their Story (A Conversation with Dr Brendan Nelson, Director of the Australian War Memorial)', The Growth Faculty, 7 November 2018, <www.thegrowthfaculty.com/blog/DrBrendanNelsonToleadpeoplehavetoknowyourstory>, viewed online 12 February 2019.

20. Making sense of the Great War centenary

1. J Burke, 'Patriotic Drama: Arts Undaunted by Anzac Fatigue', *Australian*, 18 April 2015, <www.theaustralian.com.au/arts/review/patriotic-drama-arts-undaunted-by-anzac-fatigue/news-story/7ba4d886fca56c9f7c25128db8b396c5>, viewed online 16 February 2019.
2. A Sharp, 'Gallipoli a Big Defeat for Channel 9 with David Gyngell Calling it "Disappointment of the Year"', *Daily Telegraph*, 27 February 2015, <www.dailytelegraph.com.au/entertainment/sydney-confidential/gallipoli-a-big-defeat-for-channel-9-with-david-gyngell-calling-it-disappointment-of-the-year/news-story/7c10c63190c0eb6c8b2711f9f1a7a6bb>, viewed online 16 February 2019.
3. 'Woolworths Apologises over Anzac "Fresh in our Memories" Website', 15 April 2015, *The Australian*, <www.theaustralian.com.au/business/media/woolworths-apologises-over-anzac-fresh-in-our-memories-website/news-story/8b559732955cc5bfd256105b4976c631>, viewed online 7 April 2019; F Chung, 'Gruen Transfer Panellists Review Woolies' "Fresh in Our Memories" Anzac Campaign', news.com.au, 15 April 2015, <www.news.com.au/finance/business/retail/gruen-transfer-panellists-review-woolies-fresh-in-our-memories-anzac-campaign/news-story/221fed33040e7e9169c057816b99477c>, viewed online 18 February 2019.
4. K Aubusson, 'Woolworths Anzac Campaign Hijacked by Internet Memes', *Sydney Morning Herald*, 15 April 2015, <www.smh.com.au/national/woolworths-anzac-campaign-hijacked-by-internet-memes-20150414-1ml4gt.html>, viewed online 19 February 2019.
5. J Hawkins, *Consuming Anzac: The History of Australia's Most Powerful Brand*, UWA Publishing, Perth, 2018, p. 127.
6. C Zielinski, 'Target Has Pulled Three Camp Gallipoli Products from Sale Following a Government Crackdown on the Use of the Word "Anzac"', news.com.au, 18 April 2015, <www.news.com.au/national/anzac-day/target-has-pulled-three-camp-gallipoli-products-from-sale-following-a-government-crackdown-on-the-use-of-the-word-anzac/news-story/669984e96ef3052aaf8a0bb45d2a145e>, viewed online 5 April 2019.
7. C Vedelago and C Houston, 'Camp Gallipoli Stripped of Charity Status Following ACNC Investigation', *Sydney Morning Herald*, 23 April 2016, <www.smh.com.au/national/camp-gallipoli-stripped-of-charity-status-following-acnc-investigation-20161223-gth2vm.html>, viewed online 5 April 2019.
8. 'Viewers' "Fatigue" of Gallipoli Retellings', *Daily Mail*, 3 March 2015, <www.dailymail.co.uk/wires/aap/article-2976812/Viewers-fatigue-Gallipoli-retellings.html>, viewed online 5 April 2019.
9. J Valentine, 'Gallipoli: The Story We All Grew Up With', *Sydney Morning Herald*, 21 April 2015, <www.smh.com.au/opinion/gallipoli-the-story-we-all-grew-up-with-20150421-1mpsew.html>, viewed online 4 April 2019.
10. A Matthews and N Grimm, '"Gallipoli fatigue" Causes Poor Ratings for WWI TV Shows as War Weary Australians Switch Off', ABC News, 24 April 2015, <www.abc.net.au/news/2015-04-22/gallipoli-fatigue-poor-ratings-for-wwi-tv-shows/6413536>, viewed online 4 April 2019.
11. 'TVs Fads and Follies of 2015', *Sydney Morning Herald*, 24 November 2015, <www.smh.com.au/entertainment/tv-and-radio/tvs-fads-and-follies-of-2015-20151123-gl5wb6.html>, viewed online 4 April 2019.
12. Matthews and Grimm 2015.

13 'Anzac Day 2015: Record Crowd of 120,000 Attend Dawn Service, 31,000 Attend National Service and March in Canberra', ABC News, 26 April 2015, <www.abc.net.au/news/2015-04-25/record-crowd-of-120,000-people-attend-dawn-service-in-canberra/6420536>, viewed online 5 April 2019.
14 Hawkins 2018, p. 127; 'Anzac Day 2015: Tens of Thousands Gather in WA to Remember Lives Lost in WWI', 25 April 2015, <www.abc.net.au/news/2015-04-25/anzac-day-kings-park-dawn-service/6415694>, viewed online 5 April 2019.
15 'SBS Presenter Scott McIntyre Sacked Over "Inappropriate" Anzac Day Tweets', 26 April 2015, *Sydney Morning Herald*, <www.smh.com.au/national/sbs-presenter-scott-mcintyre-sacked-over-inappropriate-anzac-day-tweets-20150426-1mtbx8.html>, viewed online 8 April 2019.
16 'Outspoken Muslim Presenter Slammed for Being Un-Australian', 27 April 2017, *Startsat60.com*, <startsat60.com/discover/news/muslim-activist-labels-treatment-over-anzac-day-tweet-unfair>, viewed online 7 April 2019; 'Yassmin Abdel-Magied on Becoming "Australia's Most Publicly Hated Muslim"', *Sydney Morning Herald*, 18 August 2017, <www.smh.com.au/lifestyle/yassmin-abdelmagied-on-becoming-australias-most-publicly-hated-muslim-20170816-gxxb7d.html>, viewed online 7 April 2019.
17 'The Anzac Post, Outrage and a Debate About Race', BBC News, 10 August 2017, <www.bbc.com/news/world-australia-40712832>, viewed online 7 April 2019.
18 K Inglis, in J Lack (ed.), *Anzac Remembering: Selected Writings by KS Inglis*, Department of History, University of Melbourne, Melbourne, 1998, p. 3.
19 *Canberra Times*, 13 April 1965, p. 3.
20 'Can Anzac Day Survive? Fifty Years after Gallipoli a Panel Debates', *Sydney Morning Herald*, 17 April 1965.
21 C Holbrook, *Anzac: The Unauthorised Biography*, NewSouth, Sydney, 2010, pp. 173–79.
22 D Stephens, 'Why Is Australia Spending so Much More on the Great War Centenary than Any Other Country?', *Pearls and Irritations*, 20 June 2015, <johnmenadue.com/david-stephens-why-is-australia-spending-so-much-more-on-the-great-war-centenary-than-any-other-country/>, viewed online 7 April 2019.
23 C Holbrook, 'Anzac Offers a New Way to Join Team Australia', *The Age*, 19 April 2016, <www.smh.com.au/opinion/anzac-season-turning-war-memory-into-a-nationalist-festival-is-wrong-20160418-go8uhe.html>, viewed online 5 April 2019.

CONTRIBUTORS

Kathryn Avery

Kathryn Avery is a PhD candidate in the Collaborative Research Centre in Australian History at Federation University Australia. Her PhD thesis focuses on the Australian government's anxieties over Japanese influence in Portuguese Timor prior to the outbreak of the Pacific War. Kathryn's broad research interest is Australian foreign policy history, with a particular focus on Australian-Japanese and Australian-British relations. Kathryn teaches in the School of Arts at Federation University Australia.

Joan Beaumont

Joan Beaumont is Professor Emerita in the Strategic and Defence Studies Centre, Coral Bell School of Asia Pacific Affairs, Australian National University. Her publications include the jointly edited *Serving Our Country: Indigenous Australians, War, Defence and Citizenship* (2018) and *Broken Nation: Australians in the Great War* (2013). *Broken Nation* was 2014 winner of the Prime Minister's Literary Award (Australian History), the 2014 NSW Premier's Prize (Australian History), the 2014 Queensland Literary Award for History, and the Australian Society of Authors' 2015 Asher Award. She is currently writing a history of Australians in the aftermath of World War I and during the Great Depression.

Anne Beggs-Sunter

Anne Beggs-Sunter is a historian in the Collaborative Research Centre in Australian History at the Ballarat campus of Federation University. Her major interests are in Australian social, cultural and political history. Her special interests relate to Ballarat and its heritage conservation, the significance of the Eureka Stockade and the Irish in Australia.

Frank Bongiorno

Frank Bongiorno is Professor of History and Head of the School of History at the Australian National University. His most recent book, edited with Benjamin T Jones and John Uhr, is *Elections Matter: Ten Federal Elections That Shaped Australia (2018)*. His other books include *The Eighties: The Decade That Transformed Australia (2015)* and *The Sex Lives of Australians: A History* (2012). He is a Fellow of the Academy of Social Sciences in Australia.

Martin Crotty

Martin Crotty studied History at undergraduate level in New Zealand before taking on postgraduate studies in Australia at Monash University and the University of Melbourne. He has since worked as a historian at the University of Newcastle and at the University of Queensland. His research interests have evolved through sports history, masculinity, the RSL and the treatment of veterans. He has authored or co-edited five monographs or edited collections as well as numerous book articles and chapters. He is currently completing a co-authored study into veteran policy globally, and is embarking on a new project regarding Australian soldiers sentenced to death in the First World War.

Honae Cuffe

Honae Cuffe is a PhD candidate at the School of Humanities and Social Science, University of Newcastle. Her research is on the Australian foreign policy tradition from the interwar period until the early Cold War, with a particular focus on the peculiarities of Australia's cultural heritage and regional reality and the subsequent efforts to integrate these divergent national interests within the changing Asia-Pacific order. Her recent publications on Australian foreign and defence policy in the interwar period include articles in *History Australia* and the *Flinders Journal of History and Politics*.

Romain Fathi

Romain Fathi is a Lecturer in History at the College of Humanities, Arts and Social Sciences at Flinders University in Adelaide and an Affiliated Researcher at the Centre d'Histoire de Sciences Po in Paris. His research interests are concerned with war commemorations, the First World War and Australian war memorialisation in Northern France. Dr Fathi publishes in French and English and has taught at several universities, including Sciences Po in France, Yale in the United States, and the University of Queensland. His book *Our Corner of the Somme. Australia at Villers-Bretonneux* was published in 2019.

Geoffrey AC Ginn

Geoffrey AC Ginn is a historian at the University of Queensland, with teaching and research interests in nineteenth century social policy, colonialism, urban history, public history, museums and cultural heritage. His book *Culture, Philanthropy and the Poor in Late-Victorian London* was published in 2017, with a paperback edition scheduled for 2019. His earlier biography of the quirky antiquarian, museums pioneer and mystic JSM Ward, *Archangels and Archaeology: JSM Ward's Kingdom of the Wise* appeared in 2012. Geoff has been a member of the Board of the Queensland Museum (2008–13, 2017–present), a member of Australian Dictionary of Biography Editorial Board and a judge in the Queensland Literary Awards. He is presently developing a monograph on the intimate politics of the Edwardian 'New Liberals' and a major digital humanities project examining religious and social experience in Queensland's past and present.

Meleah Hampton

Meleah Hampton is a historian in the Military History Section at the Australian War Memorial, where she has worked since March 2013. She is a graduate of the University of Adelaide and completed her PhD with a thesis on the 1916 battles for Pozières and Mouquet Farm. Her primary interest is in the operational conduct of the First World War on the Western Front. She is the author of *Attack on the Somme: 1st Anzac Corps and the Battle of Pozieres Ridge, 1916* (2016) and numerous book chapters and articles.

Carolyn Holbrook

Carolyn Holbrook is an Australian Research Council DECRA Fellow in the Contemporary Histories Research Group at Deakin University, and Director of the Australian Policy and History network. She is the author of *Anzac: The Unauthorised Biography* (2014). Her current research examines the history of attitudes to the Australian federation since 1901. She is also co-authoring with James Walter a history of political decision-making in Australia.

Margaret Hutchison

Margaret Hutchison is a lecturer in History in the School of Arts at the Australian Catholic University, Brisbane. Her research focuses on the history of war, culture and memory. She is the author of *Painting War: A History of Australia's First World War Art Scheme*, published in 2018. She is co-editor of a collection of essays, *Portraits of Remembrance: Painting, Memory and the First World War*, to be published in 2019.

Marilyn Lake

Marilyn Lake DLitt AO is Professorial Fellow in History at the University of Melbourne. She has published several books, journal articles and book chapters on the impact of the First World War on Australian society, including *The Limits of Hope: Soldier Settlement in Victoria*

1915–38 (1987). Her most recent book is *Progressive New World: How Settler Colonialism and TransPacific Exchange Shaped American Reform*, published in 2019. A volume of essays in her honour, *Contesting Australian History*, edited by Joy Damousi and Judy Smart, was also published in 2019. Professor Lake is a Fellow of both the Academies of Humanities and Social Sciences in Australia and former President of the Australian Historical Association.

David McGinniss

David McGinniss is a PhD student at the Collaborative Research Centre in Australian History at Federation University Australia, based in Ballarat, Victoria. His research focusses on institutional and cultural histories in the social services sector, particularly Children's Homes and Orphanages. David has worked for two decades in Commonwealth, State and Local government and the community sector, and is particularly interested in developing the role of historical inquiry, memory and commemoration in enhancing community and government services.

Keir Reeves

Keir Reeves is a professor of history at Federation University Australia and is the foundation director of the Collaborative Research Centre in Australian History. His previous teaching and research positions have been at the University of Melbourne where he was an Australian Research Council Post-doctoral Fellow and Monash University. His research concentrates on cultural heritage, public history, Australian history as well as tourism and travel. Keir has held fellowships at King's College London and Clare Hall Cambridge and is a 2019 visiting professorial fellow at Utrecht University. He was a contributing author to *Anzac Journeys: Returning to the Battlefields of World War Two (2013)*, which was shortlisted for the 2014 Ernest Scott Prize.

Henry Reynolds

Henry Reynolds has published twenty books and more than sixty journal articles and book chapters. Among his most influential books are *The Other Side of the Frontier*; *The Law of the Land*; *This Whispering in Our Hearts*; *Fate of a Free People*; *Why Weren't We Told?*; *North of Capricorn*; *Forgotten War*, which won the Victorian Premier's Literary Award for non-fiction in 2014; *Drawing the Global Colour Line*, co-authored with Marilyn Lake; and *Unnecessary Wars*. He was a co-author of *What's Wrong with Anzac?*, published in 2010. Henry is an Honorary Research Professor at the University of Tasmania.

Thomas Rogers

Thomas Rogers is a historian in the Military History Section at the Australian War Memorial, where he researches colonial Australian history, the South African (Boer) War, and the First World War. His research interests include colonial Australian and British Empire history, Indigenous history, frontier violence, and military and political history. Tom is the author of *The Civilisation of Port Phillip: Settler Ideology, Violence, and Rhetorical Possession* (2018), which considers the early years of British settlement in the state of Victoria, and the relationships between settler rhetoric and frontier violence.

Bruce Scates

Professor Bruce Scates FASSA is based in the School of History at the Australian National University. He is the author or lead author of several books on war and memory, including *Return to Gallipoli*; *A Place to Remember*; *Anzac Journeys*; *The Last Battle*; and *World War One: A History in 100 Stories*. His imagined history of Gallipoli, *On Dangerous Ground*, retraces the search for the 'Missing' and considers the politics of remembrance. He served as the Chair of the Military and Cultural History panel advising the Anzac Centenary

Board and leads the 100 Stories project at the ANU. Bruce advised government on the shape and content of the Sir John Monash Centre at Villers-Bretonneaux.

David Stephens

David Stephens is the editor of the Honest History website (honesthistory.net.au) and was secretary of the Honest History coalition 2013–19. He has postgraduate degrees from Monash University and the Australian National University, and has published a number of articles, many of them on the Honest History website, and a novel. With Alison Broinowski, he co-edited *The Honest History Book* (2017). During the Vietnam War he was a conscientious objector and National Service Act defaulter. He was an Australian public servant for nearly 20 years, then a consultant and lobbyist. From 2010 to 2012 he campaigned against the construction of war memorials that would have competed with the Australian War Memorial, but in 2018–19 he has campaigned against the proposed extensions to the Memorial.

David Sutton

David Sutton is a historian in the Military History Section at the Australian War Memorial in Canberra, where he researches the interwar period, the Second World War, and Australian peacekeeping and humanitarian operations. Before joining the Memorial, he taught twentieth-century world history and completed his PhD at the University of Wollongong. His thesis was a historiographical examination of English and Russian language histories of Operation Barbarossa, Hitler's invasion of the Soviet Union in 1941.

Richard Trembath

Richard Trembath is a Senior Honorary Research Fellow at Federation University Australia. A historian, he has taught in several

Victorian universities and regards teaching as both a pleasure and a privilege. He has written books and articles on various aspects of Australian military and social history, the most recent of which was *Defending Country: Aboriginal and Torres Strait Islander Military Service Since 1945* (with Noah Riseman), which was published in 2016. Currently, he is researching the rise of complementary medicine in Australia, its relationship with orthodox medicine and its status within the health system. Richard would also like to write a biography of the Australian musician, Margaret Sutherland, whom he thinks has not yet received sufficient acknowledgment as a modernist composer.

Bart Ziino

Bart Ziino is Senior Lecturer in history at Deakin University. He has published widely on the politics of commemoration and on private experiences of the First World War. He is author of *Australians, War Graves and the Great War* (2007) and editor of *Remembering the First World War* (2015). He is currently writing a history of private sentiment in Australia during the First World War.

INDEX

Abbott, Tony 219
Abdel-Magied, Yassmin 249
Aboriginal Australians *see* Indigenous Australians
Adam-Smith, Patsy 3, 251
Advocate (Melbourne) 22, 28
Age (Melbourne) 34
Agnew, Vanessa 200
AIF *see* Australian Infantry Force
All Hallows College, Dublin 22
ALP *see* Australian Labor Party
anxiety 33–34, 37–38, 40
Anzac
 alternatives to military narrative 15, 32–33, 42–44, 180–82, 232–33, 250–52, 253
 'Anzackery' 17, 232–33, 235–37, 241–43
 as 'birth of a nation' 91, 96–98, 220–22, 224, 229–30
 commercialisation of 5, 8, 18, 245–47
 as faith 6, 18, 240–41, 249–50, 253
 forces 12, 91, 94, 96
 and historical erasure 12–13, 91–92, 94, 238–39, 253
 historiography of 2–3, 5–10, 17–18, 179–81, 224–27
 and national sentiment 1–4, 251–53
 omission of Indigenous soldiers 13, 114
 privilege of battlefront experience 6–7, 15, 33, 176–78, 180–81, 195–97, 226–30
 see also Anzac Day; centenary commemorations; Gallipoli
Anzac Day
 comparison to Remembrance Day 212, 219–23
 dawn services 4–5, 6, 219, 248, 252, 253
 and national identity 227–28, 230, 250
 popularity of 2, 6–8, 167, 218, 219, 246–53
 see also centenary commemorations
Anzac Girls 244
The Anzacs 3
arbitration, industrial 92, 93, 97
Archdale, Betty 250–51
Argus (Melbourne) 122, 171
Ariotti, Kate 152
Armistice
 anticipation of 34–35
 and civilian experience of war 33–34, 42–44
 and mourning 32, 37, 40–41
 political reaction to 11, 35–39, 41, 76–77
 public reaction to 11, 34–36, 39–42, 212–14
 see also Armistice Day; repatriation
Armistice Day 212–16, 276n2
 see also Remembrance Day
art *see* war art schemes
artistic representations
 film and television 17–18, 244–45, 246–47, 252–53

 museum exhibits 150–51, 194–202
 novels 61, 101
 paintings 167–69, 175–78
 plays 15, 182–85, 188–92, 251
Ashenden, Dean 238
Australasia 12–13, 92–99, 262n4
Australia
 as colonial power 12, 75–78, 79, 81–82, 84, 88
 Department of External Affairs 156–58
 Department of Repatriation 114
 Department of Veterans Affairs 8, 196, 201–202, 226, 246
 national security 76–77, 79–88, 158–59, 260n2
 as part of British Empire 3, 104, 161
 relationship with Japan 79–81, 84–86, 121, 158, 260n2
 and United Nations 160–63
 see also Federal Government; imperialism; nationalism; state governments; individual states by name
Australian Aborigines' League 109
Australian Army Medical Corps (AAMC) 73
Australian High Commission 168–69
Australian Infantry Force
 as Anzacs 12, 91, 94, 96
 composition 21, 102, 113
 engagements 126–28, 137–39, 151, 155, 177–78
 over-representation in official accounts 177, 195
 war artists 168–69, 171, 176–77
 see also repatriation; veterans
Australian Labor Party
 and conscription 103
 impact of war on 3, 100, 228–29
 party politics 104, 110–11
 stance on Anzac 16, 239–40
Australian War Memorial
 centenary expansion of 16, 18, 182, 226
 exhibitions at 150–51, 180
 and frontier violence 237–38
 function of 233
 records collection 167
 Unknown Soldier 218
Australian War Records Section 169
Australian Women's Weekly 43

Baker, Herbert 202
Ballarat Star 29
Barker, Tom 197
Bartlett, Ellis Ashmead 96
Bates, Helen Page 95
Bean, Charles EW 96, 168–69, 177–78, 179–80
Beaumont, Jean 181, 187, 195
Beaverbrook, Lord 170, 173
Beazley, Kim 1

289

Bedford, Stuart 72
Behrendt, Larissa 239
Bell, George 176
Bennet, Arnold 175
Benson, George 176
Bird, David 156
Black, George 40–41
Blackburn, Maurice 111
The Blood Votes 15, 182, 188–89, 192
Bogomolov, Alexander 161
Bollard, Robert 101–102
Bolton, William 98, 102
Bongiorno, Frank 242
Boote, Mary 42
Brayley, Jack 74
Brereton, John le Gay 39
Briscoe, Billy 132
Britain
    Australian troops in 50–56
    commemorations 214–16, 222
    foreign affairs 80–81, 85–87, 158–59
    imperial ties to Australia 3–4, 36–37, 76, 96–98, 252–53
    and Irish Home Rule 25, 28–30
    and Pacific colonies 70–71, 74–75, 77, 85–87
    treatment of veterans 63–64, 66
    war art scheme 172, 175
    see also imperialism
The Broken Years 2, 251, 262n4
Brooker, Ben 181, 182
Brooks, Frederick 128–29
Brown, James 181
Bruce, Stanley 102–103, 106, 109–10, 158
Bryant, Charles 176
Bullard, Steven 75

Camp Gallipoli 246
Canada
    treatment of veterans 64
    troops from 46, 52, 53–54
    war art scheme 170, 172, 173, 175, 177
Canberra
    Anzac celebrations in 220
    memorials 233–34
    see also Australian War Memorial
Carmichael, Campbell 103–104
Carr, EH 234
Carson, Edmund 25, 30
Casey, Richard 158
Cassin, Réne 161
Catholics
    and conscription 10, 23, 187, 228
    in politics 104, 111
    sectarianism 10, 22–23, 31, 104, 228
    support for Irish Home Rule 22, 24
centenary commemorations
    celebrations 219–20, 246–47
    challenges to dominant narratives 181–82, 186–88, 234, 242–43, 248–49
    commercialisation of 245–46
    expansion of War Memorial 16, 18, 182, 226

expenditure on 16, 18, 167, 193, 237, 252
historiography of 17–18
see also Sir John Monash Centre
chaplains *see* Long, George; O'Donnell, Thomas
Chauvel, Harry 157
Chifley, Ben 163
Chifley government 121, 123, 216
civilians
    emotional burden of war 33–35, 37–39
    experience of war 32–34, 42–44, 64–65
    see also home front
civil war, Irish 31
Clark, Manning 225
Clark, Victor S 95–96
Clendinnen, Inga 7–8
Cochrane, Peter 236
Colebatch, Hal 101
Collier, Philip 38
colonialism 70–76, 82–83, 88, 97–98
    see also imperialism
combat *see* military service; trauma
commemoration *see* remembrance
Commons, John 93
Commonwealth Art Advisory Board 173–74
Commonwealth Electoral Act 1949 123
Communist Party 111
Coniston Massacre 14, 124, 126, 128–29, 130, 132–34
    see also Murray, William George
conscription
    impact on veteran benefits 64–65
    opponents of 31
    plays about 15, 186–92
    political debates on 41, 103, 176, 203, 228
    supporters of 10, 23, 103
conservatism 3, 6–7, 13, 96–98, 100–103, 109–10, 226–29, 240
Convergence Associates 193–94, 198–99, 202
Cook, Joseph 82, 86, 239
Cooper, William 108
Cossington Smith, Grace 175–76
Country Party 13, 100, 105–106, 112
court martials 21, 27–28
Cowan, Edith 108
Crawford, RM 224–25
Crotty, Martin 102
Crozier, Frank 169, 176
culture wars 17, 225–26
    Daily Telegraph (Sydney) 249
    see also historiography

Damousi, Joy 7, 42
Davidson, Bessie 172
Davison, Graeme 8
dawn service *see* Anzac Day
Deadline Gallipoli 245
Deakin, Alfred 92–93, 100
Dean, Percy 82
de Groot, Jerome 199
Dekker, Kat 189
demobilisation *see* repatriation
democracy, progressive 13, 93, 95–99, 229

Index

Democratic Party 104
Denoon, Donald 92
Department of External Affairs 156–58
Department of Repatriation 114
Department of Veterans Affairs 8, 196, 201–202, 226, 246
de Plevitz, Zoe 183
depression (mental health) 142, 143–45, 240
  see also suicide; trauma
depression, economic 147–50
de Valera, Éamon 25, 28
Diamant, Neil 65
documentaries 244–45
Dodds, Thomas Henry (General) 48
Donaldson, Carina 7
Donnelly, Daley 183, 184, 185
Downer, Sidney 126
Dukes, Charles 161
Dunn, John James 117
Dyett, Gilbert 102
Dyson, Ruby 172
Dyson, Will 168, 176

economic recovery 48, 50, 58–59
Edele, Mark 64, 65
education
  on Anzac 182–83, 185–86, 196–97, 206–207, 234–35
  of troops and veterans 50–51, 53, 60
  see also museums
Edwards, Peter 157
Elliot, Harold 14, 102, 135, 137–38, 143–51
Elliot, Kate 143, 146
Ely, Richard 95
empire see imperialism
Encounter see HMAS Encounter
Evatt, Herbert 162, 163
Evening Echo (Ballarat) 24–25

Fantome see HMAS Fantome
Federal Government
  and Anzac 1–5, 7–8, 16–17, 98, 167, 181–82, 225–27, 262
  foreign affairs 12, 76–77, 79, 81–88
  party system 100, 105–106, 107, 112
  reaction to Armistice 36–37
  and repatriation 47, 48–50, 53
  veterans in 102–103, 135–36, 156–58
  welfare 61–64, 106–107, 114
fiction see artistic representations
Fiji 73, 74
films 18, 252–53
  see also television
First Nations People see Indigenous Australians
Fisher, Andrew 168, 171, 239
Foelsche, Paul 131
Fort Lytton National Park 183–84, 186
Fox, Chris 246
France
  Australian troops 46–47, 168, 203–205, 214
  commemorations 214–15, 218–19, 221, 252
  memorials in 16, 193–201, 205–207, 219
Frances, Rae 206
frontier violence
  and policing 14, 125–26, 128–34
  remembrance of 225–26, 237–39
Fry, Arthur 32, 41
Fullwood, Henry 176
Fussell, Paul 221
Futcher, Michael 188, 189

Gallipoli
  as 'birth of a nation' 3, 36, 91, 98, 220–21, 226–27, 253
  fictional representations of 18, 168–69, 177, 184, 189, 244–47, 252–53
  pilgrimages to 1–2, 4–7, 9, 219, 252
  wartime service at 54, 127, 133, 137, 138, 150–51, 155
Gallipoli (film) 3, 18, 252, 253
Gallipoli (TV series) 244, 246
Gammage, Bill 2, 251, 262n4
Garland, John 38
Garran, Robert 82
Garrison, Ellen Wright 93–94
Garton, Stephen 63, 153
George, WJ 40
George V 96, 214
Germany
  centenary commemorations 252
  loss of colonial territories 72, 75–77, 79, 80–83
  post-war foreign affairs 158–59
  treatment of prisoners of war 205
  treatment of veterans 65–66
  see also Paris Peace Conference
Goldstein, Vida 93–94
Gordon, David 37–38
Gower, Steve 91
Grant, Douglas 116, 117
Graupner, David 251
Great Depression 147–50
Greenwood, Gordon 224
Griffith, Arthur 26
Gromyko, Andrei 162
Gruner, Elioth 172–73
Gyngell, David 244

Haggard, Henry Rider 97
Hall, Bill 1
Hall, Dianne 22
Hallenstein, Reuben 40
Hasluck, Paul 157
Hawke, Bob 1, 252
Hawker, Charles 14, 135–36, 140–41, 145–48, 151
Hawkins, Jo 8
Hay, R 115–16
health care
  domestic 62–63, 106–107
  overseas 72–75, 203–204
Herald (Melbourne) 27

291

Heysen, Nora 172
Higgins, HB 97
Historial de la Grande Guerre 16, 195, 197–98, 200–201, 207
historiography
    of Anzac 2–3, 5–10, 17–18, 179–81, 224–27
    of Australia 224–25, 230–31
    see also history
history
    as a discipline 205–206, 232, 234, 236–37
    Honest History association 17, 232–36, 237, 239, 242–43
    militarisation of 7–8, 17, 224–27, 230–31, 232–33, 250–51
    and national identity 94, 224–25
    repression of select narratives 91–92, 94
    see also historiography
HMAS *Encounter* 12, 69, 72–75
HMAS *Fantome* 12, 69, 70, 71, 73
Hodgson, William Roy 14–15, 154–63
Holman, May 108
Holman, William 104
home front
    and Armistice 34–42, 212–14
    representations of 15, 172–76, 178, 180–81, 195–97
    see also civilians
Home Rule, Ireland see Irish Home Rule
Honest History association 17, 232–36, 237, 239, 242–43
Honi Soit 251
Hood, John 157
Howard, John 4–5, 7, 17, 225–26, 252
Hughes, W (Corporal) 145
Hughes, William (Billy)
    conscription 15, 23, 186–87, 190–91, 228
    Paris Peace Conference 12, 79, 81–84, 88
    party politics 65, 97, 103, 104–105
    repatriation of troops 48, 53
    and Thomas O'Donnell 23, 26
Humphrey, John 161

immigration 81, 82–83, 84, 85, 93, 97, 110, 261n14
imperialism
    attachment to British empire 3, 36–37, 76–78, 96–98, 104, 155, 185–86, 228–29
    Australian operations in Pacific 69–75
    and Ireland 30–31
    see also nationalism
Indigenous Australians
    and Anzac narrative 13, 114
    and Australian history 17, 225–26, 237–39
    Coniston Massacre 14, 124, 126, 128–29, 130, 132–34
    dispossession 109, 116, 117, 134
    frontier violence 17, 126, 130–34, 225–26, 237–38
    in the military 113–14, 120–21, 238
    politics and voting rights 108–109, 119–20, 122–23
    veterans and the RSSILA 13, 113–23
industrial action 101, 102

influenza 72–73, 107
Inglis, Ken 7–8, 219, 221–22, 241, 249
internationalism 163–64, 202–203
    see also United Nations
Irish-Australians 21, 24
    see also sectarianism
Irish Home Rule 21–22, 23, 24–25, 30

Japan 12, 79–81, 84–86, 121, 158–59, 260n2, 261n14
Japanangka, Bullfrog 129, 133
Jellicoe, John 86–87
John, Cecelia 190
Jones, Ada 41
Jones, John Percy 38
Jones, William 39
Jupurrurla Kelly, Francis 133

Kangaroo 101, 103
Keast, Rose 40
Keating, Paul 3, 4
Kellett, Susan 188
Kelly, Francis Jupurrurla 130
Kernaghan, Lee 246
Kildea, Jeff 21
Kingston, Allen Charles 204–205
Kitchener, Horatio 186
Konody, Paul 170, 173

labour laws 92, 95, 97, 207, 229
Lake, Marilyn 7, 22, 72, 215, 226, 228
Lake War Memorials Forum 233–34
Lambert, George 176, 177
Lane, Ernie and Mabel 190
Lang, Jack 110
Larsson, Marina 61, 152
Latham, John 81, 82, 83–86
Launceston Examiner 28–29
Lawrence, DH 101
    see also *Kangaroo*
Lawson, Harry 37, 41
League of Nations 82–83, 84, 159, 260n7, 260n8
Leist, Fred 176
Liberal Party 100, 252
    see also Nationalists
Lindsay, Norman 172–73
Lloyd, Henry Demarest 93
Long, George 50–51
Longstaff, John 176
Longstaff, Will 176, 178
A Lost Story From the Great War 15, 183–86, 192
Luckins, Tanya 42
Luytens, Edwin 193, 198, 202

Mackay, Hugh 240
Mackennal, Bertram 169–70
Malcolm, Elizabeth 22
Malekula, Vanuatu 69–71
Malik, Charles 161
Malua see Malekula, Vanuatu

Index

mandate system 83–85, 261n14
Manifold, Walter 39
Mannix, Daniel 23, 24, 27, 28–29, 31, 228
massacres *see* Coniston Massacre; frontier violence
Maynard, Fred 109
McCready, Walter 117
McCubbin, Louis 176
McGregor, Catherine 237
McIntyre, Scott 248
McKay, Jim 8
McKenna, Mark 6, 7
McKernan, Michael 206
McMullin, Ross 206
McQueen, Humphrey 76
media coverage
    of Anzac Day commemorations 2, 5, 234, 246–49
    of Anzac troops 96, 236
    of Armistice 34, 43
    of Australasian democracy 92–93, 95
    of Australian actions in Pacific 71, 75
    of conscription 23, 187, 188
    of Indigenous Australians 122–23, 131
    of Irish nationalism 24–25, 28–30
    of Thomas O'Donnell 27–28
    of war art scheme 171
medical care *see* health care
Mein Smith, Phillipa 92
Middleton, Sydney 51–52
memorials 193, 198, 211, 218, 233–34
    see also Australian War Memorial
Memorials Development Committee 233–34
memory *see* remembrance
migration *see* immigration
military intelligence 81, 156
military service
    of Charles Hawker 140
    fictional portrayals 61, 183–85, 198–200, 244–45, 252
    of Harold Elliot 137–38, 143, 150
    of Hugo Throssell 138–39, 143, 150–51
    in museum exhibits 150–51, 180, 194–200
    paintings of 15, 167–70, 171, 176–78
    privilege of in war narrative 15, 33, 176–78, 180–81, 195–97, 226–30
    of Ray Stanley 183–84
    of Thomas O'Donnell 23–24
    trauma from 14, 59–61, 124–25, 133–34, 143–53, 184–85
    and violence 124–26, 133–34, 200
    of William George Murray 126–28
    of William Roy Hodgson 154, 155–56
    see also Australian Infantry Force; veterans
Millen, Edward 36
Ministry of Shipping (Britain) 48–49
Mitchel, John 26
Monash, John 46, 52–56, 144–45
    see also Sir John Monash Centre
Morton, William 129, 132
mourning 16–17, 38–40, 197, 211, 220–21, 227, 250
    see also remembrance

Muirhead, Hannah 42–43
Munro Ferguson, Ronald Munro 24
Murray, William George 14, 124–28, 129–30, 132–34
museums 16, 150–51, 168–69, 178, 180, 193–202, 206–7
    see also memorials
myths 180, 196, 232, 234–35, 240–41, 251–53
    see also Anzac

nationalism
    and Anzac 91, 96–98, 195–97, 220–22, 224, 229–30, 248–50
    Australian political 2, 88, 94
    Irish 21–22, 24–25, 31
    see also patriotism
Nationalists 24–25, 65, 100–104, 107–108
National Parks and Wildlife Service, Queensland 183
naval expansion 85–87, 158, 261n16
navy *see* Royal Australian Navy
Nehru, Jawaharlal 163
Nelson, Brendan 16, 237, 238, 241
Nelson, Elizabeth 61
New Guinea, German 80–81, 85
New Guinea, Papua *see* Papua New Guinea
New Hebrides *see* Vanuatu
New South Wales
    and Indigenous veterans 115, 116, 118–19
    reactions to Armistice in 35–36, 38–41
    repatriation of troops to 49
    state politics 103–104, 107, 108, 110
New Zealand
    and Anzac Day 220, 222
    and Australasian democracy 92–93, 95–96, 98–99, 229
    as colonial power 72–74, 75–76
    erasure from Anzac narrative 12–13, 91–92, 94, 262n4
    treatment of veterans 64
    troops in WWI 46, 127
Nikolic, Andrew 234
Northern Territory
    frontier policing 125–26, 130–33
    and Indigenous soldiers 120–21
Northern Territory Times 131
novels 61, 101
Nungarrayi, Rosie 129–30

O'Donnell, Thomas 10, 21–24, 25–31
O'Farrell, Patrick 21
Office of Australian War Graves 196, 204
The One Day of the Year 251
O'Neill, Erill 273n14
Oppenheimer, Melanie 152–53

Pacific territories
    and Australian national security 76–77, 79–88, 158–59, 260n2

and colonial power 12, 69–72, 74–78
German loss of 75–77, 79, 80–83
medical aid to 72–75
World War Two conflicts 3–4, 121
pacifism 188–89, 215
Page, Earle 105–106
paintings 167–69, 175–78
Palstra, Jacoba 39
Pankhurst, Adela 190
Papua New Guinea 4, 75–76
Paris Peace Conference 12, 79, 82–83, 88, 160, 212
Parkes, Isabell 34
parliaments *see* Federal Government; state governments
patriotism
  and Anzac sentiment 7, 220, 242–43, 248–49
  and military service 180–81, 187, 215, 226–27
  see also nationalism
peace *see* Armistice; pacifism; Paris Peace Conference
Peake, Archibald 37
Pearce, George 173
Pen-Chun Chang 161
Pensalfini, Rob 189
pensions 63–64, 152, 258n9
People's Party of Soldiers and Citizens 103–104
Piesse, EL 81
plays 15, 182–85, 188–92, 251
Poland 219
policing, frontier 125–26, 128, 130–31, 134
politics *see* Federal Government; state governments; individual political parties by name
Pope Benedict XV 29
poppies 214–15, 220
post-traumatic stress disorder (PTSD) 150, 151–52, 268n18
  see also trauma
Power, Septimus 176
The Power of Ten 245
Poynter, JR 83
Prior, Robin 206
Pritchard, Katherine Susannah 136, 139–40, 146, 147–48, 149–50
Proctor, Thea 171
Prost, Antoine 215
protests 29, 118–19, 215
  see also riots
PTSD *see* post-traumatic stress disorder (PTSD)

Queensland
  annexation of Papua 76
  conscription 190–91
  and Indigenous veterans 115, 118–19
  reactions to Armistice in 42
  repatriation of troops to 50
  state politics 13, 107, 108, 110
  University of 186–88
  see also A Lost Story From the Great War; The Blood Votes
Quinn, James 176

Rae, Arthur 202–203
Rae, Iso 172
Red Cross 42
Redmond, John 25
Reeves, W Pember 92, 93
religion
  Anzac as faith 6, 18, 240–41, 249–50, 253
  Catholicism 10, 22–24, 31, 104, 111, 187, 228
  as personal support 142, 147–48, 211
  sectarianism 10, 22–24, 29, 31, 104, 228
remembrance
  Armistice Day 212–16, 276n2
  civilian experiences 32–33, 42–43
  competing narratives 60–61, 98, 168, 173–74, 195–96, 206–207, 250–53
  memorials and shrines 193, 198, 211, 218, 233–34
  mourning 16–17, 38–40, 197, 211, 220–21, 227, 250
  museums 16, 150–51, 168–69, 178, 180, 193–202, 206–207
  official collections 15, 167–69, 177–78, 179–81
  public expressions 33–34, 63, 138, 214–15
  see also Anzac Day; Australian War Memorial; centenary commemorations; history; Remembrance Day; trauma
Remembrance Day
  comparison with Anzac Day 220–23
  evolution of 16–17, 211–12, 215–19, 276n2
  see also Armistice Day
Remembrance Sunday 216–17
repatriation
  logistics of 11, 45–50, 52–53, 54–56, 59–60
  terminology 47
  troop activities during 50–52, 53–55
  see also veterans
Repatriation Commission 62
resilience 14, 141–43, 149, 152–53, 164
Returned and Services League of Australia (RSL) 113–14, 250
  see also Returned Sailors' and Soldiers' Imperial League of Australia (RSSILA)
Returned Sailors' and Soldiers' Australian Democratic League 98
Returned Sailors' and Soldiers' Imperial League of Australia (RSSILA)
  and conservatism 101–102
  establishment 98, 113
  and Indigenous veterans 13, 114–23
  and repatriation benefits 62, 65, 66–67
Reynolds, Henry 7, 72
riots 11, 54, 59, 101, 190
  see also protests
Ritchie, George 38
Rix Nicholas, Hilda 171, 176, 178
Robins, John Francis 69, 71
Robinson, Arthur 38
Ronaldson, Michael 241
Roosevelt, Eleanor 161, 271n39
Rosenthal, Charles 103
Rout, Ettie 203–204

Index

Royal Australian Navy 69–75, 77–78
  see also naval expansion
Royce, Josiah 92–93, 95
RSSILA *see* Returned Sailors' and Soldiers' Imperial League of Australia (RSSILA)
rural Australia 105–106
Russia *see* Soviet Union
Ruxton, Bruce 113

Santa Cruz, Hernan 161
Saunders, Reg 121
Saxby, Jack 132, 133
Scarlett, Philippa 117
Scates, Bruce 6, 152–53
Scott, Ernest 49, 96
Scott, James 176
Scullin, James 24–25
Seal, Graham 180
sectarianism 10, 22–24, 29, 31, 104, 228
security, national 76–77, 79–88, 158–59, 260n2
sedition 26, 31
self-determination
  arising from World War One 29–30, 71–72, 83–84
  Ireland 21–22, 24–25, 27–31
  see also mandate system
Sémelin, Jacques 133
sexually transmitted diseases 203–4
Seymour, Alan 251
Shaw, AGL 224
Sherington, Guy 47–50
shipping 48–49
Shorten, Bill 239–40
Shrine of Remembrance 211, 248
silence 200–201, 214, 218
Singapore Naval Strategy 87
Sinn Féin 22, 24, 26, 30
Sir John Monash Centre 16, 193–97, 198–201, 205–207, 219
Smart, Henry 169, 177
Smith, Walter 130
socialism 92–95, 101–102, 111, 139, 147–48
social media 245, 248, 249
soldier settlement 62, 97–98, 106, 116–17, 152–53
soldiers *see* military service; veterans
Somme *see* Historial de la Grande Guerre; Sir John Monash Centre
South Australia
  Anzac celebrations in 219–20
  frontier policing 130–31
  reactions to Armistice in 37–39
  repatriation of troops to 50
  state politics 108
Soviet Union
  foreign affairs 161–62
  treatment of veterans 64–65, 66
Spanish flu *see* influenza
Spence, Catherine 93
Spencer, Baldwin 169–70
sport 51–52

SS *Talune* 72–73
Stafford, Randal 128–29, 132
Stanley, Millicent Preston 108
Stanley, Peter 234
Stanley, Ray 183–85
state governments
  post-war innovations 13, 104, 107–109, 110–11
  reactions to Armistice 11, 35–39, 41, 76–77
  veterans in 103–104, 138
  women in 107–108
Stephens, David 182
Sternberg, Jason 246
Stevens, Bertram 172
Stirling, Alfred 158
Street, Jessie 36
Streeton, Arthur 170, 176
suffrage movement 93–94, 108
suicide
  considered by Charles Hawker 145–46
  of Harold Elliot 135, 145
  of Hugo Throssell 136, 139, 144, 149–50
  see also trauma

Target 246
tariffs 105, 109–10
Tasmania
  and Indigenous veterans 115, 116
  repatriation of troops to 50
  see also O'Donnell, Thomas
television 17–18, 244–45, 246–47
theatre *see* plays
Theodore, Ted 110
Thomson, Alistair 152, 206
Thorp, Margaret 15, 42, 188, 190
Thring, Hugh 73
Throssell, George 138
Throssell, Hugo 14, 136, 138–40, 143–44, 146, 147–51
Throssell, Ric (brother of Hugo) 143
Throssell, Ric (son of Hugo) 138–39, 140, 146
Tippett, Maria 175
Tonga 73, 74
trade unions *see* unions
Trahair, William 174
Traill, Jessie 172
trauma
  from military service 14, 59–61, 124–25, 133–34, 143–53, 184–85
  theories of 8–9, 141–43, 150, 200
  see also civilians, emotional burden of war; resilience
Tregear, Edward 95–96
Treloar, John 169, 177
troops *see* military service; veterans
Turkey *see* Gallipoli
Turnbull, Malcolm 248, 249
Twomey, Christina 8, 61, 151

UHDR *see* Universal Declaration of Human Rights, United Nations (UHDR)

unions 92–93, 102, 187, 190, 229
United Nations 15, 160–63
United States of America
    forces in World War One 37, 46
    foreign affairs 159, 161–62, 189
    treatment of veterans 11, 64–66, 219
Universal Declaration of Human Rights, United Nations (UHDR) 15, 154, 161, 162
University of Queensland 186–88
Unknown Soldier 218
Ure Smith, Sydney 174

Valentine, James 246–47
Vanuatu 69–71
Versailles Peace Conference *see* Paris Peace Conference
veterans
    commemorations by 5, 138, 214–15, 251
    Gallipoli pilgrimages 1–2, 252
    Indigenous Australians 13, 113–23
    political influence of 64–65, 67, 98, 104, 113–14
    as politicians 14–15, 102–103, 135–36, 138, 156–64
    post-war benefits 11, 61–67, 97–98, 106–107, 114, 116, 152
    protests and unrest 11, 54, 59, 101, 215
    and trauma 14, 59–61, 67–68, 124–25, 133–34, 143–53, 184–85
    see also Department of Veterans Affairs; repatriation; Returned Sailors' and Soldiers' Imperial League of Australia (RSSILA)
Victoria
    assistance to Indigenous veterans 115
    conscription 23
    and Indigenous veterans 115–17, 122–23
    reactions to Armistice in 34, 37–41, 213
    repatriation of troops to 49–50, 101
    state politics 100, 108, 110, 112
victory *see* Armistice
Villers-Bretonneux
    Australian forces at 203–5
    memorial at 193, 198, 218
    see also Sir John Monash Centre
voting systems 13, 107–8

Walker, Edmund 173
Wannan, William 122–23
war art schemes
    Australian 15, 167–74, 176–78
    British 172, 175
    Canadian 170, 172, 173, 175, 177
    depictions of home front 172–75
    women artists 171–72, 175–76
Warburton, Peter Egerton 131
Ward, Stuart 6
Warlpiri people 129–30
war pensions *see* pensions
War Precautions Act 24–25
Watson, Don 3, 235
Watt, William 37, 76–77, 86, 173
Weber, Max 242
Weir, Peter *see Gallipoli* (film)
welfare 17, 62–64, 106–108, 110, 114–15, 152, 229
Wellington, Jennifer 180
Western Australia
    Anzac celebrations in 248
    reactions to Armistice in 35, 38
    repatriation of troops to 50
    state politics 108, 123, 228
Western Samoa 72–74
What's Wrong with Anzac? 7–8
White, Brudenell 96, 157
Williams, Tom 117
Wilson, Woodrow 82–83
    see also self-determination
Windshuttle, Keith 226
Winter, Jay 195, 197, 200–201
women
    artists 171–72, 175–76
    and politics 13, 93–94, 107–108
    wartime experience 33, 42, 199, 203–204
Women's Peace Army 190
Woolworths 245–46
World (Hobart) 30
World War Two
    commemoration of 3–4, 216, 233–34
    impact on remembrance of World War One 33, 42–43, 216–17, 222, 251
    Indigenous soldiers 114, 120–21
    treatment of veterans 64, 65–66, 114
Wright, Clare 247

www.ingramcontent.com/pod-product-compliance
Lightning Source LLC
LaVergne TN
LVHW040408260326
834688LV00033B/447